GAMBLING — CRIME OR REC...

INFORMATION PLUS®
WYLIE, TEXAS 75098
© 1978, 1980, 1982, 1984, 1992, 1996, 1998
ALL RIGHTS RESERVED

EDITORS:
ABBEY M. BEGUN, B.A.
MARK A. SIEGEL, Ph.D.
NANCY R. JACOBS, M.A.

CHAPTER I

GAMBLING — AN AMERICAN TRADITION

COLONIAL PASTIME

Gambling was a popular pastime in North America long before there was ever a United States. Playing cards and dice were brought over by both the British and the Dutch. By the end of the seventeenth century, just about every county seat in colonial America had a lottery wheel. Cockfighting flourished throughout the colonies, especially in the South. Bear-baiting (an old form diversion in which dogs were made to torment a chained bear) was also a popular sport, but the Puritans banned it "not because it gave pain to the bear, but because it gave pleasure to the spectators." While strict New Englanders considered gambling a "disorder to God" and levied fines and whippings against gamblers, gambling was much less of a moral issue in other parts of the country.

European visitors to America, from English soldiers during the Revolutionary War period to the writer Frances Trollope in the nineteenth century, commented on the American affinity for gambling. George Washington was an avid, though mediocre, card player and wisely limited his betting. Benjamin Franklin printed and sold playing cards. The controversial Stamp Act levied a one-shilling tax on every pack of cards, raising perhaps as much ire as the tax on tea, since every well-furnished colonial home possessed a card table. In the South, the planter-aristocrat, with his thoroughbred horses, had the opportunity and the wealth to enjoy leisure time pursuits — horse racing being a favorite.

LOTTERIES HELP FINANCE THE GROWTH OF A NATION

During the Colonial Period, lotteries were a popular means of raising funds. English lotteries provided most of the funding to establish the colony of Virginia, and the original Jamestown settlement was financed by a lottery conducted by the Virginia Company in London, England. In 1748, young Ben Franklin organized a lottery to pay for military supplies to defend Philadelphia from attack by Indian tribes and French soldiers.

In 1777, the Continental Congress held a $5 million lottery to help finance the Revolutionary War. Unfortunately, all winnings over $50 were to be paid in promissory notes (to be collected at some future date). The lottery was mismanaged, and several scoundrels abused the trust of their fellow revolutionaries. The lottery was a disaster, and most people holding winning tickets never received their winnings.

Lotteries were also held to raise money for county treasuries, to build bridges, assist churches and schools, and establish relief funds. Lottery proceeds contributed to the establishment of such prestigious Ivy League schools as Harvard, Yale, Columbia, Princeton, and Dartmouth.

ENTERTAINMENT DURING THE JACKSONIAN ERA

President Andrew Jackson believed that a person's destiny should be controlled by the individual, rather than by elected officials. During his administration (1829-1837), popularly known as the era of "the common man," gambling was a form of entertainment enjoyed by large numbers of people, as well as public officials. President Jackson was an avid gambler (he once reportedly bet all of his clothes during a game of chance). During his presidential campaign, Jackson's eventual successor, Martin Van Buren (1837-1841), wagered a new suit, along with $40,000, on his victory in the elections.

During this period, Americans were well known for their eager and continued interest in all forms of gambling. A northern traveler in the South commented on the heavy betting at cockfights, which were attended by people from all levels of society. A flatboat merchant who plied the Ohio River observed that Kentuckians were completely absorbed in horse racing and gambling. One could hardly talk to a Kentuckian, he wrote, without hearing the phrase, "I'll bet you."

Along the Mississippi and Ohio Rivers, notorious gamblers earned their keep on the riverboats that sailed down the rivers to New Orleans, a gambler's paradise. The first formal casino in New Orleans opened in 1827, and it soon became a model for other "carpet joints," as the lavishly decorated casinos were called. Riverboat gambling continued after the Civil War but never regained its antebellum (pre-Civil War) dash and glamour.

Urban areas were also centers of gambling activity during the Jacksonian Era. While the countryside and riverfront facilities relied on visitors from outlying areas to attend their cockfights, horse races, or casinos, urban areas had a ready-made customer base. New York City was an early gambling center. By 1850, it had approximately 6,000 flourishing gambling houses, an astounding ratio of one gambling house for every 85 New Yorkers.

THE REFORM MOVEMENT

During the 1840s, a reforming spirit swept across America. Societies formed to combat tobacco use, profanity, and the transit of mail on Sunday. The first women's rights movement was organized, and temperance crusaders preached against alcohol use. The abolitionist movement against slavery gained significant momentum during these years.

Many reformers attacked gambling. They were most successful in their fight against the flourishing lottery business. During the 1830s, some newspapers began publishing accounts of corrupt lotteries and their harmful effect on individuals who could not really afford to buy tickets, but did so anyway. As a result of this negative publicity, the number of lottery permits decreased, and lotteries were abolished altogether in most northern states by 1840. The increasing rate of profiteering by lottery middlemen eventually incited public indignation in the South and West as well. By 1860, every state in the nation except Delaware, Kentucky, and Missouri had enacted constitutional or statutory prohibitions against lotteries.

Although illegal in most states by this time, gambling occurred openly in such cities as New York, Chicago, and New Orleans. In reaction to reform efforts, operators of gambling establishments fought to save their lucrative businesses by paying members of local police forces for protection. Policemen staged prearranged raids for appearance's sake, but they were careful not to damage furniture, and they usually returned the gamblers to their places of business after booking them. The very fact that gambling was illegal seemed to add to its popular appeal as an exciting form of entertainment. Any attempts to legalize gambling probably would have been opposed by gamblers, operators, and corrupt police and public officials alike.

During the mid- and late-1860s, the financial demands of the Civil War and Reconstruction once again led to an interest in lotteries in the southern and western states. However, because of their reputation for breeding corruption and a lack of uniform state regulation, federal legislation against lotteries was introduced. Lottery operators mounted efforts to get around anti-lottery laws by forming "gift companies," which operated in essentially the same manner as lotteries.

THE WILD WEST — HONKY-TONKS AND THE GOLD RUSH

The opening of the Far West after the Civil War gave gambling in America a second life. Far from both government controls and the moral interference of reform groups in the East, gambling became so popular and widespread that monte (a card game) tables were often set up in the street in the middle of town. Professional gamblers, rumored to earn as much as $20,000 per month, were glad to relieve hard-working miners of their gold nuggets. Losses were usually taken philosophically. For the unlucky miners, a quick return to their gold mines in the hills would usually replenish whatever they lost at the gaming tables. Gambling houses could easily be found in Kansas City, Dallas, Denver, and San Francisco, as well as nearly every small town located near mining camps, railroad towns, and major cattle trails.

THE LOUISIANA LOTTERY

As noted above, dishonesty and fraud were common in lottery operations during the 1800s. The Louisiana Lottery, however, took these characteristics to such extremes that, by the turn of the century, gambling and political corruption would be forever linked in the minds of many people.

In 1864, 1868, 1872, and 1876, federal laws were passed to stop the expansion of lotteries by taxing them and limiting the activities they could conduct by federal mail. Louisiana was the only state still operating a lottery. In 1865, a New York-based gambling syndicate (a group of individuals or corporations formed to undertake an activity, usually one that requires substantial financial backing) applied for approval to operate a lottery in Louisiana. In return for granting a sales monopoly to the syndicate, the Louisiana state treasury would receive $40,000 annually for 25 years to finance the Charity Hospital in New Orleans. The use of profits from gambling for charitable causes became an established tactic to promote the acceptance of gambling within the community.

The approval of the Louisiana Lottery was assured by rigged elections that kept out candidates opposed to the lottery and by bribing legislators to grant licenses. From its inception, the Louisiana Lottery controlled legislatures, newspapers, banks, and governors. It continued operating despite prohibitions by federal laws because enforcement officials would not prosecute lottery managers. Players around the country participated in the Louisiana Lottery by mail, bringing the lottery's profits to an average $13 million per year, a huge sum of money at the time.

Mounting Criticism

National criticism grew as the Louisiana Lottery extended into every state, with the syndicate receiving more than 90 percent of its income from outside Louisiana. Reformers, labor and farm organizations, newspapers, and churches all demanded federal action against the Louisiana Lottery. As a result, the state legislature canceled the lottery, but using the considerable number of dollars at its disposal, the syndicate forced an extension through a Louisiana constitutional convention.

Finally, in 1890, the U.S. Congress passed legislation banning postal delivery of all items dealing with lotteries and prohibiting the conduct of operations through an agent or representative, such as the New Orleans National Bank. For the first time, violations of this law became punishable by imprisonment. A new provision was also

4

enacted making the offense triable by a court in any jurisdiction through which lottery material had been transported, thereby making it harder for the lottery operators to avoid conviction by bribing local jurors.

The Louisiana Lottery Company moved to Honduras in Central America to avoid postal regulations. In 1895, Congress authorized the Postmaster General to withhold delivery of lottery-related mail and to deny any person representing a lottery company the use of the postal service. Interstate transportation of lottery materials and the use of express mail became illegal in 1895. The anti-lottery laws deprived the Louisiana Lottery Company of the methods by which it had evaded state and federal laws for years, and it had to close. The combined effect of several federal statutes enacted between 1890 and 1895 eliminated lotteries for the next 70 years.

THE PROGRESSIVE ERA — A SECOND PERIOD OF REFORM

Between 1900 and 1917, a reform-minded group of people called the "Progressives" dedicated themselves to exposing corruption in big business and municipal governments, correcting social evils, and improving living conditions for women, children, and the poor. Progressive reformers had two main goals: to use state power to curb unscrupulous business trusts and to stem the threat of socialism.

Reformers attacked red-light (prostitution) districts, saloons, and alcoholism. Francis E. Willard founded the Anti-Saloon League to crusade against these establishments, considered to be dominated by crooked city officials and political bosses who supported "booze interests," counted poker chips by night, and miscounted ballots by day. Progressive reformers were also instrumental in closing gambling houses and race tracks, as well as policy (see Chapter X) and bookmaking operations. By 1915, only seven states permitted horse racing.

ORGANIZED CRIME

In 1920, Congress instituted Prohibition, which outlawed the manufacture, transportation, and sale of alcoholic liquors in the United States. However, while Congress could make alcohol illegal, it could not curb Americans' appetite for alcohol. With its potential for huge profits, the manufacture and sale of alcoholic beverages became the domain of the underground world of gangsters. Subsequently, organized crime moved on to other profitable and illicit activities, such as gambling.

During the Prohibition Era (1920-1933), illegal gambling was organized into an authoritarian regional and national system. Responsibility for the syndication of gambling is usually attributed to Arnold Rothstein (1881-1928), who invented the inner-city layoff (in which gambling organizations in one city helped those in other cities cover heavy, potentially risky bets). Rothstein is also known for masterminding the "Black Sox" Scandal in which the White Sox threw the 1919 World (Baseball) Series to the Cincinnati Reds to assure gambling profits.

Organized crime no longer possesses the glamorous reputation it enjoyed in movies during the 1920s and 1930s. Findings by the Special Senate Committee to Investigate Organized Crime in Interstate Commerce, headed by Senator Estes Kefauver in 1950, and the McClellan hearings in 1963-64 revealed the brutal activities of the underworld and instigated more vigorous attempts at reform and containment. Most illegal slot machines and walk-in bookie joints disappeared from sight. They still existed, of course, as did floating card and "crap" games — they were just less conspicuous.

LEGAL GAMBLING AGAIN BECOMES ACCEPTABLE

Since the 1970s, the United States has turned full circle in its attitude towards gambling. Three hundred years ago, the "sport," especially in the form of lotteries, was seen as a perfectly acceptable way to raise money for public purposes. During the late 1980s and early 1990s, slow economic growth, cuts in federal funding to states, and growing public needs forced many desperate state and even local governments to seek additional sources of revenue. Most states turned to lotteries, horse and dog racing, and, most recently, a growing number of states have resorted to casino gambling as a way to "painlessly" raise money for the public coffers.

While moral issues and concerns about criminal involvement usually play a part in state and local election campaigns to institute legalized gambling, they were, until recently, almost always overcome by the prospect of even less attractive alternatives: decreased social programs and/or increased taxes. Increased fiscal need and fear of increased taxes often outweigh any moral argument.

Once big business understood the unrealized potential of legal gambling in the United States, it was not long before gambling swept across the nation. While most Americans following business over the last decade have focused on the explosion in high technology, the transformation of the gambling industry has been just as dynamic. Las Vegas, the nation's fastest growing metropolitan area, has more hotels and casinos than anywhere on Earth. While the nation's gambling capital, it markets itself as a family event.

After some shaky years, Atlantic City seems to be returning to financial solvency. Well-appointed riverboats, many of them unable to sail, attract millions of Americans along the nation's waterways. Indian reservations, many of them mired in poverty, now host some of the most attractive casinos in the country. Old mining towns in Colorado and South Dakota offer visitors a chance to bet their money. (See Chapters V, VI, and VII.)

Two hundred years ago, gambling was as American as apple pie. Then, gambling went through a long period of time when it was associated with the Mafia and corrupt officials. Today, gambling has become a part of the business page in the newspaper and an everyday part of American life.

CHAPTER II

GAMBLING AND THE GOVERNMENT

LAWS, COURT CASES, LOBBYING, AND POLITICS

PUBLIC POLICY ON GAMBLING

Current gambling policies at the state and federal levels reflect the mixed feelings Americans have toward gambling. Over the years, Americans have generally held one of two or three beliefs about gambling — that it is morally and socially destructive and it must be eliminated; that its enormous popularity makes it a suitable activity for government licensing and taxation; or that it is morally destructive, but if you want to do it, that is your problem. With the nation's apparently increasing tolerance for once-prohibited activities, coupled with a growing need for state and local revenues, the lure of gambling revenues has prompted most states to reconsider and usually change their gambling policies.

TRYING TO CONTROL CRIME CROSSING STATE LINES AND BORDERS

The first modern anti-gambling legislation was passed to outlaw the use of "floating casinos." During the 1940s, gambling took place on ships off the California coast, just outside the country's three-mile limit, in order to avoid prohibitions against gambling. The federal government did not approve, and in 1948, Congress passed 18 USC 1081-1083*, which effectively halted the operation of gambling ships off the coast of the United States by prohibiting transportation to and from the ships. (Gambling ships have since become legal.)

The Kefauver Committee investigations (see Chapter I) produced a number of statutes directed at "nation-wide crime syndicates." The Johnson Act (15 USC 1171-1177), a group of statutes produced by the Kefauver Committee, prohibited the interstate transportation of illegal gambling devices. This law supported state policies prohibiting slot machines and successfully eliminated interstate traffic in coin-operated gambling machines.

Throughout the 1950s, most federal efforts to control gambling were undertaken by the Internal Revenue Service (IRS). The IRS attacked illegal gambling operations under the Wagering Excise Tax and Wagering Occupational Stamp Tax statutes (26 USC 4401 and 26 USC 4411). (See below.)

The (John F.) Kennedy Administration (1961-1963) was committed to controlling illegal gambling. During the 1960s, Congress passed statutes that attacked large gambling syndicates operating across state lines (18 USC 1081-1804 and 18 USC 1952). With the passage of these statutes, the federal government attempted to suppress large-scale interstate gambling operations by allowing local and state governments to extend their investigations across state boundaries.

The interstate transportation of wagering paraphernalia is defined under Public Law (PL)

---

* This and the following citations refer to the United States Code. The number preceding the USC is the volume. The number after the USC is the section.

91-452 (18 USC 1952-53) and contains the broadest anti-gambling provisions: it prohibits interstate travel or the use of interstate facilities to promote illegal gambling enterprises. Statutes 18 USC 1084 and 18 USC 1952 have been most effective against interstate bookmaking operations and were essential in closing down the lavish, large-scale illegal casinos that flourished in major cities during the 1940s and 1950s. Before these statutes were passed, a large interstate layoff bookmaking operation (in which a bookie turns to other bookies to help handle larger bets) existed throughout the country (see Arnold Rothstein, Chapter I) and supported bookmaking establishments in a number of states.

Federal law enforcement agencies were more effective in combating interstate gambling syndicates than were state or local governments because federal authorities could operate more easily across state lines, and they were somewhat less susceptible to payoffs. The federal effort substantially eliminated interstate bookkeeping operations controlled by organized crime and all but the two most prevalent forms of illegal gambling — the numbers game and bookmaking.

TARGETING ORGANIZED CRIME

Despite all the government's previous efforts to control syndicated gambling, congressional hearings and research revealed that gambling was still the largest single source of income for organized crime. The passage of the Organized Crime Control Act of 1970 (PL 91-452) significantly expanded federal jurisdiction over gambling.

Provision 18 USC 1955 of the Organized Crime Control Act changed the federal government's basis for attacking organized gambling. First, it defined an illegal, organized gambling operation as one that involved five or more people in the conduct, financing, directing, managing, or ownership of a gambling business doing a gross volume of $2,000 per day, or operating continually over a 30-day period, and in

violation of the law in a particular state. It also broadened the federal government's control over interstate commerce by requiring only general, rather than specific, knowledge of illegal activities as cause to apprehend lawbreakers.

Corrupt public officials often play a major role in organized crime operations. Statute 18 USC 1511 of the Organized Crime Control Act prohibits an elected or appointed public official from using his or her position to hinder an investigation of illegal gambling activity.

GAMBLING AND RACKETEERING

Statutes 18 USC 1961-68 provide civil remedies for illegal gambling activities. These provisions, enacted as part of the Organized Crime Control Act of 1970, are collectively known as the RICO (Racketeer-Influenced and Corrupt Organizations) statutes. The RICO statutes permit the federal government to act in a civil or criminal case against anyone engaged in two separate acts of "racketeering activity" (obtaining money illegally). The transmission of gambling information, interstate transportation of wagering paraphernalia, and illegal gambling businesses became offenses punishable by imprisonment.

The civil remedy provision, 18 USC 1964, does not normally involve imprisonment. However, this provision permits a court to order individuals to divest themselves of interests which are in violation of RICO statutes, to impose reasonable restrictions on future activities and investments of such persons, and to order the dissolution or reorganization of such enterprises involved in racketeering activities. These long-term preventive actions, while not putting the violator in jail, can sometimes provide more practical protection from racketeering activity than criminal punishment.

An extremely important part of statute 18 USC 1964 is that if a defendant violates a court order, he or she must show cause why he or she should not be held in contempt of court, while the government must only show that the order has been violated. This lowers the government's burden of proof and thereby allows a rapid response to any violations of the court's order. Finally, in a civil case, the government need only prove by "a preponderance of the evidence" (or the bulk of the evidence) that the defendant is likely in the future to engage in conduct that violates the law. This means that a violator can be put in prison, not because he or she has been guilty "beyond a reasonable doubt," as in all criminal proceedings, but because "a preponderance of the evidence" shows that a court order has been violated.

The RICO statutes have had great success in stemming illegal gambling in the United States, but many civil libertarians question the use of this law, which has been used as an easy way to prosecute alleged lawbreakers, ranging from those charged with pornography to those arrested for picketing abortion clinics.

TAXABLE EARNINGS

Since the Prohibition Era (1920-1933), tax laws have been used to control organized crime. In fact, Al Capone was booked for income-tax evasion even before the investigation of his illegal bootlegging activities was completed, and he went to jail for failing to pay his taxes, not for his many other criminal activities. On the other hand, some tax laws have contributed to the success of illegal gambling operations and thereby promoted organized crime.

Section 61 of the Internal Revenue Service code describes as taxable income "any accretion to wealth ... unless specifically exempt," which means gambling winnings are taxable. Since most persons wager or bet for entertainment, few small winners coming home from a moderately successful trip to Las Vegas or Atlantic City are likely to declare their winnings. Few gamblers are net winners during a given year or, for that matter, during their gambling careers, but most gamblers think that at some time they will become big winners.

Winners who properly declare their gambling income are not permitted to carry back or carry forward losses from previous or later years as a deduction against their current winnings (an economic disadvantage), as they would in the case of normal investment earnings. Consequently, the tax laws tend to encourage patronage of illegal games. Furthermore, a big winner knows that a legal gambling establishment will report his or her winnings to the IRS, while the winner in an illegal game can safely assume that the operator will not file a report of his business activities.

Certainly one of the most controversial recommendations made by the Commission on the Review of the National Policy Toward Gambling in 1976 was to repeal taxes on gambling winnings in order to take away a major edge held by illegal gambling. Some experts believe that if taxes on gambling were repealed, it could have a significant impact in eliminating illegal gambling operations. A change in the tax policy, however, is most unlikely.

In 1951, in an attempt to raise money, Congress passed the Wagering Excise Tax (26 USC 4401) and the Wagering Occupational Stamp Tax (26 USC 441). Originally, for those engaged in gambling activities, the excise tax was 10 percent of earnings plus a $50 charge for the occupational stamp required for each person involved in gambling operations. On December 1, 1974, Congress changed these requirements to 2 percent and $500, respectively, in an effort to enable legal bookmakers who pay the taxes to compete more effectively with their illegal competitors. This wagering tax applies only to sports, horse bookmaking, and numbers games; it does not apply to pari-mutuel betting, coin-operated machines, state lotteries that base winnings on horse race results, or casino games.

Although the laws discussed here were intended to limit illegal gambling activity, not much money or manpower has been devoted to their enforcement. In fact, these laws have hurt legal state-sanctioned gambling operations because legal operators are far more likely to pay taxes than illegal operators; hence, they are unable to offer the same return on a wager as the illegal operations. Therefore, the Commission on the Review of the National Policy Toward Gambling recommended that the excise and occupational taxes be eliminated, as well as the $250 Occupational Tax on Coin-Operated Devices (26 USC 4411), passed in 1941. None of the tax recommendations made by the commission has yet been instituted.

State Gambling Taxes — Some Examples

States have a variety of ways to collect gambling taxes. Nevada and New Jersey have taxed gambling for many years, since they have been gambling meccas longer than any other states. Colorado, Illinois, Indiana, Iowa, Louisiana, Mississippi, and South Dakota are more recent gambling-tax collectors.

Nevada levies a tax on each admission fee to a or casino. The state also imposes extensive gambling license fees. There are 10 categories of annual state licenses, depending on the number of games that are being played in an establishment. Nevada collects different quarterly license fees for small (fewer than 10 games) operators and large (more than 10 games) operators. In addition, Nevada imposes monthly county license fees based on the number of games and devices being operated in a gambling house. A $250 annual tax is imposed on each slot machine over and above any other license fee and gaming tax.

New Jersey charges an annual 8 percent tax gross revenues from its casinos. In addition, an initial fee of at least $200,000 is required for a casino license. The annual renewal for this license is a minimum of $100,000.

Arkansas taxes all admission charges for bingo games and on gross receipts from any apparatus used in playing the game. (No admission tax is levied on charitable or non-profit organizations.) Arkansas also imposes a "dog racing privilege tax" of 3 percent of all money gambled.

Florida takes in 7.6 percent of the gross proceeds from betting pools. Florida also taxes horse racing with a harness horse tax of 1 percent per race. A 3 percent thoroughbred horse tax is levied from January 10 through March 1, which coincides with Florida's heaviest tourist season. The popular sport of jai-alai is taxed at a rate of 5.5 percent per performance.

New York has a complex horse racing tax structure, which includes 17 categories of taxes on both regular and multiple bets. The state taxes pari-mutuel winnings at between 2.5 percent and 7.5 percent of the total pool. New York also taxes admissions to race tracks. Licensed simulcasts (programs being broadcast as they occur on television or radio or both) of races are taxed on earned money equal to 1.5 percent. Any city in the state of New York with a population of 1 million or more people may collect gambling taxes up to 5 percent of bets at off-track facilities located in that city.

ADVERTISING FOR LOTTERIES

Title 18 USC Para. 1302 prohibits the mailing of any "publication of any kind containing any advertisement of any lottery, gift enterprise, or scheme of any kind offering prizes dependent in whole or in part upon lot or chance, or containing any list of the prizes drawn or awarded by means of any such lottery, gift, enterprise, or scheme." This law dated back to the 1940s, when lotteries were illegal. By the 1980s, most states had a lottery, and many wanted to advertise the lottery through promotions sent out directly through the mail and/ or in newspapers, which are often sent through the mail.

The Minnesota Newspaper Association challenged the law, and a federal district court, in *Minnesota Newspaper Assn., Inc. v. Postmaster General* (677 F. Supp. 1400, 1987), ruled the law valid as it applied to advertisements but unconstitutional as applied to prize lists, since the law could prevent the publication of prize lists in news reports, and that would be a violation of the freedom of the press.

The case was appealed all the way to the U.S. Supreme Court. However, before the Supreme Court could hear the case, the U.S. Congress reached a legislative remedy to this problem. Congress passed and President Ronald Reagan signed into law the "Charity Games Advertising Clarification Act of 1988" (PL 100-625). This law indicates that the existing federal law should not apply to advertisements or radio broadcasts concerning lotteries prepared by either state or non-profit organizations, which are published or broadcast in a state that conducts a lottery. The law also applies to private companies that use a lottery as a promotional activity ("but only a promotional activity and only occasional[ly]").

Based on this new law, the Postmaster General agreed that the law no longer applied to the noncommercial publishing of prize lists. The Supreme Court, in *Frank, Postmaster General of the United States v. Minnesota Newspaper Association, Inc.* (490 US 225, 1989), finding there was no longer a controversy, declared the case moot and referred it back to the lower court to be dismissed.

SPORTS GAMBLING

During the late 1980s and early 1990s, several states tried to introduce sports betting, either as part of the lottery (similar to a sports pool) or as sports bookmaking. Attempts to introduce sports bookmaking in California to counter the sports bookmaking operations across the Mexican-American border in Northern Baja California, Mexico, have failed, as have attempts in New York, Illinois, and New Jersey. Oregon has tied sports betting with its lotteries.

Fear of Gambling in the Sports Industry

Nonetheless, the leaders of the nation's sports industry, including the National Basketball Association (NBA), the National Football League (NFL), and Major League Baseball, were concerned that the states in their desperation to raise monies might begin to tie sports betting with their lotteries. They began to put strong pressure

on state legislatures not to introduce sports betting. The sports industry also started lobbying Congress, and as a result, several bills have been introduced in the U.S. Congress to limit the growth of sports wagering, either as part of a lottery or as sports bookmaking. The most notable were two similar bills, one (S 474) proposed by then-Senator Dennis DeConcini (D-AZ) and the other (HR 74) by former Representative John Bryant (D-TX).

Gambling Is Bad for Sports

At hearings on HR 74, representatives from the NBA and the NFL strongly supported the bill. They believed that legal gambling on sports would threaten the integrity of their games. Any missed basketball shot or field goal that hooked away from the goal posts would be suspect. Had the player missed the shot or the kick because some gambler had paid him money? What about a terrible call by the referee? Was the game fixed? These were questions the sports leagues believed could threaten their businesses. (See Chapter XI for a discussion of public attitudes as to whether various sporting events are fixed.)

NFL Commissioner Paul Tagliabue declared that

We do not want our games used as bait to sell gambling. Sports gambling should not be used as a cure for the sagging fortunes of Atlantic City casinos or to boost public interest in state lotteries. We should not gamble with our children's heroes.

NBA Commissioner David Stern added that

Sports betting alters the interest of spectators from that of fans, who are principally interested in the ultimate outcome of the game, to that of gamblers, who are principally interested in beating the point spread and winning their bets.

Finally, some legislators believed that sports gambling could be a bad influence on young people. Former Senator DeConcini indicated that

The spread of legalized sports gambling threatens to lure our youth into all types of gambling. It threatens the very foundation of professional and amateur sporting events, which is to provide wholesome entertainment for all ages.

Sports Is Just Another Opportunity for Gambling

Opponents of the bills, mainly representatives from the various states which were considering such gambling possibilities in order to raise money, plus the North American Association of State & Provincial Lotteries (NASPL), believed the sports leagues were being hypocritical. They wondered why the sports businesses were willing to accept sports betting in Nevada but would not accept it in other states that need the money just as badly. Furthermore, they argued, the sports leagues were aware that billions of dollars were bet illegally on sporting events, so that the opportunity for gamblers' influence on players and referees already existed.

NASPL President James Hosker observed,

More than $1.5 billion is wagered annually on sports in Nevada and an estimated $15 billion to $20 billion nationwide. The leagues have long been aware of this activity and have taken virtually no action to prevent it. If this has not undermined the integrity of professional sports, state-sponsored sports lotteries will not do so.

Similarly, Oregon Lottery Director James Davey observed,

The leagues have long known of extensive wagering in Nevada and the publication of point spread in virtually every major newspaper and have done nothing.... The leagues' attempts to ban carefully regulated, state-run sports pool lotteries cannot be justified.

Proponents further pointed out that the various pre-game sports shows (usually for football games) featured the point spreads (see Chapter VIII) that the sports leagues knew were used for betting on the games. Apparently stung by such criticism, the National Football League (NFL) has tried to pressure the networks carrying their games not to discuss the odds or point spread on these pre-game shows, although without success. Moreover, virtually every sports page in every newspaper carries the point spread and other odds attached to the game. The National Basketball Association (NBA) sued the Oregon Lottery Commission to forbid them from using the scores of basketball games as the basis of their lottery's sports lottery game. The NBA and the commission settled out of court, with the commission agreeing not to offer betting on professional basketball games for the next five years.

The Professional and Amateur Sports Protection Act of 1992

On October 28, 1992, former Senator DeConcini's and then-Representative Bryant's bills were enacted into law as the Professional and Amateur Sports Protection Act of 1992 (PL 102-559). The law forbids betting on professional and collegiate sports but exempts all existing sports betting in Delaware, Nevada, Oregon, and Montana. New Jersey had until January 1, 1994, to introduce sports betting should it choose, which it did not. Horse racing, dog racing, and jai-alai were in no way affected by this law.

GAMBLING ON CRUISE SHIPS

When ships are three miles off the coast of the United States, there generally has been no regulation over the gambling that may or may not take place on board. In 1992, Congress approved a general maritime law (PL 102-251) that included a section permitting gambling on cruise ships. The law allowed U.S. flag ships within the 3-mile limit to operate gambling facilities on board as long as the gambling was not the sole purpose of the cruise. Gambling was permitted only on international and interstate (between states) voyages. This law actually applied to very few cruise ships since, of the 100-plus cruise ships that dock at American ports, barely 2 percent are registered in the United States.

Any gambling that took place in ports located within a single state would be regulated by that state. "Cruises to nowhere," gambling trips in which the ship sails out into international waters and then cruises around while the passengers gamble, would be controlled by the state from which the ship left port. Currently, only Florida, Georgia, and Texas allow "cruises to nowhere," although California and South Carolina are considering such options.

Some cruises leaving Los Angeles stopped at other California ports (Catalina and San Diego). Up until the passage of the new legislation, foreign ships had been operating casino games as they traveled between California ports, such as Los Angeles, Catalina, and San Diego. Dan Lungren, attorney general of California, decided to reconsider the situation in light of the new legislation, which allowed the individual states to regulate such intrastate cruises operated by foreign owners.

As a result, in 1992, California passed a new law (AB3769) banning gambling on both American and foreign registered ships traveling between ports in the state. The law also reemphasized the state's ban on "cruises to nowhere." Faced with a loss of gambling revenue, several cruise lines cancelled stops in Catalina and San Diego, whose tourist industry lost many millions of dollars in revenue. Currently, the cruise lines are fighting to have the new law reconsidered or reinterpreted in such a way that would permit the resumption of gambling on their ships when they travel between California ports.

The cruise ship industry was dealt another severe blow in Alaska. Cruises up the coast to Alaska have become very popular, offering travelers the opportunity to see some of the most beautiful scenery in the world, along with whales and polar bears. Up until recently the ships have been sailing the inland passages and waterways of Alaska with the casinos open and producing revenues. Then, in 1993, the Federal Bureau of Investigation (FBI) ruled that these cruise ships had been violating the law because they were sailing in Alaska waters, and Alaska did not permit casino gambling. The FBI ordered the casinos closed when they were in Alaskan waters.

As a result, the Alaska state legislature quickly passed a bill that would allow the casinos to operate in Alaskan waters. After all, tourism is the state's number one industry, and cruise ships are an important part of that business. Much to the surprise of many, former Governor Walter Hickel vetoed the bill, claiming he was "fundamentally opposed to gambling, because it adds nothing to civilization." This was an economic blow to the cruise industry since the casinos will now likely be open perhaps one day each way as they travel through international waters to and from Alaska.

GAMBLING ON AIRCRAFT

Gambling has become so widespread that some legislators were concerned wagering would be introduced in the nation's commercial airliners. In the early 1990s, many airlines were suffering financially, and lengthy international flights in jumbo jets that can be reconfigured to include small gambling areas were considered an opportunity to earn additional revenue.

The Federal Aviation Administration Authorization Act of 1994 (PL 103-305) forbad the use of "any gambling device on board an aircraft in foreign air transportation." At the same time, the law required the secretary of transportation to consider three issues. The first question concerned the potential safety risks represented by the effects of electronic gambling machines on the navigational and other electronic equipment of the aircraft. The second appraised the competitive implications of permitting foreign air carriers, but not American air carriers, to install gambling devices on international flights. Finally, the third question considered whether gambling should be allowed on international flights.

GAMBLING ON NATIVE AMERICAN RESERVATIONS

Gambling on Indian reservations can be found in almost half the states in the country. However, today's widespread Indian gambling did not just happen. It is the product of a three-decade long effort by Native Americans to develop an industry most of them believe will benefit their people and their reservations.

Because of historical tribal treaties, Native American reservations have been under exclusive federal jurisdiction and thereby exempt from the laws of the state in which they are located. However, under PL 83-280, passed in 1968, Congress granted civil and criminal jurisdiction over reservations to the states, as long as the move was approved by tribal consent. This statute was passed with the understanding that federal supervision would gradually be eliminated and state jurisdiction would prevail. The most controversial issue arising from PL 83-280 concerns taxation — it prohibited the states from collecting a tax on Indian activities. Nevertheless, many state governments, searching for additional sources of revenue, have shown an interest in collecting such taxes, but their efforts, so far, have failed.

Turning to Bingo

Like the states, Native American tribes saw their federal funding cut back during the 1980s, and they began looking for another source of income. Many tribes decided to take advantage of their unique sovereign status and set up gambling (mainly bingo) operations on their reservations. By the end of the 1980s, Native American tribes were sponsoring over 100 gambling operations, most of them high-stakes bingo games, which were producing more than $100 million in revenues annually for the tribes. Some bingo games became so big that prizes reached $100,000.

Wanting a Part of the Take — Trying to Tax the Income

Not surprisingly, many states with these reservations wanted to regulate and, perhaps, tax the income from the gambling. The state of Florida wanted to regulate bingo games played on Seminole land, but the Fifth Circuit Court of Appeals, in *Seminole Tribe of Florida v. Butterworth* (658 F.2d 310, 1981), ruled that the state could not regulate bingo on the reservation if the game were legal in the state. The Supreme Court denied *certiorari* (would not hear) (455 US 1020, 1982), letting the lower court decision stand. (*Barona Groups of Captain Grande Band of Mission Indians v. State of Wisconsin* [694 F.2d 1185, 1982] and *Oneida Tribe of Indians v. State of Wisconsin* [518 F. Supp. 712, 1981] produced similar rulings.)

In 1987, the U.S. Supreme Court, in *California v. Cabazon of Mission Indians* (480 US 202), ruled that states generally may not regulate gaming on Native American reservations, but that the federal government does have the authority to regulate or forbid Native American gaming enterprises and to delegate authority to the states.

In 1986, the Bureau of Indian Affairs (BIA) reversed a long-standing policy by notifying Indian tribes that the BIA must approve bingo management contracts with outside companies. This ruling was an attempt by the federal government to become involved in what had previously been a state-regulated gambling industry. The federal government was concerned about the possibility of organized crime controlling gambling on Native American reservations and the possibility that large gambling winnings might go unreported, since tribal revenues are unaudited and cannot be taxed.

The Indian Gaming Regulatory Act

Meanwhile, Congress had already begun to try to resolve the problem. Like many controversial issues, it took a long time (six years) to reach a compromise that would satisfy the competing factions. The federal government claimed to be concerned that organized crime would take over the Native American games, the states were offended by any gambling activities within their borders that they did not regulate, and the Native Americans resented any intrusion on their lands or tribal rights.

In 1988, Congress passed, and President Ronald Reagan signed into law, the Indian Gaming Regulatory Act (IGRA, PL 100-497) which permits

> Indian tribes [to] have the exclusive right to regulate gaming activity on Indian lands if the gaming activity is not specifically prohibited by Federal law and is conducted within a State which does not, as a matter of criminal law and public policy, prohibit such gaming activity.

The law creates three different categories of gambling. "Class I gaming" refers to "social games solely for prizes of minimal value or traditional forms of Indian gaming" which would be regulated only by the tribe. "Class II gaming," which includes bingo, lotto, and other games similar to bingo (and specifically does not include baccarat, chemin de fer, or blackjack), would be under the regulation of a National Indian Gaming Commission set up by the law. "Class III gaming" refers to all other forms of gambling, including casinos, slot machines, and horse and dog racing. These gambling activities would not take place on Native American lands unless they were permitted in the state and unless the tribe reached an agreement with the state.

A "grandfather clause" would permit certain card games, most notably blackjack, to be continued to be played in the states of Michigan, North Dakota, South Dakota, and Washington, since they were already in operation.

The National Indian Gaming Commission consists of three full-time members, the chairman appointed by the president of the United States with the advice and consent of the Senate, and the other two appointed by the secretary of the interior. No more than two members can come from the same political party, and at least two members have to be enrolled in a Native American tribe.

The commission has the power to regulate Class II and Class III gambling on Native American lands, although Class III gambling is also controlled by agreements between the tribe and the state within which the reservation is located. Finally, the states could not tax the Native American earnings from gambling, and, in fact, the law specifically states that a court "shall consider any demand by the State for direct taxation of the Indian tribe or of any Indian lands as evidence that the State has not negotiated in good faith."

State-Tribal Compacts

As a result of the law, states and tribes have entered compacts to permit gambling facilities to be developed on Native American lands. By December 1997, 147 tribes in 24 states had reached 158 compacts with the governments in the states within which their lands were located. Many of these compacts have already led to very successful casino operations, and more will develop in the near future. (See Chapter VII.)

Not Always Easy

Nonetheless, the procedure of making state compacts has not always been easy. Some states, including California and New Mexico, have been reluctant to negotiate with Native Americans. On the other side, many Native American leaders resent having to deal with state officials. In the past, they have only had to deal with federal officials. In addition, many Native American leaders believe that having to reach a compact agreement with states compromises their authority as sovereign nations.

Several states have gone to court in order to avoid reaching a compact with a Native American tribe. The states claimed the Tenth Amendment reserves to the states all powers not delegated to the federal government by the Constitution.* They also argued that the Eleventh Amendment declares that a state may not be sued by individuals based on federal legislation (unless clearly so stated by Congress). In many states, including Washington, North Carolina, Arizona, New Mexico, and Massachusetts, state and tribal authorities have clashed. In Alaska, the state passed a law banning Monte Carlo nights so that they would not have to agree to permit casino gambling on land belonging to the Klawock Band of Tlingit Native Alaskans.

THE STATES AND NATIVE AMERICANS GO TO COURT OVER IGRA

Several courts of appeals have reached mixed findings on these questions, and the resolution of the issue will have to await the rulings of the U.S. Supreme Court.

Cheyenne River Sioux Tribe v. South Dakota

In *Cheyenne River Sioux Tribe v. South Dakota* (3 F.3d 273, 1993), the Eighth Circuit Court of Appeals held that the Indian Gaming Regulatory Act (IGRA) did not violate either the Tenth or the Eleventh Amendments of the United States Constitution. The Cheyenne River Sioux had gone to court claiming that South Dakota had refused to negotiate in good faith with them. The tribe had wanted to offer keno because the Cheyenne River Sioux claimed that the state permitted video keno. The state claimed the games were quite different, and the circuit court agreed, indicating that South Dakota did not have to

permit keno because it did not allow keno in the state. Furthermore, the state could impose a $5 betting limit on Indian gambling because "bet limits are established by state law" and covered all other betting in the state.

However, the court ruled that IGRA did not violate the Tenth Amendment because (quoting from an earlier case) "Congress, when acting pursuant to the Indian Commerce Clause, has the power to abrogate (invalidate) the States' [Eleventh Amendment] immunity."

Concerning the Tenth Amendment, the circuit court ruled that IGRA did not force states to negotiate since the states can refuse to respond. There are a number of options, and if the state refuses to negotiate, a mediator can choose to accept the tribe's proposed compact. Obviously, negotiating is in the best interest of the state, but it does not have to do it. "Therefore," declared the court, "we hold the IGRA does not force the state to compact with Indian tribes regarding the Indian gaming and does not violate the Tenth Amendment."

Rumsey Indian Rancheria of Wintun Indians v. Wilson, Governor, State of California

In *Rumsey Indian Rancheria of Wintun Indians v. Wilson, Governor, State of California* (41 F 3d 421, 1994), the Ninth Circuit Court of Appeals agreed with the Eighth Circuit. The Rumsey Indian tribe had asked permission to have casino games, such as slot machines and blackjack. The tribe noted that the state already permitted video lottery terminals, pari-mutuel horse racing, and poker, which were "functionally similar" to the games the tribe wanted.

The Ninth Circuit Court did not agree. The games that the Rumsey tribe wanted were different from the ones already permitted in the state.

---

*"The Judicial power of the United States shall not be construed to extend to any suit in law or equity, commenced or prosecuted against one of the United States by Citizens of another State, or by Citizens or subjects of any Foreign State."

Simply because a state permitted some gambling did not mean it had to permit all types of gambling. "We agree with the approach taken by the Eighth Circuit," said the court.

> IGRA does not require a state to negotiate over one form of a gaming activity simply because it has legalized another, albeit similar, form of gaming. Instead, the statute says only that, if a state allows a gaming activity "for any purpose by any person, organization, or entity," then it also must allow Indian tribes to engage in that same activity. In other words, a state need only allow Indian tribes to operate games that others can operate, but need not give tribes what others cannot have.

Seminole Tribe of Florida v. Florida

When the State of Florida refused to negotiate with the Seminole Tribe of Florida, the tribe took the state to court to compel them to negotiate under the terms of the Indian Gaming Regulatory Act (IGRA). The State of Florida countered that they were under no obligation to negotiate because the Eleventh Amendment of the U.S. Constitution granted the state sovereign immunity from being sued. The Eleventh Circuit Court of Appeals, in Seminole Tribe of Florida v. Florida (11 F.3d 1016, 1994), agreed with the State of Florida and said that the Seminole tribe did not have the right to sue the State of Florida.

The court agreed with the earlier cases that the Congress had, indeed, clearly intended to void the state's Eleventh Amendment immunity. On the other hand, unless the state had consented to be sued, which they had not, "Congress, when it enacted IGRA pursuant to the Indian Commerce Clause, lacked the power to abrogate (void) the states' sovereign immunity" and, therefore, the state could not be sued. The court recognized the right of the states, under certain circumstances, to be sued under the Interstate Commerce Act, but the Indian Commerce Act was not the Interstate Commerce Act and did not apply. Consequently,

the court concluded, "The principles of federalism and sovereign immunity exemplified in the Eleventh Amendment prevent Congress from abrogating the states' immunity."

The court closed, noting that

> Nevertheless, we are left with the question as to what procedure is left for an Indian tribe faced with a state that not only will not negotiate in good faith, but also will not consent to sit. The answer, gleaned from the statute, is simple. One hundred and eighty days after the tribe first requests negotiations with the state, the tribe may file suit in district court. If the state pleads an Eleventh Amendment defense, the suit is dismissed, and the tribe ... then may notify the Secretary of the Interior of the tribe's failure to negotiate a compact with the state. The secretary then may prescribe regulations governing class III gaming on the tribe's lands. This solution conforms with IGRA and serves to achieve Congress' goals....

This case was appealed to the U.S. Supreme Court, and in Seminole Tribe of Florida v. Florida (64 LW 4167), the High Court upheld the findings of the Eleventh Circuit Court of Appeals. The Court noted that

> Notwithstanding Congress' clear intent to abrogate the States' sovereign immunity, the Indian Commerce Clause does not grant Congress that power, and therefore ... cannot grant jurisdiction over a State that does not consent to be sued.

The High Court concluded that

> The Eleventh Amendment prohibits Congress from making the State of Florida capable of being sued in federal court.

The Seminoles' claim against the state of Florida was dismissed.

However, while it might have appeared that Indian tribes had suffered a defeat, some Indian observers thought the decision might work to their benefit. The Supreme Court had not resolved the issue of whether the Indian tribes could go directly to the Department of Interior as recommended in the court of appeals ruling (see above). Tom Wapato, National Indian Gaming Association Executive Director, observed that "the result ... is that the case returns the tribes to pre-IGRA time where the interior secretary is responsible for completing gaming agreements with tribes."

Apparently the states, instead of having at least some power to control the development of Indian gambling casinos within their state borders, may now be left out of the process. Decisions in which they had had at least some input would now be decided by federal authorities in Washington. Many Indian leaders believe that they will get better treatment from the Department of the Interior than they had received from some reluctant states. The states, on the other hand, might have achieved a Pyrrhic victory (a too costly victory). While they might have won their case, they may not be better off. (See Chapter VII for political problems that have developed.)

Spokane Tribe of Indians v. Washington State

The Spokane Tribe of Indians and the state of Washington met a number of times from 1989 through 1991 in an unsuccessful attempt to reach a mutually acceptable compact. Unsatisfied, the tribe filed a complaint against the State of Washington claiming the state had failed to negotiate in good faith and asking for an injunction ordering the parties to conclude a compact within 60 days. The State of Washington claimed that the suit had no validity because the state had immunity based on the Eleventh Amendment of the U.S. Constitution. The Ninth Circuit Court of Appeals, in *Spokane Tribe of Indians v. Washington State* (28 F.3d 991, 1994), did not agree.

Concerning whether Congress intended to abrogate the state's immunity, the court observed

Our discussion of congressional intent need not be lengthy. Every federal court that has considered the issue has concluded that the IGRA's language reveals a clear intent to abrogate the states' Eleventh Amendment immunity.

Concerning the Indian Commerce Clause and the Interstate Commerce Clause, the court observed that it

Cannot agree ... that the differences between the Indian and the Interstate Commerce Clauses support state immunity from tribal suit where, as here, Congress has authorized such suits. Congress' power over both Indian and interstate commerce is set forth in Article I, ¶ 8:

The Congress shall have power, ...

3. To regulate commerce with foreign nations, and among the several states, and with the Indian tribes.

... Congressional power pursuant to the Indian Commerce Clause, then, cannot be less than its authority under the Interstate Commerce Clause.

The Ninth Circuit Court concluded that

Congress tried to fashion a plan (IGRA) that would enable the states to have a choice in how tribal gaming should operate and to enforce to some degree the states' own laws. The states' immunity from suits under the Eleventh Amendment should not frustrate that goal. Indeed, principles of state sovereignty are singularly out of place in such a scheme, where the federal government is tailoring a limited grant of power to the states. In this case, sovereign immunity would undermine rather than remove the assertion of state interests.

The court strongly disagreed with the Eleventh Circuit Court's conclusion in *Seminole Tribe of Florida v. Florida* (see above) that the case could always be referred to the secretary of the interior. The secretary of the interior, said the Ninth Circuit Court, should be only "a matter of last resort." The compact should be reached through negotiations between the state and the tribe so that resolution benefitting both sides can be reached. Using the secretary of interior as the expected, eventual arbitrator of the issue "would turn the Secretary of the Interior into a federal czar, contrary to the congressional aim of state participation."

National Indian Gaming Commission

Finally, after several years, the National Indian Gaming Commission (NIGC) reached full membership and began to prepare long overdue guidelines to provide some oversight for the Native American gambling industry. Beginning in 1993, the National Indian Gaming Commission began daily oversight of Class II gaming (mainly bingo) and, with approval of management, contracts, and tribal rules on Class III gaming (casinos, slot machines, etc.). Most regulation on Class III gaming, however, will be established in the state-tribe compacts.

Many tribal leaders resent NIGC having any control over them. They feel they have had two hundred years of oversight by federal agencies, most notably the Bureau of Indian Affairs, and it has done them little good. They further think they are fully capable of running their reservations and the business done on those reservations, and they do not need NIGC looking over their shoulders. The tribal leaders know that certainly some of them will fail, and others may be cheated by unscrupulous business people, but these circumstances happen in all sorts of business

endeavors, and there is no reason they should be singled out for oversight.

On the other hand, Tony Hope, former Chairman of the National Indian Gaming Commission, believed that regulation would actually promote the profitability for gambling on Indian reservations. When customers know that the Indian casinos are regulated, they will have more faith in the integrity of the games and will, therefore, be more likely to go to the reservations to gamble. Hope believed that regulation is not an issue of tribal sovereignty, but a matter of sound business. His successor, Harold Monteau, also indicated his desire to take "a leadership role in encouraging in the development of strong tribal regulatory structures."

There are approximately 300 tribes in the United States, and it will not be easy for the NIGC to find agreement among this large group. Like any group of hundreds of different sovereign entities, they have hundreds of different positions and needs. Just as there is no single generic nation in the world, there is no single generic Native American tribe. The NIGC faces a considerable challenge and will have to recognize this diversity and learn to work with this wide variety of opinions and situations.

The rapid growth of casino gambling on Native American reservations has led to the introduction of several proposed pieces of legislation designed to change the Indian Gaming Regulatory Act (IGRA). In 1993, Representative Robert Torricelli (D-NJ) and Senator Harry Reid (D-NV) introduced similar bills on the same day calling for the limiting of Class III Native American gambling. Representative Torricelli's bill, the Gaming Integrity and State Enforcement Act of 1993, and Senator Reid's proposal, the Indian Gaming Regulatory Act Amendments, both prohibited Native American gambling compacts unless the state permitted the gaming as part of a commercial, for-profit enterprise within the state. In addition, just because a state permitted one type of Class III gaming, most notably a lottery, did not mean that it had to permit other forms of Class III gaming, such as a casino.

Both bills also proposed to make the state a more equal power in the preparation of the compact and less subject to the threat that they were not bargaining in good faith. Both congressmen claimed that Native American gaming had gotten out of control. Meanwhile, Senator Daniel Inouye (D-HI), Chairman of the Senate Indian Affairs Committee, had spent a great deal of time meeting with Native American leaders and government officials in an effort to reach a compromise that would essentially leave IGRA intact. Neither bill ever became law.

In the following 104th Congress (1995), advocates of stricter control of Native American gambling in the Senate introduced a bill (S 487) that would require Native American tribes to license games, conduct strict background checks on important casino workers, and provide the federal government with periodic accounting of gambling revenues and profits. Initially, the bill had included provisions that allowed tribes to bypass states which refused to negotiate compacts. Tribes in many states had been blocked in their efforts to draw up compacts and introduce gambling on their reservations.

Despite all of the other proposals which the tribal authorities had considered offensive, this provision was considered so important that it had led many Indian leaders to support S 487. Native American leaders found that their support was considered unnecessary since this provision was removed from the bill before it won approval from the Senate Committee on Indian Affairs.

In the House of Representatives, legislators proposed a bill calling for the federal government to tax Indian gaming. Thinking they would be more successful in the Senate, Native American representatives lobbied Senate leaders to oppose the House bill when it reached the Senate for consideration. Their efforts focused upon then-Senate Majority Leader Robert Dole (R-KS). They reminded him that tribal governments have never been taxed before, that much of the money earned is being used for social needs, that this is the only successful economic activity on Indian reservations, and finally, that the Republicans had promised no new taxes, and this pledge should include Native Americans. Senator Dole, through a spokeswoman, indicated that he opposed the tax and would fight to keep it out of the Senate budget. The proposal, however, never made it out of House committee.

Using Tribal Winnings to Replace Tribal Allocations

Native American tribes receive Tribal Priority Allocations (TPA) from the Department of Interior to provide educational and social services on their reservations. These fundings are essential for the operation of the reservations. In 1995, the Senate Interior Appropriations Committee proposed that the secretary of the interior, the administrator responsible for providing funding to Indian reservations, use a "means test" to determine how much funding each tribe should get. Initially, the draft bill indicated, "Notwithstanding any other provision of law, the secretary of the interior may reduce the funds provided in this act for tribes receiving gaming revenues in order to minimize the need for funding reductions for other tribes." This meant that those tribes earning monies from gambling would receive less money, an amount likely equal to their earnings from gambling.

Although this provision was eventually removed from the funding bill, this attitude still likely prevails. Congress is looking everywhere to cut spending, and Native Americans have relatively little political clout in Congress. In addition, the success of gambling on many Indian reservations has led many people to think that Native Americans are rolling in money. While many Indian casino ventures have proved quite successful, most have not earned enough to lift their reservations out of the economic hardship that characterizes most reservations.

DEALING WITH STATE GOVERNMENTS

In the recent past, when the nation's major concern was to control illegal gambling, the federal government was the main enforcement level of government. Gambling was illegal almost everywhere in the country. Gambling laws were designed to control gambling and catch bookies, operators of illegal card games, and the members of criminal syndicates who dominated illegal gambling. Gambling was a criminal matter, and federal laws were designed to put those who ran the illegal operations behind bars. Even in the few places where it was legal, most notably Las Vegas, it was thought, quite correctly, that criminal elements played a major role in gambling operations.

During the past several years, the political landscape has been turned upside down. Few people are arrested for illegal gambling (see Chapter III), and many Americans tolerate gambling as readily as they accept other forms of entertainment, such as the movies and sporting events. While the federal laws are still on the books, they seem to have little applicability to the modern gambling industry.

Gambling has become a major part of the entertainment industry. Companies offering gambling are like any other businesses in the entertainment industry. Like so many businesses, expansion has been the order of the day. Unlike the growth in many industries, most political issues have not passed through Washington, DC, but rather through state capitals such as Jackson, Mississippi; Jefferson City, Missouri; Baton Rouge, Louisiana; Des Moines, Iowa; and Denver, Colorado.

Making Gambling Interests Heard

The state legislatures decide if gambling will become legal in the individual states. Currently, some form of gambling is legal in all states except Hawaii and Utah. While success is never assured, revenue-hungry state governments are virtually always willing to give gambling interests a hearing.

Like any industry, gambling companies want their interests to be heard in the state capitals. They hire lobbyists and donate to political campaigns. While major donations do not necessarily buy votes, they usually earn the right to be heard. In 1996, gambling interests saturated the state of Arkansas with one of the industry's largest campaigns for casino gambling. Arkansas rejected the proposal. Six other states — Ohio, Washington, Colorado, Iowa, Nebraska, and Louisiana — also rejected wagering proposals on election day. Only Michigan voters passed a proposal to permit casinos in economically depressed Detroit. (Louisiana rejected one gambling proposal, but passed two others.)

Political contributions by gambling corporations have led to scandals in Louisiana, Missouri, Arizona, Kentucky, South Carolina, and West Virginia. For example, it is suspected that video poker operators in Louisiana had bribed state legislators to kill proposed anti-gambling legislation. (As a result of that scandal, in 1996, Louisiana voters voted to end video poker in 33 of the state's 34 parishes.) The attorney general of Pennsylvania pleaded guilty to hiding contributions from operators of illegal video poker games. Legislators in Arizona, Kentucky, South Carolina, and West Virginia have been convicted of taking bribes from gambling interests. When so much money is involved, there is always the chance for corruption.

Modern gambling is generally a well-regulated business. Virtually every state that permits casino gambling or pari-mutuel betting has a state racing or gambling commission to monitor gambling activities. While today's gambling industry is big business run by huge corporations, virtually every state regulatory commission feels it must show it is making sure that no underworld or syndicate figures play a role in its state gambling activities. The commissions also control other activities, such as how late casinos may stay open and whether there will be limits on betting. Since these regulations are usually determined by state legislatures, it is only natural that gambling companies try to influence their decisions through lobbyists and political donations.

At the same time, however, although the gambling business is now controlled by major entertainment corporations, they still must bear the stigma of their history. Gambling money was once mob money. Twenty years ago, if a legislator was found to have accepted money to handle a gambling matter, it was assumed that it was syndicate money, and the legislator's career was likely in jeopardy. Today, although gambling has become just another matter handled by state legislatures, gambling money still appears as tainted money to some.

Some Money Still Goes to Washington

Although state capitals have become more important than the federal capital in regulating gambling, it does not mean that the gambling industry has forgotten the federal government. For example, The Center for Public Integrity, a Washington-based research organization, reported that gambling interests had contributed more than $200,000 to Bob Dole's presidential campaign and $60,000 to President Clinton's campaign by 1996. The amount of these contributions were eight times more than the industry had ever donated previously to a presidential election. The Center for Responsive Politics, a nonpartisan watchdog organization, reported that the gambling industry donated more than $130,000 to Republican congressional candidates and $53,000 to Democratic congressional candidates in 1995.

OPPOSITION TO GAMBLING

The rapid expansion of gambling across the United States has not been well received by all Americans. The failure of many gambling initiatives over the past few years indicates an opposition powerful enough to either influence state legislators to drop proposed legislation allowing various forms of gambling in their state or to garner enough votes to defeat initiatives that would do the same thing.

Varied Reasons for Opposition

Opposition to gambling can include a wide variety of interests. Some business people might fear that a casino could draw spending away from their restaurants or hotels. Many point out that gambling casinos rarely bring in as much income to the area or tax revenues to the government as gambling promoters claim. Others fear that crime will increase as more people are drawn to gambling. One gambling interest might oppose another gambling interest. For example, horse and track owners often oppose the introduction of casino gambling, as do owners of "cruise ships to nowhere," which leave ports in New York and Florida and sail into international waters so that passengers can gamble on the casinos onboard.

A Moral Issue

Many who oppose gambling consider it morally or theologically wrong. The domestic violence and crime that might result from compulsive gambling could lead to the breakdown of the family and divorce. Gambling, especially the lotteries, contributes to the attitude that a person can get something for nothing, a belief many people consider particularly harmful to the nation's morality. The states, by administering the lotteries, have become party to this. By sanctioning gambling, government authorities have contributed to making gambling publicly acceptable. Many opponents believe that government and community leaders have had a choice between money and morality and, in all too many cases, have chosen money. Not only have they degraded their own integrity, but they have also debased the values of their communities.

Some people consider gambling a social and economic, as well as a moral, issue. In many instances, poorer people will spend a higher

TABLE 2.1

THE CASE AGAINST LEGALIZED GAMBLING

1. **Gambling creates no new wealth.** It redistributes wealth on an inequitable basis. It enriches the few and impoverishes the many. Gambling is non-productive. It performs no useful or necessary services. Gambling is parasitic.

2. **Gambling depresses legitimate business,** siphoning off money from the regular business community. It dislocates the purchasing dollar. Business leaders are reluctant to invest money in areas that sustain large gambling enterprises because of the ensuing bad debts, delinquent time payments, and bankruptcy. Gambling disrupts the normal checks and balances of a well-ordered community. Gambling restricts business.

3. **Gambling increases welfare costs.** Gambling weakens the stability of family life. Gambling lowers the standard of living and necessitates a larger welfare burden, thus raising taxes. Increased revenue from gambling means larger claims for welfare.

4. **Gambling increases crime.** Gambling always attracts racketeers and mobsters. Gambling increases the number of murders, assaults, robberies, crimes of violence of all kinds, etc. The underworld thrives on gambling. Police costs increase.

5. **Gambling corrupts government.** Gamblers always seek to increase their odds and to buy protection. Gamblers are soul-less in attempting to corrupt police, judges and legislators. Instead of the state controlling legalized gambling, the professional gamblers often end up in control of the state.

6. **Gambling produces human desperation.** Gambling victimizes the poor. Gambling leads to embezzlement, bribes, extortion, treason, suicide, and corruption of college and professional athletes. Crime often results from victims trying to recoup gambling losses. Those who can least afford it usually gamble the most. Gambling exploits the weaknesses of individuals. Gambling and poverty go hand in hand. Inner-city residents are hurt the most by expanded gambling.

7. **Gambling is a sophisticated form of legalized stealing.** In winning, one obtains the wages that another person has earned without giving anything in exchange. The larger the winnings, the more someone else had to lose.

8. **Gambling produces the wrong attitudes toward work.** It promotes the idea that a person can live by his wits and luck without making any contribution to society.

9. **Gambling contradicts social responsibilities.** Mature adults try to minimize the risks in life. Gambling seeks to maximize risks. Responsible societies attempt to build security into life, gambling undermines security. Gambling deliberately creates artificial and unnecessary risks. Gambling militates against the highest values of human welfare. History shows that a major increase in gambling has signified the decline of a nation.

10. **Gambling revenues violate all the sound theories of taxation.** Gambling revenue is regressive, inequitable, variable and unpredictable. To make public services dependent upon erratic gambling "taxes" is irresponsible. Public service should be soundly financed.

11. **As a source of state revenue, gambling has a consistent record of failure.** Proponents promise huge government income from legalized gambling, but only a trickle of money results. Even in Nevada, only about one-third of the state's budget comes from gambling. Lotteries have been discredited as a source of school funds.

12. **Gambling is socially disintegrating,** politically corrupt and morally dangerous. Gambling is bad business, bad politics and bad morals. The State cannot gamble itself rich.

Source: National Coalition Against Legalized Gambling, Birmingham, AL

proportion of their income on gambling. A gambler might gamble away a paycheck, or even the family savings. The family might end up on welfare, costing the government money. A gambler might steal from the job in order to pay off gambling debts and get fired for stealing, or might become indebted to a loan shark who will charge extremely high interest and harm him if he does not pay. Under pressure from debts, he might beat his wife and/or children. The gambler, deep in debt, the whole world crumbling around him, might commit suicide.

Increased Addiction

An estimated 0.7 percent of Americans are addicted to gambling. The spread of lotteries and casino gambling has increased the opportunities for those already addicted to gamble more, and for those who have the potential to become addicted, but who have never been exposed to gambling, to become hooked. Observers estimate that with the increased opportunities to gamble, the proportion of compulsive gamblers has increased to 2 to 5 percent of those who gamble. They consider this a significant percentage, certainly high enough to make anyone think twice about introducing gambling into his area. In the long run, opponents claim, the treatment of compulsive gamblers and their families, the effects of increased crime, and the loss of business in other areas will cost far more than any revenues produced by the casinos or lotteries.

THE NATIONAL COALITION AGAINST LEGALIZED GAMBLING

The National Coalition Against Legalized Gambling (Washington, DC) believes that "this surge toward legalized gambling must stop before it destroys our communities." The National Coalition supports the passage of legislation to study the social and economic effects of gambling on the United States. Undoubtedly, the National Coalition hopes that the results of this study will either slow down or stop the expansion of gambling and lead to federal regulation that might even roll back some of the gambling already in existence.

The National Coalition also hopes to stop the development of interactive gambling on the Internet or cable television. "The Case against Legalized Gambling," a Coalition release, summarizes the arguments against gambling (Table 2.1). In 1996, the National Coalition opened up an office in Washington, DC to lobby Congress more effectively.

The Reverend Tom Grey, Executive Director of the National Coalition Against Legalized Gambling, in testimony before the House Judiciary Committee (September 29, 1995), summed up the Coalition's position when he observed,

> to many Americans, government's promotion of gambling is a cop-out and a double-cross. We see public officials sacrificing our communities to a predatory enterprise — for money. Citizens see government living off gambling profits, taken from the poorest and weakest of our citizens, instead of facing up to rational choices regarding budgets and taxes.

The National Coalition (its president and executive director are both ministers) receives considerable support from conservative Christian groups, such as Focus on the Family and the Christian Coalition, as well as many mainline churches. This backing gives the organization considerable grassroots support and the ability to mobilize letters to congressmen or votes in ballot initiatives. The National Coalition claims to have played a major role in the defeat of dozens of proposed gambling casinos.

THE AMERICAN GAMING ASSOCIATION

In order to present the best image of the industry to state and federal governments and to the public, the gambling industry has established the American Gaming Association (AGA) as an industry trade group. Frank J. Fahrenkopf, Jr., former national chairman of the Republican Party and former lawyer in Reno, Nevada, was chosen as the group's first president. One of his main responsibilities is to see that the federal government is aware of the gambling industry's position on whatever gambling issues the federal government might consider. In addition to lobbying the federal government concerning the needs and position of the nation's gambling industry, the AGA also intends to educate the public about the industry and to act as a clearinghouse for information about the industry.

The industry believes that American consumers want to enjoy gambling as a form of entertainment. Certainly the huge increases in gambling revenues show both that the American marketplace wants gambling and that need has not yet been filled. Gambling brings employment as has been shown by the many tens of thousands of workers employed at gambling casinos and riverboats.

The industry considers syndicate control of gambling very much a thing of the past. Gambling is now a major entertainment industry operated by publicly owned companies that are monitored by the Securities and Exchange Commission (SEC). The mob probably could not raise the many hundreds of millions of dollars needed to develop a new resort complex.

The industry does not accept the argument that gambling does not produce anything. They note that, in the same sense, Disneyland or Disney World do not produce anything either. People go to Las Vegas and Disneyland to be entertained and have fun. It is not appropriate to compare a Las Vegas casino or Disney World with a manufacturing plant, such General Motors or Gateway Computers. One is a service or entertainment industry; the other is a manufacturing industry. People go to a casino or to Disneyland to have fun. If they have a good time, then they have gotten their money's worth.

Supporters of gambling claim that increased crime does not accompany gambling. State gaming commissions work very hard to make sure that casino ownership and management not have any links to organized crime. Local crime increases proportionately no more than the growth in the population caused by the gambling casino. The crime rate in Orlando, Florida (where Disney World is located), is significantly higher than that in Las Vegas, Nevada, yet no one would claim that Mickey Mouse and Donald Duck contribute to crime.

The industry recognizes that for a small percentage of gamblers, addiction is a real problem. The industry has been supporting many states in the creation of agencies to help those people needing assistance. The industry also works hard to make sure that those under 18 years old do not gamble at casinos.

Finally, while some people may feel that gambling is morally unacceptable, they do not have the right to force their moral or religious views on others. If they do not want to gamble, they do not have to gamble. However, if their neighbor wants to gamble, that should be his or her choice.

See Chapters XII and XIII for a more complete debate on the issue of gambling.

THE NATIONAL GAMBLING AND POLICY COMMISSION

A bill creating a commission to study the impact of legalized gambling was signed into law by President Bill Clinton on August 3, 1997 (HR 497 — PL 104-169). The legislation, sponsored by Frank R. Wolf (R-VA) in the House and Paul Simon (D-IL) in the Senate, creates a nine-member federal commission to investigate all facets of gambling in America, including casinos, lotteries, sports betting, and Indian gambling. The purpose of the bill is to give policy makers advice on how to bring gambling into a state or community, or whether to bring it in at all.

The commission, which has the power to subpoena documents, has two years to submit a report to Congress, which shows the economic impact of gambling on an area's families and businesses. The report will also include the commission's findings on American Indian gambling, gambling on the Internet, and if there is any relationship between gambling and crime.

The commission was formed in response to the rapid nationwide growth in legalized gambling from 1976, when only two states permitted legal gambling, to 1996, when 48 states had some form of legalized wagering. Supporters of the bill claim that the surge in gambling has brought many problems with it, including a rise in crime and gambling addiction. However, opponents of the commission say that gambling regulation is the responsibility of the states and fear that the study will lead to more federal intervention.

GAMBLING — HERE TO STAY?

People in the United States are still torn between the perceived evils of gambling and its potential for raising money for social needs, such as education and care for the elderly. Politicians see it as a way to avoid raising taxes. Many Americans consider it just plain fun. Nonetheless, despite moral misgivings, the United States has become far more tolerant of gambling in recent years. Most states now operate lotteries, and an ever-growing number of states and communities are turning to some form of casino gambling to generate income.

CHAPTER III

AN OVERVIEW OF GAMBLING*

Of all the entertainment engines, right now gambling is humming the fastest.
Business Week, March 14, 1994

SOME DEFINITIONS

As with any industry or occupation, gambling has its own vocabulary. Following are a few terms that have a specific meaning in the gambling industry:

• Gaming — same as gambling.

• Wager — same as "bet," that is, the amount of money a person spends on a gambling activity.

• Handle — the total amount of money bet by all bettors on a specific gambling event or activity.

• Take-out — the percentage of the handle that is taken out by the operator of the gambling activity (the race track operator, for example) and by the state (in the form of taxes and license fees, etc.).

• Pay-off — the amount of money left over after the take-out; the amount which is distributed among the winning bettors.

TYPES OF LEGAL GAMBLING

There are five principal forms of legal gambling in the United States: bingo, lotteries, pari-mutuel betting, off-track betting, and casinos. According to the Organized Crime Control Act of 1970 (PL 91-452), the term gambling includes, but is not limited to, pool-selling; bookmaking; maintaining slot machines, roulette wheels, or dice tables; conducting lotteries, policy, bolita, or numbers games; or selling chances to these games. Legal gambling operations can be conducted by either a state or a private enterprise. Gambling operations must follow federal statutes but are generally regulated by state governments.

In 1997, some form of legal gambling was either operating or authorized to operate in 48 states plus Washington, DC, and the jurisdictions of Puerto Rico and the U.S. Virgin Islands. The only states that have no form of legal gambling either authorized or operating are Hawaii and Utah (which permits quarterhorse racing but no pari-mutuel gambling). North Carolina permits only charitable bingo.

Bingo is the most common form of legalized gambling (46 states, Washington, DC, and Puerto Rico). Forty-three states (although not necessarily operating), Puerto Rico, and the Virgin Islands permit thoroughbred horseracing. Lotteries are allowed in 37 states, Washington, DC, Puerto Rico, and the Virgin Islands. Twenty-two states and Puerto Rico permit casino gambling. Table 3.1

---

* Most of this chapter has been based upon "The United States — 96 Gross Annual Wager," *International Wagering Gaming and Business*, August 1997, prepared by Eugene Martin Christiansen and Will E. Cummings of Christiansen/Cummings Associates, Inc. Note that the industry uses the word "gaming" instead of gambling. This Information Plus publication has used the word gambling since its inception in 1979. To change the use of the term might indicate a lack of balance in the presentation, and therefore, this publication will continue to use the word gambling.

TABLE 3.1

United States Gaming at a Glance

	Charitable bingo	Charitable games	Card rooms	Casinos & gaming	Non-casino devices	Indian casinos	Indian bingo	Sports betting	Lottery operated games					Parimutuel wagering							
									Video lottery	Keno games	Instant/pulltabs	Lotto games	Numbers games	Greyhound	Jai-alai	Harness	Quarter Horse	Thoroughbred	Inter-track wagering	Off-track wagering	Telephone wagering
Alabama	●						●							●		◆	■	■	●		
Alaska	●	●					●														
Arizona	●	●				●	●				●	●		●			●	●	●	●	
Arkansas	●													●			◆	●	●	●	
California	●	●	●			☆	●			☐	●	●	●	●		●	●	●	●	●	
Colorado	●	●	●	●		●	●			●	●	●		●		●	●	●	●	●	
Connecticut	●	●				●	●			●	●	●	●	●	●	◆	◆	◆	◆	●	●
Delaware	●	●							●		●	●	●	●		●		●	●		
D.C.	●	●									●	●	●								
Florida	●	●	★			●	●			●	●	●	●	●	●	●	●	●	●	●	
Georgia	●						●			●		●	●								
Hawaii																					
Idaho	●	●				☆	●				●	●				■	●	●	●	●	
Illinois	●	●		●							●	●	●			●	◆	●	●	●	
Indiana	●	●		●							●	●	●			●	◆	●	●		
Iowa	●	●		●	●	●	●				●	●		●		●	●	●	●	●	
Kansas	●	●				●	●				●	●		●		●	●	●	●		
Kentucky	●	●									●	●	●			●	●	●	●	●	●
Louisiana	●	●		●	●	●	●				●	●	●	●		■	●	●	●	●	
Maine	●	●					●				●	●		●		●		■	●		
Maryland	●	●	●		●						●	●	●	●		●	●	●	●	●	◆
Mass.	●	●								●	●	●	●	●	●		●	■	●	●	
Michigan	●	●		◆		●	●				●	●	●	●		●	●	●	●	●	
Minnesota	●	●				●	●				●	●	●			●	●	●	●		
Miss.	●	●		●		●										●	●	●	●		
Missouri	●	●		●							●	●	●	●		■	■	■	◆	◆	
Montana	●	●	●	▼	●	●	●	●			●	●				◆	●	●	●	●	
Nebraska	●	●				▲	●			●	●	●				●	■	●	●		
Nevada	●		●	●	●	●	●	●						■	■	■	●	●	●	●	●
New Hamp.	●	●									●	●		●		◆		●	●	●	
New Jersey	●	●	●	●							●	●	●			●		●	●	●	
New Mexico	●	●			◆	●	●			●	★					●		●	●	●	
New York	●	●				▲	●			●	●	●	●	●		●	●	●	●	●	●
N. Carolina	●					●	●														
N. Dakota	●	●	●			●	●				●	●				■	●	●	●	☐	
Ohio	●	●						●			●	●	●			●	●	●	●	◆	●
Oklahoma	●	●				☆	●				●	●				◆	●	●	●	●	
Oregon	●	●				●	●		●	●	●	●	●	●		●	●	●	●		
Penn.	●	●							●		●	●	●			●	■	●	●		●
R. Island	●	●							●	●	●	●	●	●	●	■		■	●		
S. Carolina	●			▼	●																
S. Dakota	●	●	●	●		●	●		●		●	●				■	●	●	■	●	
Tennessee	●										●	●				◆	◆	◆	◆	◆	
Texas	●	●					●			●	●	●					●	●	●		
Utah																	○				
Vermont	●	●									●	●		■		●		■	◆		
Virginia	●	●									●	●				◆	◆	◆	◆	◆	
Wash.	●	●	●	▼		▲	●			●	●	●		●		■	●	●	●	●	
W. Virginia	●	●							●		●	●	●	●		◆	■	●	●		
Wisconsin	●	●				●	●				●	●	●	●		◆	◆	◆	●		
Wyoming	●	●					●									◆	●	●	●		
Puerto Rico	●			●								●	●						●	●	
Virgin Islands				◆						●									●	●	

● Legal and operative
★ Implemented since June 1996
▲ Table games only (no slots)
◆ Authorized but not yet implemented
▼ Commercial bingo, keno, or pulltabs only

■ Permitted by law and previously operative
○ Operative but no parimutuel wagering
☐ Previously operative but now not permitted
☆ Compacts signed for non-casino gaming, such as parimutuel wagering & lottery; however, casino games may be operating

Source: "North American Gaming at a Glance," *International Gaming and Wagering Business*, New York, New York, September 1997

TABLE 3.2

Canadian Gaming at a Glance

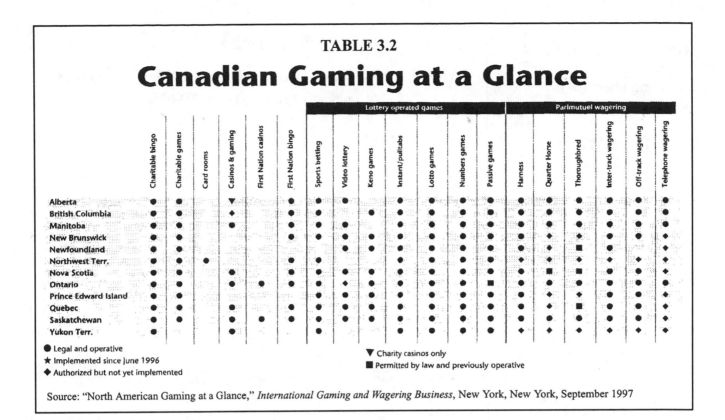

- ● Legal and operative
- ★ Implemented since June 1996
- ◆ Authorized but not yet implemented
- ▼ Charity casinos only
- ■ Permitted by law and previously operative

Source: "North American Gaming at a Glance," *International Gaming and Wagering Business*, New York, New York, September 1997

shows the types of gambling activities available throughout the United States and its jurisdictions and their operating status. Table 3.2 shows the same information for provinces and territories in Canada.

A BIG BUSINESS

Gambling is big business with dramatic changes occurring over the past few years. Casino gambling, which was once limited to two states, is now legal in 21 states. At one time, only bingo parlors could be found on Native American reservations. Today, almost 100 casinos are operating in 21 states. States without lotteries are now the exception and even many southern states, such as Texas and Georgia, which were once reluctant to have lotteries, now aggressively market them.

As a result, horse and dog racing has generally suffered during this period of rapid change as gamblers bet their money elsewhere. Many states have permitted off-track betting and simulcasting (see Chapter IV) to maintain betting on these races, and many racetrack operations have introduced other forms of gambling to their tracks.

In 1996, a record $47.6 billion was earned by legal gambling companies (earnings came from the gamblers' losses), a 5.6 percent increase from just the year before. Most of the earnings came from casinos (40 percent) and lotteries (34 percent). (See Table 3.3.) This was almost four times the amount earned by gambling only a dozen years before.

To understand how extensive gambling has become, the revenues from gambling ($47.6 billion) dwarf the revenues from such mainstays of American life as movies ($5.9 billion), spectator sports such as football, baseball, and basketball ($6.3 billion), theme parks ($7.2 billion), video games ($7.1 billion), and recorded music ($12.5 billion). Revenues from all the publications sold were $49.3 billion.

If the total $47.6 billion in revenue earned by gambling were represented as the sales revenue for one single company, that company would have been the eleventh largest company in the 1996 Forbes Sales 500 for the year, up from number 19 just four years before in 1992.

GROSS WAGERS (THE HANDLE)

In 1996, Americans bet $586.5 billion on legal gambling in the United States, more than four times as much as the $125.7 billion bet in 1982. Nearly 3 out of 4 dollars (74 percent) were wagered at casinos, mostly in Las Vegas, Nevada, or Atlantic City, New Jersey. Most of the remainder was bet at games on Indian Reservations (11 percent) or on the lotteries (7 percent). (See Table 3.4.)

From 1982 to 1996, the amount bet in non-Nevada/New Jersey card rooms (places where gamblers get together and play card games for money) rose 886 percent, while the amount wagered on lotteries increased 950 percent. (The take from card rooms in Las Vegas and Atlantic City are included in their table games.) The amount bet on legal bookmaking (where the gambler bets on sporting events or horseraces) rose 385 percent over the same period, virtually all of the increase attributable to sports books. Gambling at the slot machines in Nevada and New Jersey rose 781 percent over this period, while the wagering at the

TABLE 3.3

1996 gross gambling revenues by industry and change from 1995

(in millions)

	% retained	1996 Gross revenues (expenditures)	Increase/(decrease) in gross revenues (expenditures)	
			Dollars	Percent
Parimutuels				
Horses				
On-Track	20.5%	$815.1	-$132.5	-14.0%
ITW	21.1%	1,273.1	114.7	9.9%
OTB	21.3%	1,063.0	89.6	9.2%
TOTAL	21.0%	$3,151.3	$71.8	2.3%
Greyhounds				
On-Track	22.0%	335.6	-98.3	-22.7%
ITW	21.5%	146.8	10.2	7.4%
OTB	21.2%	22.3	-0.4	-1.8%
Total	21.8%	$504.7	-$88.5	-14.9%
Jai Alai	22.7%	54.0	-12.4	-18.7%
TOTAL PARIMUTUELS	21.1%	$3,710.0	-$29.2	-0.8%
Lotteries				
Video Lotteries	9.8%	884.3	265.6	42.9%
Traditional Games	45.2%	15,335.6	611.2	4.2%
TOTAL LOTTERIES	37.8%	$16,219.8	$876.9	5.7%
Casinos				
Nevada/NJ Slot Machines	5.7%	7,292.1	199.9	2.8%
Nevada/NJ Table Games	2.1%	3,775.9	-80.4	-2.1%
Deepwater Cruise Ships	7.1%	234.0	5.3	2.3%
Cruises-to-nowhere	7.1%	200.0	20.0	11.1%
Riverboats	5.3%	5,543.3	891.3	19.2%
Other Land-Based Casinos	5.9%	454.6	14.4	3.3%
Other Commercial Gambling	36.4%	158.4	-0.7	-0.4%
Non-Casino Devices	10.3%	1,482.5	76.7	5.5%
TOTAL CASINOS	4.4%	$19,140.9	$1,126.5	6.3%
Legal Bookmaking				
Sports Books	3.1%	76.4	-3.0	-3.8%
Horse Books	7.7%	10.1	-12.1	-54.4%
TOTAL BOOKMAKING	3.3%	$86.5	-$15.1	-14.8%
Card Rooms	6.9%	679.3	10.4	1.5%
Charitable Bingo	23.6%	952.2	-28.6	-2.9%
Charitable Games	26.0%	1,475.3	14.5	1.0%
Indian Reservations				
Class II	30.0%	627.5	29.3	4.9%
Class III	7.5%	4,731.3	555.4	13.3%
TOTAL INDIAN RESERVATIONS	8.2%	$5,358.8	$584.7	12.2%
GRAND TOTAL	7.7%	$47,622.7	$2,540.03	5.6%

Note: Column may not add to totals due to rounding.

Christiansen/Cummings Associates, Inc.

Source: "The United States — 96 Gross Annual Wager," *International Gaming and Wagering Business*, New York, New York, Supplement to August 1997

TABLE 3.4
Trends in gross wagering (handle), 1982-1996

(in millions)

	1982 gross wagering (handle)	1995 gross wagering (handle) (revised)	1996 gross wagering (handle)	1982-1996 increase/(decrease) in gross wagering (handle) dollars	percent	Average annual rate 1982-1996
Parimutuels						
Horses						
On-Track	$9,990.6	$4,628.5	$3,972.1	-$6,018.6	-60.24%	-6.38%
ITW		5,612.0	6,043.4		N/A	N/A
OTB	1,707.3	4,529.8	4,981.5	3,274.3	191.78%	7.95%
TOTAL	$11,697.9	$14,770.3	$14,997.0	$3,299.1	28.20%	1.79%
Greyhounds						
On-Track	2,208.6	1,989.8	1,522.8	-$685.7	-31.05%	-2.62%
ITW		633.9	682.9		N/A	N/A
OTB		106.2	105.3		N/A	0.00%(1)
Total	$2,208.6	$2,729.9	$2,311.1	$102.5	4.64%	0.32%
Jai Alai	622.8	296.4	237.8	-385.0	-61.82%	-6.65%
TOTAL PARIMUTUELS	$14,529.2	$17,796.5	$17,545.8	$3,016.6	20.76%	1.36%
Lotteries						
Video Lotteries		6,124.4	9,017.5	9,017.5	N/A	N/A
Other Games	4,088.3	32,308.1	33,909.5	29,821.2	729.43%	16.31%
TOTAL LOTTERIES	$4,088.3	$38,432.5	$42,927.0	$38,838.7	950.00%	18.29%
Casinos						
Nevada/NJ Slot Machines	14,400.0	121,295.7	126,840.8	112,440.8	780.84%	16.81%
Nevada/NJ Table Games	87,000.0	185,575.0	178,719.9	91,719.9	105.43%	5.28%
Deepwater Cruise Ships		3,221.8	3,295.9	3,295.9	N/A	N/A
Cruises-to-nowhere		2,535.2	2,816.9	2,816.9	N/A	N/A
Riverboats		88,083.8	104,418.1	104,418.1	N/A	N/A
Other Land-Based Casinos		7,309.9	7,717.9	7,717.9	N/A	N/A
Other Commercial Gambling		433.8	435.1	435.1	N/A	N/A
Non-Casino Devices		12,861.8	14,436.2	14,436.2	N/A	N/A
TOTAL CASINOS	$101,400.0	$421,317.1	$438,680.9	$337,280.9	332.62%	11.03%
Legal Bookmaking						
Sports Books	415.2	2,428.6	2,480.5	2,065.4	497.48%	13.62%
Horse Books	122.8	167.6	130.7	7.9	6.43%	0.45%
TOTAL BOOKMAKING	$538.0	$2,596.2	$2,611.2	$2,073.3	385.38%	11.95%
Card Rooms	1,000.0	9,440.9	9,863.7	8,863.7	886.37%	17.76%
Charitable Bingo	3,000.0	4,132.7	4,042.5	1,042.5	34.75%	2.15%
Charitable Games	1,200.0	5,648.4	5,676.2	4,476.2	373.01%	11.74%
Indian Reservations						
Class II		1,994.0	2,091.7	2,091.7	N/A	N/A
Class III		55,669.3	63,083.9	63,083.9	N/A	N/A
TOTAL INDIAN RESERVATIONS		$57,663.3	$65,175.6	$65,175.6	N/A	N/A
GRAND TOTAL	$125,755.5	$557,027.8	$586,523.0	$460,767.5	366.40%	11.63%

Note: Lottery handles for 1982 are for the twelve months ending June 30th
   Columns may not add to totals due to rounding.
   (1) Average annual rate from 1984 to 1995

Christiansen/Cummings Associates, Inc.

Source: "The United States — 96 Gross Annual Wager," *International Gaming and Wagering Business*, New York, New York, Supplement to August 1997

tables at these two gambling centers rose only 105 percent. Gambling on Native American reservations, which hardly existed in 1982, and was estimated at $1.3 billion in 1990, soared to an estimated $65 billion in 1996. (See Table 3.4.)

On the other hand, the amount of pari-mutuel wagering (betting on horses, greyhounds, and jai-alai) rose only 21 percent. Without off-track betting (OTB) and inter-track wagering (ITW), it would have actually dropped. In 1982, pari-

TABLE 3.5
Trends in gross revenues (consumer spending), 1982-1996

(In millions)

	1982 Gross revenues (spending)	1995 Gross revenues (spending) (revised)	1996 Gross revenues (spending)	1982-1996 Increase/(decrease) in gross revenues (spending) dollars	percent	Average annual rate 1982-1996
Parimutuels						
Horses						
Tracks	$1,850.0	$947.6	$815.1	-$1,034.9	-55.9%	-6.0%
ITW		1,158.5	1,273.1	1,273.1	N/A	N/A
OTB	400.0	973.4	1,063.0	663.0	165.7%	7.2%
TOTAL	$2,250.0	$3,079.5	$3,151.3	$901.3	40.1%	2.4%
Greyhounds						
Tracks	430.0	433.9	335.6	-94.4	-22.0%	-1.8%
ITW		136.7	146.8	146.8	N/A	N/A
OTB		22.7	22.3	21.2	N/A	32.8%(1)
Total	$430.0	$593.2	$504.7	$74.7	17.4%	1.2%
Jai Alai	112.0	66.4	54.0	-58.0	-51.8%	-5.1%
TOTAL PARIMUTUELS	$2,792.0	$3,739.1	$3,710.0	$918.0	32.9%	2.1%
Lotteries						
Video Lotteries		618.7	884.3	884.3	N/A	N/A
Other Games	2,170.0	14,724.3	15,335.6	13,165.6	606.7%	15.0%
TOTAL LOTTERIES	$2,170.0	$15,343.0	$16,219.8	$14,049.8	647.5%	15.5%
Casinos						
Nevada/NJ Slot Machines	2,000.0	7,092.3	7,292.1	5,292.1	264.6%	9.7%
Nevada/NJ Table Games	2,200.0	3,856.3	3,775.9	1,575.9	71.6%	3.9%
Deepwater Cruise Ships		228.8	234.0	234.0	N/A	N/A
Cruises-to-nowhere		180.0	200.0		N/A	N/A
Riverboats		4,652.0	5,543.3	5,543.3	N/A	N/A
Other Land-Based Casinos		440.3	454.6	454.6	N/A	N/A
Other Commercial Gambling		159.1	158.4	158.4	N/A	N/A
Non-Casino Devices		1,405.7	1,482.5	1,482.5	N/A	N/A
TOTAL CASINOS	$4,200.0	$18,014.4	$19,140.9	$14,940.9	355.7%	11.4%
Legal Bookmaking						
Sports Books	7.7	79.4	76.4	68.7	889.0%	17.8%
Horse Books	18.0	22.2	10.1	-7.9	-43.9%	-4.0%
TOTAL BOOKMAKING	$25.8	$101.6	$86.5	$60.8	235.9%	9.0%
Card Rooms	50.0	668.9	679.3	629.3	1,258.6%	20.5%
Charitable Bingo	780.0	980.8	952.2	172.2	22.1%	1.4%
Charitable Games	396.0	1,460.8	1,475.3	1,079.3	272.5%	9.8%
Indian Reservations						
Class II		598.2	627.5	627.5	N/A	N/A
Class III		4,175.9	4,731.3	4,731.3	N/A	N/A
TOTAL INDIAN RESERVATIONS		$4,774.1	$5,358.8	$5,358.8	N/A	N/A
GRAND TOTAL	$10,413.8	$45,082.7	$47,622.7	$37,209.0	357.3%	11.5%

Note: Lottery handles for 1982 are for the 12 months ending June 30th. Columns may not add to totals due to rounding.
   (1) Average annual rate from 1984 to 1995.

Christiansen/Cummings Associates, Inc.

Source: "The United States — 96 Gross Annual Wager," *International Gaming and Wagering Business*, New York, New York, Supplement to August 1997

mutuel betting had accounted for about 12 percent of all money wagered; by 1996, it accounted for barely 3 percent. Betting on the horses at the racetrack fell 60 percent from 1982 (and 14 percent from 1995), and wagering on jai-alai, a game in which the players hurl a small ball against the walls of the court using a curved basket attached to one arm, tumbled 62 percent. On-track betting for greyhound racing posted a 31 percent loss over this period (and dropped 23 percent from just the year before). Most experts agree that pari-mutuel wagering has been the most affected by the expansion of lotteries and casino gambling. Wagering on charitable games is up 373 percent, while charitable bingo has leveled off with an increase of only 35 percent from 1982 to 1996. (See Table 3.4.)

HOW MUCH DOES THE HOUSE KEEP?

Of the $586 billion wagered in 1996, the United States gambling industry kept $47.6 billion in gross revenues, or about 7.7 percent of the amount bet. Nevada/New Jersey table games and slot machines, Native American casinos, cruise ships, riverboats, and card rooms throughout the country kept less than 8 percent of the amount bet, while traditional lotteries retained almost half (45.2 percent) of all the money bet. Operators of charitable bingo, and other charitable games kept about one-fourth of the amount bet. (See Table 3.3.) Pari-mutuel games kept about one-fifth.

Gross Revenues (The Take)

Not surprisingly, the gross revenues (the amount the house has after giving out the winnings) rose (or fell) right along with the increase (or decrease) of the total wagering. As shown in Table 3.4, total gross wagering for most forms of gambling increased from 1982 through 1996, so it should not be surprising that gross revenues also rose. Gross revenues more than quadrupled over this period, increasing from $10.4 billion in 1982 to $47.6 billion in 1996. (See Table 3.5.)

From 1982 through 1996, non-Nevada/New Jersey card rooms (up 1,259 percent), lotteries (up 647.5 percent), and casinos (up 356 percent) showed the greatest increases. Non-bingo charitable games (up 272.5 percent) and slot machines and other types of gambling machines (up 265 percent) also saw large growth. Gambling on Native American reservations, virtually

	1995 Revenue market shares	1996 Revenue market shares	Increase
TABLE 3.6			
Market shares (revenues)			
1995 vs. 1996			
Riverboats	10.32%	11.64%	1.3%
Class III Indian	9.26%	9.93%	0.7%
Video Lotteries	1.37%	1.86%	0.5%
Horse ITW	2.57%	2.67%	0.1%
Horse OTB	2.16%	2.23%	0.1%
Cruises-to-nowhere	0.40%	0.42%	0.0%
Greyhound ITW	0.30%	0.31%	0.0%
Greyhound OTB	0.05%	0.05%	0.0%
Non-Casino Devices	3.12%	3.11%	0.0%
Class II Indian	1.33%	1.32%	0.0%
Sports Books	0.18%	0.16%	0.0%
Deepwater Cruise Ships	0.51%	0.49%	0.0%
Other Commercial Gambling	0.35%	0.33%	0.0%
Other Land-Based Casinos	0.98%	0.95%	0.0%
Horse Books	0.05%	0.02%	0.0%
Jai Alai	0.15%	0.11%	0.0%
Card Rooms	1.48%	1.43%	-0.1%
Charitable Games	3.24%	3.10%	-0.1%
Charitable Bingo	2.18%	2.00%	-0.2%
Greyhound Tracks	0.96%	0.70%	-0.3%
Horse Tracks	2.10%	1.71%	-0.4%
Nevada/NJ Slot Machines	15.73%	15.31%	-0.4%
Other Lottery Games	32.66%	32.20%	-0.5%
Nevada/NJ Table Games	8.55%	7.93%	-0.6%
TOTAL INDIAN RESERVATIONS	10.59%	11.25%	0.7%
TOTAL CASINOS	39.96%	40.19%	0.2%
TOTAL LOTTERIES	34.03%	34.06%	0.0%
TOTAL BOOKMAKING	0.23%	0.18%	0.0%
HORSE TOTAL	6.83%	6.62%	-0.2%
GREYHOUND TOTAL	1.32%	1.06%	-0.3%
TOTAL PARIMUTUELS	8.29%	7.79%	-0.5%

Christiansen/Cummings Associates, Inc.

Source: "The United States - 96 Gross Annual Wager," *International Gaming and Wagering Business*, New York, New York, Supplement to August 1997

unknown a dozen years ago, brought in $5.4 billion. Similarly, riverboats and other commercial casinos such as those in Colorado, which did not exist in 1982, brought in $5.5 billion and $455 million in 1996, respectively. (See Table 3.5.)

At the same time, reflecting betting trends indicated earlier, not all forms of gambling showed such vigorous growth. Revenues from pari-mutuel betting increased barely 40 percent over this period, while jai-alai revenues actually dropped 52 percent. If horsetrack owners had to depend on money earned solely from returns at the track (track owners also receive money from off-track betting and simulcasting), they would be in even deeper trouble than some of them are as revenues dropped 56 percent over the 1982-1996 period. The popularity of charitable bingo (up only 22 percent) seems to have leveled off. (See Table 3.5.)

SHARE OF THE GAMBLING MARKET

Casinos took in the largest market share (40 percent) of gross revenues, most of which came from the slot machines and casino tables of Las Vegas and Atlantic City (23 percent of all gambling revenues). Just a few years ago almost all casino revenues came from Las Vegas and Atlantic City. In 1996, riverboats (11.6 percent of all gambling revenues) also accounted for a significant proportion of the revenues earned from casino gambling. (See Table 3.6.)

Lotteries (34 percent) were the second largest proportion of the market. Total pari-mutuel betting on horses, greyhounds, and jai-alai brought in about 1 of every 12 gambling dollars (8 percent), while charitable games (3 percent) and charitable bingo (2 percent) accounted for most of the rest. Gambling on Native American reservations brought in about 11 percent, most of which came from newly built casinos. (See Table 3.6 and Figure 3.1.)

The makeup of the gambling market has changed dramatically over the past dozen years. In 1982, the pari-mutuels, betting on horses and dogs, accounted for 1 of every 4 dollars earned; in 1996, barely 1 in 12 dollars. Twelve years ago, gambling on Native American reservations played no role in the market; in 1996, it earned 1 in 9 gambling dollars. In 1982, lotteries earned about one-fifth of total revenues; in 1996, they made over one-third. Casinos earned about 2 in 5 gambling dollars in 1982 and in 1996. Lotteries, casinos, and Native American gambling have all helped drive the huge increase in gambling in the United States. Pari-mutuel gambling has not.

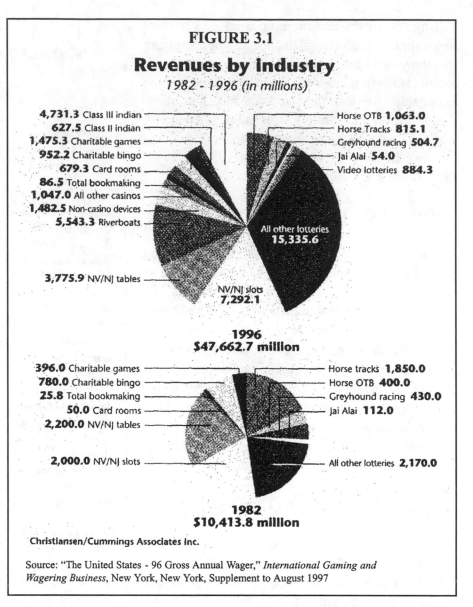

FIGURE 3.1

Revenues by Industry
1982 - 1996 (in millions)

4,731.3 Class III indian
627.5 Class II indian
1,475.3 Charitable games
952.2 Charitable bingo
679.3 Card rooms
86.5 Total bookmaking
1,047.0 All other casinos
1,482.5 Non-casino devices
5,543.3 Riverboats
3,775.9 NV/NJ tables

Horse OTB **1,063.0**
Horse Tracks **815.1**
Greyhound racing **504.7**
Jai Alai **54.0**
Video lotteries **884.3**

All other lotteries **15,335.6**

NV/NJ slots **7,292.1**

1996
$47,662.7 million

396.0 Charitable games
780.0 Charitable bingo
25.8 Total bookmaking
50.0 Card rooms
2,200.0 NV/NJ tables
2,000.0 NV/NJ slots

Horse tracks **1,850.0**
Horse OTB **400.0**
Greyhound racing **430.0**
Jai Alai **112.0**

All other lotteries **2,170.0**

1982
$10,413.8 million

Christiansen/Cummings Associates Inc.

Source: "The United States - 96 Gross Annual Wager," *International Gaming and Wagering Business*, New York, New York, Supplement to August 1997

ILLEGAL GAMBLING

International Gaming and Wagering Business, the monthly magazine which covers the gambling industry and the data source for much of this chapter, no longer includes illegal gambling when it counts gambling revenues. Eugene M. Christiansen, who prepares *International Gaming and Wagering Business's* annual review of gaming, has noted that there are not enough reliable data to make an estimate. (See Chapter X for a further discussion of estimates of illegal gambling.) In 1989, *International Gaming and Wagering Business* estimated that Americans lost about $6.7 billion at illegal gambling, about 22 percent of all gambling losses at the time.

GAMBLING ON NATIVE AMERICAN RESERVATIONS

As discussed in Chapter II, the Indian Gaming Regulatory Act (PL 100-497) permits Native American tribes to introduce gambling on their reservations. Many tribes had already been holding bingo games on their reservations, but the new law opened up the possibility that other forms of gambling could be played on Native American lands. It also meant that the Native American tribes would play a major role in the large expansion of gambling that was occurring throughout the country.

While returns from bingo, the major form of gambling that was being played on reservations, were beginning to level off, many Native American tribes recognized that

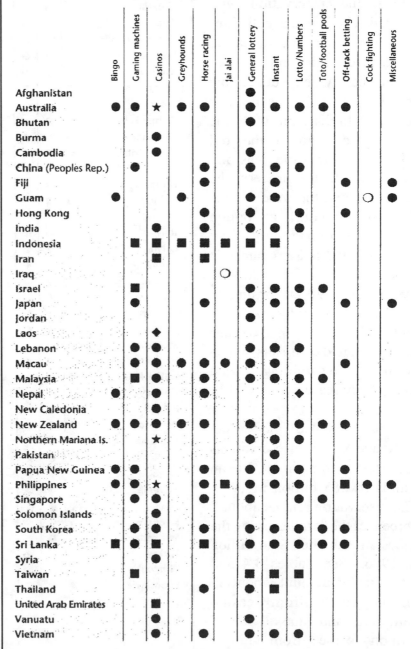

TABLE 3.7

EXPLANATION OF SYMBOLS

- ● Legal and operative
- ▲ Legalized and implemented in 1996-1997
- ★ Additional new operation(s) in 1996-1997
- ◆ Authorized but not yet implemented
- ■ Previously operative, currently inactive
- ○ Previously operative, current status not confirmable

Asia Pacific, Middle East

	Bingo	Gaming machines	Casinos	Greyhounds	Horse racing	Jai alai	General lottery	Instant	Lotto/Numbers	Toto/football pools	Off-track betting	Cock fighting	Miscellaneous
Afghanistan							●						
Australia	●	●	★	●	●		●	●	●	●	●		
Bhutan													
Burma			●										
Cambodia			●										
China (Peoples Rep.)		●			●		●	●	●		●		●
Fiji					●		●	●			●		●
Guam	●											○	●
Hong Kong					●		●	●			●		
India			●		●		●	●	●				
Indonesia		■	■	■	■	■	■	■					
Iran			■				■						
Iraq							○						
Israel		■					●	●	●	●			
Japan		●			●		●	●			●		●
Jordan							●						
Laos			◆										
Lebanon		●	●				●	●					
Macau		●	●	●	●		●	●	●		●		
Malaysia		■	●		●		●	●	●		●		
Nepal	●	●	●							◆			
New Caledonia													
New Zealand	●	●		●	●		●	●	●		●		
Northern Mariana Is.			★				●	●	●				
Pakistan									●				
Papua New Guinea	●	●					●	●			●		
Philippines	●	●	★		●	■	●	●			■	●	●
Singapore		●			●		●	●	●				
Solomon Islands		●											
South Korea		●	●		●		●	●	●		●		
Sri Lanka	■	●	■		●		●	●	●		●		
Syria			●										
Taiwan		■					●	■	■				
Thailand					●		●	■					
United Arab Emirates		■											
Vanuatu		●	●				●						
Vietnam					●		●	●	●				

Continued on the following page.

casino games were being offered in more places throughout the United States. (See Chapter VII.) They saw this as an opportunity to bring some prosperity to their reservations.

The Indian Gaming Regulatory Act permitted the tribes to conduct any type of gambling on their reservation which was permitted in the state where the reservation was located. The law also called for the tribe and the state to negotiate agreements or "compacts" which would allow this gambling. The state was required to bargain with the tribes in good faith. If they did not, or if the tribe was not satisfied with the process, the law permitted the tribe to take the issue to court, an option Native Americans have frequently used. (See Chapter II for a complete discussion.) By December 1997, according to the Bureau of Indian Affairs, almost 147 tribes in 24 states had negotiated compacts, which permit casino gambling, a trend likely to increase.

The amount of money bet on Native American reservations rose from nothing in 1982 to an estimated $65 billion in 1996. The reservation retains about 8 percent of the handle, giving the tribes an estimated $5.4 billion in 1996. (See Tables 3.4 and 3.5.) Of this amount, about $5 billion came from casino gambling and about $627.5 million came from bingo. Gambling revenue from

TABLE 3.7 (Continued)
Europe

	Bingo	Gaming machines	Casinos	Greyhounds	Horse racing	Jai alai	General lottery	Instant	Lotto/Numbers	Toto/football pools	Off-track betting	Cock fighting	Miscellaneous
Albania							●		●	●			
Austria		●	●		●		●	●	●	●	●		▲
Belarus													
Belgium		●	●	●	●		●	●	●	■	●		
Bulgaria		●	●		●		●	●	●		●		
Croatia		●	●				●	●	●	●			
Cyprus		●	●		●		●	●	●				
Czech Republic		●	●	●			●	●	●	●	●		
Denmark		●	●		●		●	●	●	●	●		
Estonia		●	●				●	●	●				
Finland	●	●	●				●	●	●	●	●		●
France		●	●	●	●		●	●	●	●	●		
Germany		●	★	●	●		●	●	●	●			
Gibraltar	●	●					●		●	●			
Great Britain	●	●	●	●	●		●	●	●	●	●		
Greece		●	●		●		●	●	●	●			
Hungary		●	●		●		●	●	●	●	●		
Iceland	●	●					●	●	●	●			
Ireland	●			●	●		●	●	●	●	●		●
Italy		●	●	●	●		●	●	●	●	●		
Latvia		●	●				●	●	●				
Lithuania		●	◆				●	●	●	●			
Luxembourg		●	●				●	●	●				
Macedonia		●	●				●	●	●		●		
Madeira		●	●				●		●				
Malta	●	●	●		●		●	●	●		●		
Moldova							●		●				
Monaco		●	●								●		
Netherlands	●	●	●	●	●		●	●					
Norway		★					●	●	●	●	●		
Poland		●	★		●		●	●	●	●	●		
Portugal	●	●	●				●	●	●	●	●		
Romania		●	●		●		●	●	●	●	●		
Russia		●	★		●		●	●	●	●	●		
Slovakia		●	●				●	●	●	●			
Slovenia		●	●				●	●	●				
Spain	●	●	●		●	●	●	●	●	●	●		
Sweden	●	●	●		●		●	●	●	●	●		●
Switzerland		●	★				●	●	●	●	●		
Turkey		●	●		●		●	●	●	●	●		
Ukraine							●		◆				
Yugoslavia	●	●	●		●		●	●	●	●			

Continued on the following page.

reservations has been increasing rapidly, with income more than tripling from 1992 alone. In all likelihood, these numbers will continue to increase. (See Chapter VII for a more complete discussion of gambling on Native American reservations.)

SPORTS GAMBLING

Sports gambling is legal and operating in Montana, Nevada, North Dakota, and Oregon, and is legal, but not operative, in Delaware. Bookmaking is legal statewide only in Nevada, while it takes place in limited localities in Montana and North Dakota and is used in Oregon as part of its lottery program. Sports betting is also legal in a number of locations in Baja, California, Mexico, which borders California. The overwhelming majority of bettors visiting these border locations are Americans, mainly Californians who cross the border. (For illegal sports betting, see Chapter X.)

Almost all the money wagered legally on sports books is bet in Nevada. In 1996, $2.5 billion was wagered on sports in Nevada with about $76.4 million retained by the house. This is a retained percentage of 3 percent, much less than the 5.7 percent take in 1994. The 1994 revenues were inordinately high, and sports bettors will have to be very unlucky to allow the house to continue to earn that high rate of return in the future.

TABLE 3.7 (Continued)

North America, Central America and the Caribbean

	Bingo	Gaming machines	Casinos	Greyhounds	Horse racing	Jai alai	General lottery	Instant	Lotto/Numbers	Toto/football pools	Off-track betting	Cock fighting	Miscellaneous
Antigua	●	●	●		●		●						
Aruba	●	●	●		●							○	●
Bahamas		●	●				◆						
Barbados	●	●		■	●		●	●	●		●		
Bélize							●						
Bonaire		●	●										
Canada	●	★	★				●	●	●		★		
Costa Rica	●		●				●	●	●				
Curaçao	●	●	●				●	●					
Dominica							■						■
Dominican Republic	●	●	●	■	●		●				●	○	
El Salvador							●						
Grenada	●				■							■	
Guadeloupe	●				●		●	●	●			○	
Guatemala	●						●	●	●				
Guyana	●				●		●				●		
Haiti		●	●	■			●					○	
Honduras	●	●	●				●		●			○	
Jamaica	●				●		●		●		●		
Martinique	●				●		●	●	●	●	●	○	●
Mexico					●	●	●	●	●		●	○	
Netherlands Antilles							●						
Nicaragua	●		■				●	●					
Panama		●	●		●		●	■			●	○	
Puerto Rico	●	★	★		●		●		●		★	○	
St. Kitts	●	●	●										
St. Lucia	●						●						
St. Maarten (Dutch)	●	●	●				●	●					
St. Vincent	●	●	●										
Trinidad & Tobago	●				●		●	●	●	■	●		
United States	●	★	★	●	★	●	●	●	●	●	★		
U.S. Virgin Islands					●		●	●	●				

Continued on the following page.

GAMBLING IN THE FUTURE HIGH-TECHNOLOGY WORLD

The gambling industry is studying how to develop ways to allow Americans to wager using the Internet or cable television. Craig Fields, former director of the Defense Advanced Research Projects Agency, the agency which developed cutting edge technology for the Pentagon (to include the communications system now called the Internet), has become vice-chairman of Alliance Gaming Corporation, a major gaming company. He plans "to do something in the entertainment and gaming industries because they're now the greatest users of advanced technologies." Sega, the high-technology video game company, is entering the gambling business, as are Apple Computer, Inc., and Philips Electronics NV.

The technology is available. The issues are legal and political. In order for a significant amount of gambling to occupy the worldwide web, laws restricting gambling on the Internet or cable television will likely have to be changed. This will have to be done through state and federal legislatures, which will undoubtedly lead to regulation of high technology gambling. It may also involve a political conflict as some of those opposed to gambling see the Internet and cable television as the issue upon which to make their stand to try to stop the spread of gambling in the United States.

Currently, it is illegal to gamble on the Internet because it violates the Interstate Wire Act. Nonetheless, lotteries are looking into ways that bettors could buy tickets on the Internet. Internet Casinos operates out of the tiny island nation of Turks and Caicos (near the Bahamas in the Atlantic Ocean) and claims to have over 25,000 registered players. The New York Racing Commission and Cablevision offer a gambling program on television. The gambler, watching the race on television at home, can pick up the phone and place a bet with the state's OTB (off-track betting) system. Churchill Downs in Louisville, Kentucky, is experimenting with a similar system that allows the gambler to bet via television and a telephone without leaving home.

In 1997, there were nearly 500 gambling sites on the Internet. About 10 of them permitted bettors to wager real money. "Cyber casinos," as they are called, offer a wide variety of games to play, and include lotteries, virtual slots, table games, and sports books. Such gambling sites are easy to start up, do not require much start-up capital, and have low operating expenses. They also have millions of potential customers. Congress, however, is concerned about such matters as consumer protection, effects on legal gambling establishments, underage gambling, and gambling addiction. Therefore, Internet gambling will be included as an issue to be studied by the National Gambling Impact and Policy Commission. (See Chapter II.)

Minnesota was the first state to file suit against an Internet operation. The state's attorney general, Hubert Humphrey III, sued Granite Gate Resorts, which is based in Las Vegas, Nevada. (Most Web casinos are based off-shore, making it difficult to control them.) The state sued Granite Gate for

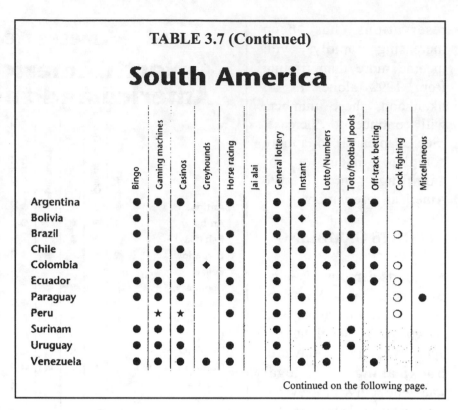

TABLE 3.7 (Continued)

South America

	Bingo	Gaming machines	Casinos	Greyhounds	Horse racing	Jai alai	General lottery	Instant	Lotto/Numbers	Toto/football pools	Off-track betting	Cock fighting	Miscellaneous
Argentina	●	●	●		●		●	●	●	●	●		
Bolivia	●						●	◆					
Brazil	●				●		●	●	●	●	●	○	
Chile		●	●		●		●	●	●	●	●		
Colombia	●	●	●	◆	●		●	●	●	●	●	○	
Ecuador	●	●	●		●		●	●				○	
Paraguay	●	●	●		●		●	●				○	●
Peru		★	★		●		●	●				○	
Surinam	●	●	●				●						
Uruguay	●	●	●		●		●			●	●		
Venezuela	●	●	●	●	●		●		●	●	●		

Continued on the following page.

38

consumer fraud and false advertising. According to Minnesota, by advertising a sports book to Minnesotans, Granite Gate was incorrectly claiming that sports gambling was legal in that state, when in fact, it is not. Granite Gate argued that Minnesota had no authority over it because its Web site was not fashioned to actively seek business in Minnesota. The court found in Minnesota's favor, ruling that Granite Gate placed an advertisement in Minnesota that was "available 24 hours a day, seven days a week, 365 days a year." This was enough contact to establish jurisdiction by the state. (Minnesota may now request an injunction requiring the site to either cease operations or forbid residents of the state from registering as players.) (*State of Minnesota v. Granite Gate Resorts, Inc.,* 568 NW 2nd 715, 1997)

INTERNATIONAL GAMBLING

This publication examines gambling only in the United States. However, the explosion in gambling is taking place worldwide. Many other countries of the world have always permitted gambling, but now gambling is becoming as common throughout the world as it has become in the United States. Just as in the United States, other industrially developed and financially strained countries

TABLE 3.7 (Continued)

Africa

	Bingo	Gaming machines	Casinos	Greyhounds	Horse racing	Jai alai	General lottery	Instant	Lotto/Numbers	Toto/football pools	Off-track betting	Cock fighting	Miscellaneous
Algeria	■				●		●	●	●	●			
Angola							●			●			
Benin		●	●				●	●	●	●	●		
Botswana	●	●	●	◆	●		●				●		
Burkina Faso							●	●			●		
Burundi							●	●					
Cameroon			●				●	●	●	●	●		
Cape Verde							○						
Central African Rep.			●				■				●		
Chad					●						●		
Comoros		●	●										
Congo			●				●	●					
Rep. of Congo		●	●				●				●		
Egypt		●	★		●								●
Ethiopia	●		●				●	●					
Gabon		●	●								●		
Gambia		●	●										
Ghana		●	●		●		●	●	●				
Guinea-Bissau										●			
Ivory Coast		●	●				●	●					
Kenya		●	●		●		●			●			
Lesotho		●	●		●								
Liberia		●	●				●		●				
Madagascar		●	●		●		●	●	●		●		
Mali							●	●			●		
Mauritius		●	●		●		●			●	●		
Morocco			●	●	●				●	●	●		
Mozambique							●		●	●			
Namibia		●	●										
Niger							●	●	●				
Nigeria		●	●		●						●		
Reunion		●	●								●		
Senegal		●	●		●		●			●			
Seychelles		●	●										●
Sierra Leone		●	●					●	●				
South Africa		●	●	●	●		●		●		●		
Swaziland		●	●							●			
Tanzania			●				●		◆				
Togo			●				●	●	●		●		
Tunisia			●		●		●				●	●	
Uganda			●				■						
Zambia	●	●	●		●			◆			●		
Zimbabwe	●	●	●		●		●	◆		●	●		●

Source: "World Gaming at a Glance," *International Gaming and Wagering Business*, New York, New York, October 1997

are considering a growing gambling market as an opportunity to increase tax revenues. Less-developed countries see gambling as a tool to increase tourism and attract more foreign dollars.

New Zealand is considering plans to open a third casino on South Island. The New Zealand government is currently drafting legislation for Internet gambling. Although it is not considered legal now, the government hopes to become an official hub for Internet gambling. A new tourist resort is scheduled to open in Phnom Penh near the Thailand border. It will have a three-story casino and a duty-free shopping arcade.

In 1997, a new casino opened in Cebu, the Philippines. There are more than a dozen casinos now operating in the Philippines. The Polish government will award 15 new casino licenses around the country. An additional 100 slot arcades will be added to the existing 115 already in operation in Poland. Table 3.7 shows which forms of gambling are permitted in the nations of the world. Other than cockfighting, these are forms of gambling generally available in the United States.

Just as in other areas of commerce, much of the development of gambling is being financed and managed by companies in the industrially developed world. Many of the companies that play a major role in the development of America's gambling market are investing in overseas markets to develop gambling in those countries. Should the American gambling market become satiated or if political opposition stops its expansion, which is a possibility, these companies will be in position to continue developing in the world market.

Reflecting this change in the gambling marketplace, the *International Gaming & Wagering Business*, the monthly publication that covers the industry, has reformatted its presentation. Not only has the magazine cover been given a facelift, but the United States, while still the most important country covered, is now one of many countries being considered. For example, the cover of the January 1998 issue leads with two

stories, one on "The New American Dream" (European casino operators investing in Las Vegas) and the other on Caixa Economica Federal (the government savings bank that holds the federal lottery monopoly in Brazil) offering new games.

Inside, articles include coverage on the Turkey casino crisis that may force all 76 of Turkey's casinos to close, and a deal permitting video lottery terminals (VLTs) in restaurants in Switzerland. There is also a report on Australia's Star City casino, and an item about a Canadian firm purchasing a casino in Aruba. Stories covering gambling in the United States lead with the dateline of the country's name, just as stories from the other countries covered. The explosion in gambling in the United States is part of a worldwide phenomenon in which many American gambling companies are playing a major role.

COMPULSIVE GAMBLERS

As can be concluded from the many surveys taken on gambling, for most people who bet, gambling is a form of recreation and fun. (See Chapter XI.) While they receive enjoyment from the game, they can take or leave it. Even when they lose, they usually look upon it as the cost of entertainment and it does not upset them.

For some people, however, gambling is a compulsion, an addiction they cannot control. These people may become addicted to gambling and, like alcoholism, it may take control of their behavior and destroy their lives. The addiction may cause them to gamble away their paychecks or go deeply into debt. It may threaten their marriages and their relationships with their children, relatives, and friends.

Characteristics of Compulsive Gamblers

The Council on Compulsive Gambling of New Jersey, Inc., "aims to reduce and prevent this insidious disease by mobilizing public support through public information and education and

TABLE 3.8

Some Statistics for 1996:

Volume of calls: 26,080 in 1996 (14,577 in 1993)

Types of gambling:
69% casino games	9% bingo
47% lotteries	4% illegal gambling
42% horse racing	1% video machines
28% sports betting	1% stocks & commodities

(These figures add up to more than 100% because many callers mentioned more than one type of gambling.)

Average gambling debt: $31,012   Average annual income: $42,474

Highest occupational categories:
25% sales	6% retired
13% service workers	5% clerical
8% unemployed	4% students
8% professionals	2% gambling industry

Age: 9% were under the age of 21; 13% were over the age of 55

Marital status:
48% were married	2% were widowed
38% were never married	3% were separated
7% were divorced	2% were living together but not married

Family size: Average family of caller had 2 children; 27% had children under the age of 10 and 40% had children over the age of 20

Gender: 76% of gamblers were male; 24% were female; in 1992, 80% were male and 20% were female; in 1990, 87% were male and 13% were female

Race/Ethnicity:
85% White	2% Asian
11% Black	2% Others
3% Hispanic/Latino	.3% American Indian

Who called: 72% of the calls were from the gambler; 28% of the calls were from someone seeking help either for the gambler or the gambler's family

Presentations: 34 high schools
12 colleges
13 senior citizen groups
 4 employee assistance program (EAP) workshops
48 prison inmate consultations
1,019 1-800-GAMBLER information packets mailed
299,761 pieces of literature distributed

Source: The Council on Compulsive Gambling of New Jersey, Inc., Trenton, NJ, n.d.

through interaction with professional groups concerned with the growing impact of pathological gambling." The agency offers a toll-free line, 1-800-GAMBLER, to provide help to compulsive gamblers.

The Council on Compulsive Gambling of New Jersey, Inc., an affiliate of the National Council on Compulsive Gambling, Inc., considers compulsive gambling "the Hidden Epidemic." The Council on Compulsive Gambling of New Jersey, Inc., annually surveys callers to the agency hotline. In 1996, 26,080 people called the 1-800-GAMBLER number, almost twice as many as the 14,577 people who phoned in 1993. Seventy-six percent were male and 24 percent were female. (In 1992, 20 percent were female, and in 1990, 13 percent were women.) The average caller had 2 children.

Those responding to the survey bet on a wide variety of games — 69 percent played casino games, 47 percent bought lottery tickets, 42 percent played the horses, 28 percent wagered on sporting events, 9 percent bet on bingo, 1 percent played the video machines, and 1 percent bought stocks and commodities. The typical caller was $31,012 in debt with an average annual income of $42,474. Of all the calls received, 72 percent were made by the gamblers and 28 percent were from people seeking help for gamblers or for members of the gamblers' families. About half (48 percent) were married. (See Table 3.8.)

In a more complete 1989 survey of 196 obsessive gamblers who had called the hotline, gamblers indicated that they were generally not happy with their situation. Seventy-eight percent had been bailed out (had their gambling debts paid off by somebody). Nonetheless, after having been bailed out, 91 percent continued to gamble. About 69 percent of the respondents said they had thoughts of suicide, and 17 percent claimed to have actually tried to kill themselves. Three-fourths (75 percent) had committed a felony because of their compulsive gambling — 35 percent stole money, 18 percent embezzled money, and 22 percent wrote bad checks.

About one-fourth (24 percent) also had other addictions. Nine percent were alcoholics, 3 percent used drugs, 6 percent were smokers, and 11 percent were overeaters. Some suffered from combinations of all these addictions. Of this group, 68 percent were getting some type of help for their addictions.

GAMBLERS ANONYMOUS

Gamblers Anonymous offers a 12-step program similar to Alcoholics Anonymous. Currently, people attend Gamblers Anonymous meetings at over 1,100 locations across the nation, up from 800 locations just four years ago. All members share two goals — to stop themselves from gambling and to help other compulsive gamblers to do the same. Gamblers Anonymous can be reached by calling (213) 386-8789, faxing (213) 386-0030, or writing Gamblers Anonymous, International Service Office, P.O. Box 17173, Los Angeles, CA 90017. It will supply the address of the nearest Gamblers Anonymous location. All information is kept confidential.

The National Council on Problem Gambling, Inc., a not-for-profit agency dedicated to addressing the issue of problem and pathological gambling, also offers a nationwide hotline for those needing assistance (1-800-522-4700).

In addition, most states that permit gambling have developed some sort of state-supported system to assist compulsive gamblers. Those needing help from these state agencies should be able to find out their phone numbers from the state gaming commission or the lottery commission. Some gambling companies have recognized the seriousness of the problem and are contributing money to some of these programs.

CHAPTER IV

PARI-MUTUEL BETTING —
HORSES, DOGS, AND JAI-ALAI

HOW PARI-MUTUEL BETTING WORKS

The term "pari-mutuel" describes a method of betting in which the persons who pick the winners in a given event divide the total amount of money bet in proportion to their wagers. Winnings, or payoffs, are paid on the win (first place), place (second place), and show (third place) categories of a given event, or on certain combinations of these categories.

The amount of the payoff depends on the total amount wagered on a given race or game. If the winners are heavily favored, the payoff per individual is much smaller than if the winners have little money wagered or "riding" on them. For example, if a horse is a 5-to-1 favorite, it means that for every dollar bet on that horse, $5 has been bet on the other entries. If the horse has negative odds, or is an "odds-on" favorite, let us say 1 to 2, it means that for every two dollars bet on that horse, one dollar was bet on all the other horses in the race. Bettors are constantly informed of the changing odds in an event (as people place their bets) by computerized totalizator machines, which flash new betting totals and odds on the "tote board" every 60 to 90 seconds.

The minimum amount for a pari-mutuel wager is $2, but the bettor may wager any additional amount in denominations of $5, $10, $50, or $100. Of the total amount wagered on a particular race, approximately 78 to 80 percent is returned to winning bettors in the form of payoffs. Before the winning bettors collect their money, a percentage of the total amount of money bet is taken by the agency conducting the betting operation, for example, the race track operator, and by the state, in the form of taxes.

In most states where pari-mutuel gambling is legal, a person must be 18 years old to wager at a racetrack, although in Illinois a 17-year-old may bet. In Birmingham and Macon County, Alabama, Nebraska, and Wyoming, the age is 19 years, while in New York, Nevada, and Texas, the legal age for wagering is 21 years. Most states do not have an age restriction on simply attending an event, although several do require that a minor be accompanied by an adult.

HISTORY OF THE PARI-MUTUEL SYSTEM

Pari-mutuel betting, the standard form of wagering on horses, was invented in France in 1865. This new method of wagering made its first American appearance in 1871 at New York's Jerome Park and became an established feature of horse racing when it was successfully used at the 1908 Kentucky Derby.

Before pari-mutuel wagering was introduced, the racetrack bookmaker was a dominant figure. The bookmaker was an agent, or professional bettor, against whom the layman (non-professional) bettor wagered his own expertise and hunches. As a competitor to the layman, the bookie held a clear advantage. With the invention of pari-mutuel wagering, the bookie's position was weakened because the pari-mutuel system allowed the bettor to wager against his peers, instead of

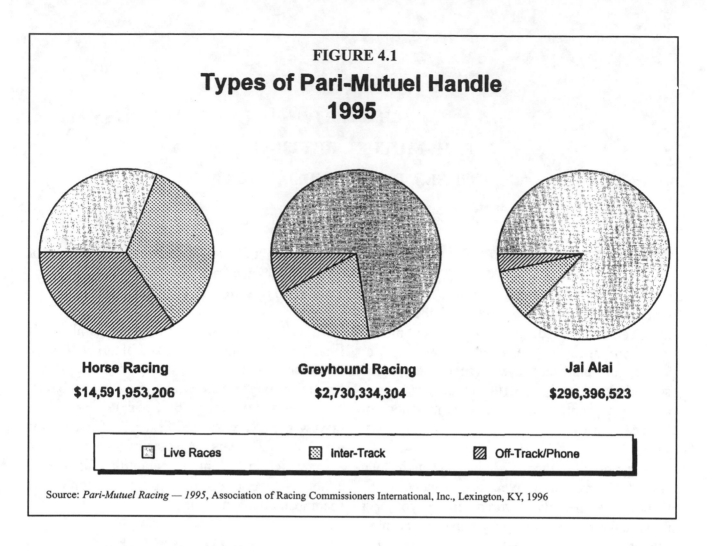

FIGURE 4.1

Types of Pari-Mutuel Handle
1995

Horse Racing	Greyhound Racing	Jai Alai
$14,591,953,206	$2,730,334,304	$296,396,523

☐ Live Races   ☒ Inter-Track   ☒ Off-Track/Phone

Source: *Pari-Mutuel Racing — 1995*, Association of Racing Commissioners International, Inc., Lexington, KY, 1996

against professional bookmakers. This system also increased the bettor's return on his investment by allowing him to receive payoffs on second and third place finishes.

PARI-MUTUEL
BETTING TODAY

Pari-mutuel wagering is the most common form of betting on horse races (thoroughbred, harness, and quarter horse), dog races, and jai-alai games. Most pari-mutuel betting is done at the race track or game site where the event is actually taking place, but in many states, bettors can also place pari-mutuel bets at off-track and simulcast sites (see below) and via telephone. Pari-mutuel wagering is legal in all but six states (Alaska, Georgia, Hawaii, Mississippi, North Carolina, and South Carolina) and Washington, DC.

AN OVERVIEW OF THE INDUSTRY

Some Real Problems

The pari-mutuel industry has been hard hit by many of the recent changes in the gambling industry. The nation's bettors have been provided with many other options. The huge growth of lotteries over the past decade has given gamblers another place to spend their money. Even more serious has been the recent explosion of casino gambling on riverboats, selected counties in a number of states, and the ever-growing number of casinos on Native American reservations. Race-tracks in Minnesota, Wisconsin, and Connecticut, where Native American casinos have been most successful, have been badly hurt.

Pari-mutuel betting has been barely holding its own over the past dozen years, a period of dramatic change in the gambling industry. As recently as 1982, pari-mutuel gambling played a dominant role in the gambling business, accounting for 27 percent of the wagering. Just 12 years later, in 1994, pari-mutuels brought in only 9 percent, and in 1996, 7.8 percent. With the nationwide spread of lotteries and casino gambling, pari-mutuel gambling has almost become a minor player in the gambling business.

In 1982, Americans wagered $14.5 billion on pari-mutuel betting; by 1995, wagering had increased to $17.5 billion, not enough to even keep up with inflation. (The figures do not account for inflation.) From 1995 to 1996, the pari-mutuel handle dropped by $250 million (down 1.41 percent). From 1982 to 1996, betting at the greyhound track fell 31 percent. It toppled 60 percent at the horse track, and plunged 61 percent at the jai-alai frontons. Without the introduction of off-track betting (OTB)*, intertrack wagering (ITW)**, and simulcasting***, pari-mutuel gam-

bling may have disappeared. (See Table 3.4 in Chapter III.) Figure 4.1 shows how OTB and ITW have become fundamental to the earnings of pari-mutuel gambling.

Revenues from pari-mutuel gambling rose from $2.8 billion in 1982, when it accounted for 27 percent of the market, to $3.7 billion in 1996. The market share dropped in one year — 1995 to 1996 — from 8.3 percent to 7.8 percent, a 0.5 percent decrease. (See Table 3.6 in Chapter III.) The decline in the fortune of pari-mutuels can also be seen in the drop in the amount of money the government collected. In 1990, state and local governments made $897 million from pari-mutuel wagering; by 1995, that figure had dropped to $625 million. (See Table 4.1.)

Despite the success of some tracks, such as Remington Park (Oklahoma), Penn National (Pennsylvania), and Churchill Downs (Kentucky), overall pari-mutuel gambling is a struggling

---

* Off-track betting (OTB) means exactly what it says — a person places a bet on a horse or dog race at some location other than the track where the race actually takes place. Off-track bets are usually placed at a track branch office or a betting shop. Some states permit a bettor to call in his or her bet over the telephone, although this has often not been successful in increasing revenues. Revenues are distributed to state and local governments and the racing industry (which includes the OTB corporations themselves, race track operators, etc.). Many observers hope that locating OTBs in attractive places, such as restaurants, special OTB theaters, or gambling casinos, will make these operations more effective. Some people associate OTB with the parlors in New York, many of which have become sleazy and unappealing.

** Intertrack wagering (ITW) is the programming of thoroughbred, harness, quarterhorse, or greyhound racing, which is shown on televisions or television projectors at a site away from the actual racetrack where the event is taking place for the purpose of parimutuel wagering. This may occur at a special betting parlor or, more likely, another racetrack. The person watching the television simulcasting is watching the race "live" and may bet on it as if he or she were at the actual track where the race was being run. In the case of ITW, the racetrack has opened solely for the purpose of showing these televised races. There is no live racing going on at the track. Both the track where the race is being run and the place where the ITW is occurring share in the revenues from the races.

*** Simulcasting is the programming of thoroughbred, harness, quarterhorse, or greyhound racing. It is shown on televisions or television projectors at a site away from the actual racetrack where the event is taking place for the purpose of parimutuel wagering in order to augment a live schedule of racing. Technically, simulcasting and ITW are the same thing, but with simulcasting, the transmitted races add to the existing show while with ITW, the transmitted races are the only show.

TABLE 4.1
PARI-MUTUEL WAGERING IN THE UNITED STATES

TOTAL PARI-MUTUEL REVENUE TO GOVERNMENT
1959 - 1995

Year	Revenue		Year	Revenue
1995	625,521,148		1976	821,311,348
1994	656,123,006		1975	871,345,367
1993	693,214,593		1974	729,533,116
1992	725,585,548		1973	657,647,137
1991	792,767,083		1972	595,253,462
1990	897,426,844		1971	572,277,744
1989	862,718,105		1970	539,742,764
1988	870,233,100		1969	508,545,672
1987	880,558,761		1968	468,077,649
1986	852,535,313		1967	432,076,514
1985	876,005,323		1966	424,252,115
1984	875,243,184		1965	402,705,421
1983	856,888,828		1964	379,914,405
1982	858,251,794		1963	343,228,047
1981	876,384,974		1962	313,438,030
1980	899,996,920		1961	287,920,639
1979	861,706,557		1960	280,090,399
1978	835,846,080		1959	262,810,999
1977	819,201,638			

(Note: Does not include jai-alai prior to 1978.)

Source: *Pari-Mutuel Racing — 1995*, Association of Racing Commissioners International, Inc., Lexington, KY, 1996

industry that likely must turn to either very innovative marketing or the introduction of new forms of gambling at the racetracks in order to survive.

HORSE RACING —
THE SPORT OF KINGS

Horse racing has changed over the centuries from a sport associated with the aristocracy into, until recently, one of the more popular pastimes in America. The first known form of horse racing was practiced by the Sumerians over 6,000 years ago and was similar to the chariot races occasionally seen in the movies. "Flat Racing," in which a rider is mounted directly on the horse instead of sitting in a rig drawn by an animal, was first popularized about 3,000 years ago. The first recorded horse race took place in Greece about 600 B.C.E. Horse racing became one of the major diversions of the British royalty between the twelfth and seventeenth centuries, and, thereafter, horse racing was known as the "Sport of Kings."

Horse racing was popular in colonial America, and, true to its English heritage, was limited to the aristocracy or "gentry." In early colonial days, concern over the lack of quality horses in America prompted colonial governors to sponsor races as a means of identifying the fastest horses for selective breeding. The first racetrack in America was the Newmarket Course, built in 1665 in Hempstead, New York.

By the 1800s, horse racing was conducted at county fairs or at gypsy (traveling) tracks, most notably in Maryland, Virginia, and Kentucky. The first big racetracks opened around the turn of the century, with New York's Belmont Park leading the way in 1905. The first American stakes race, offering a purse for the winner, was the Traveler's Stakes at Saratoga Springs, New York. In 1934, California's Santa Anita track opened. The largest track in the United States, New York's Aqueduct, opened in 1959. Racetracks are usually operated by private investors but are regulated by State Racing Commissions.

46

TABLE 4.2

Live Racing Days

	Thoroughbred	Quarter Horse	Harness	Mixed	Total
Alabama	61				61
Arizona				289	289
Arkansas	64				64
California	483	142	102	114	841
Colorado				264	264
Connecticut	No Live Horse Racing Conducted				
Delaware	129		62		191
Florida	385		200		585
Idaho				108	108
Illinois	358		652		1,010
Indiana	42		104		146
Iowa				62	62
Kansas				70	70
Kentucky	303		90		393
Louisiana	394	74			468
Maine			296		296
Maryland	259		237		496
Massachusetts	159		150		309
Michigan	181		655	91	927
Minnesota			6	55	61
Montana				58	58
Nebraska	183				183
Nevada				11	11
New Hampshire	100		12		112
New Jersey	270		440		710
New Mexico				344	344
New York	413		1,003		1,416
North Dakota				8	8
Ohio	490	4	801		1,295
Oklahoma	119			285	404
Oregon				145	145
Pennsylvania	414		368		782
Rhode Island	No Live Horse Racing Conducted				
South Dakota				15	15
Texas	206	95		183	484
Vermont			10		10
Washington	214			31	245
West Virginia	385				385
Wyoming				62	62
Totals	**5,612**	**315**	**5,188**	**2,128**	**13,243**

Source: *Pari-Mutuel Racing — 1995*, Association of Racing-Commissioners International, Inc., Lexington, KY, 1996

Growing Competition

Fifteen years ago, if a person wanted to gamble, he went to the racetrack, placed his bet, and rooted for his favorite horse or dog. The only other option was to call a bookie, who would take bets on those same dog or horse races. Today the situation has changed dramatically. The gambler can go to his local convenience store and buy a lottery ticket, visit a local truck stop and play a video lottery terminal, ride a riverboat and play casino games, cruise on a "trip to nowhere" and play roulette, or visit an old mining town in Colorado or South Dakota and play the slot machines. All of these gambling opportunities have captured many of the gambling dollars that were once bet on the horses and dogs. As a result, horse racing's popularity has been dropping over the past decade, a decline from which it may never recover.

TABLE 4.3

On-Track Attendance

	Thoroughbred	Quarter Horse	Harness	Mixed	Total
Alabama	34,423				34,423
Arizona				624,925	624,925
Arkansas	897,164				897,164
California	4,172,174	364,866	127,783	431,383	5,096,206
Colorado				158,899	158,899
Connecticut					
Delaware	384,210		61,544		445,754
Florida	1,813,963		435,740		2,249,703
Idaho				175,398	175,398
Illinois	1,535,030		1,067,052		2,602,082
Indiana	95,468		146,671		242,139
Iowa				N/A	N/A
Kansas				46,676	46,676
Kentucky	1,864,445		105,342		1,969,787
Louisiana	697,557	41,914			739,471
Maine			N/A		N/A
Maryland	2,382,008		446,101		2,830,109
Massachusetts	964,675		249,575		1,214,250
Michigan	532,404		1,198,916	10,005	1,741,325
Minnesota			1,359	226,073	227,432
Montana				N/A	N/A
Nebraska	416,096				416,096
Nevada				N/A	N/A
New Hampshire	332,366		N/A		332,366
New Jersey	1,505,042		1,794,447		3,299,489
New Mexico				715,745	715,745
New York	2,866,456		1,324,232		4,190,688
North Dakota				5,600	5,600
Ohio	1,478,483	8,067	1,757,504		3,244,054
Oklahoma	629,794			489,242	1,119,036
Oregon				N/A	N/A
Pennsylvania	966,904		538,965		1,505,869
Rhode Island					
South Dakota				N/A	N/A
Texas	831,445	254,521		343,880	1,429,846
Vermont			N/A		N/A
Washington	696,803			47,600	744,403
West Virginia	634,893				634,893
Wyoming				N/A	N/A
Totals	**25,731,803**	**669,368**	**9,257,231**	**3,275,426**	**38,933,828**

Source: *Pari-Mutuel Racing — 1995*, Association of Racing Commissioners International, Inc., Lexington, KY, 1996

Average attendance at two of the country's most famous tracks, Aqueduct and Belmont Park in New York, has decreased 40 percent in the past 15 years, and attendance is down at many other tracks. Roosevelt Raceway on Long Island, New York, one of the most famous harness racing tracks, closed in 1988. Florida's Hialeah track, a stalwart of the thoroughbred industry, shut down in 1990.

Canterbury Downs in Minnesota, built at a cost of $80 million (which saddled it with a heavy debt payment) in 1985 to be the ultimate harness track, could not compete with neighboring Indian casinos and went under in 1992. Citing competition from the newly opened riverboat at nearby Elgin, the ownership of Arlington Racetrack near Chicago decided to cancel the 1995 racing season (although they later agreed to do a shortened meet). Finally, no longer able to compete, the track shut down in October 1997. Much was expected from the Sam Houston Race Park in Houston, Texas, but it soon went bankrupt as well.

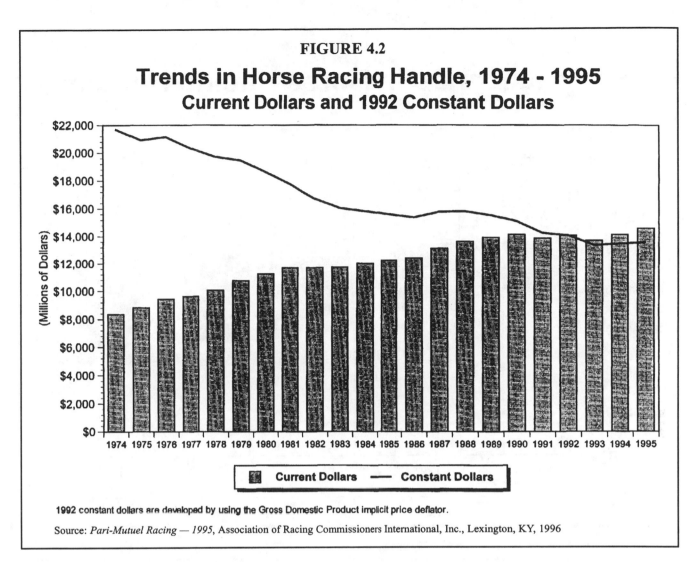

FIGURE 4.2

Trends in Horse Racing Handle, 1974 - 1995
Current Dollars and 1992 Constant Dollars

1992 constant dollars are developed by using the Gross Domestic Product implicit price deflator.

Source: *Pari-Mutuel Racing — 1995*, Association of Racing Commissioners International, Inc., Lexington, KY, 1996

Types of Horse Racing Events

There are three major forms of horse racing: thoroughbred, harness, and quarter-horse racing. In the United States, thoroughbred is, by far, the most popular form of horse-racing, followed by harness and then quarter horse racing.

Thoroughbred Racing

Anatomically, the thoroughbred horse is distinguished from other breeds of horses by its greater height and longer legs, although in order to be registered as a thoroughbred, other criteria must be met. In 1894, the prestigious Jockey Club was formed in New York for the purpose of organizing and regulating thoroughbred racing. Traditionally, a thoroughbred horse must be registered with the New York Jockey Club, and a horse may be registered only if his sire (father) and dam (mother) are already on the rolls. In other words, the lineage of all thoroughbreds must be genetically traceable back to three oriental stallions, Godolphin, Byerly, and Darley, the prototypes of the breed.

Harness Racing

In harness racing, the rider sits in a carriage (sulky) and guides the horse around the track. The horses are trained to be either trotters or pacers. On a trotter, the left-front and right-rear legs of the horse move forward almost simultaneously; then the right-front and left-rear legs move. On a pacer, both left legs move forward in unison, then both right legs move.

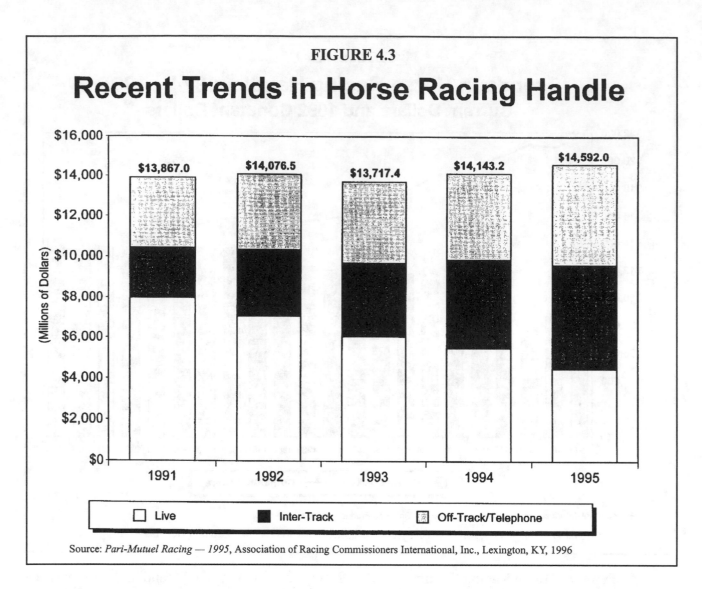

FIGURE 4.3
Recent Trends in Horse Racing Handle

(Millions of Dollars)

Year	Total
1991	$13,867.0
1992	$14,076.5
1993	$13,717.4
1994	$14,143.2
1995	$14,592.0

Legend: ☐ Live ■ Inter-Track ▨ Off-Track/Telephone

Source: *Pari-Mutuel Racing — 1995*, Association of Racing Commissioners International, Inc., Lexington, KY, 1996

Quarter Horse Racing

The quarter horse (the word quarter referring to the quarter-mile sprint it runs) evolved in colonial Virginia where breeders crossed native English horses with those of Spanish ancestry. This crossbreeding resulted in a swift horse that could outrun other breeds in short-distance races. Unlike the thoroughbred, quarter horses can also be used for farm work and transportation.

Racing Days and Number of Races

Race tracks are not open every day of the year, but rather operate for relatively short periods called "meets." A track might have two meets in a year, often one in the spring and one in the fall. State regulatory agencies usually approve the times for these meets and try to schedule them so that neighboring tracks do not have conflicting meets.

In 1995, there was a total of 13,243 racing days in the United States, down from 13,841 in 1990. New York had the greatest number of racing days (1,446), followed by Ohio (1,295), Illinois (1,010), and Michigan (847). Connecticut (0), Rhode Island (0), North Dakota (8), Vermont (10), Nevada (11), and South Dakota (15) had the fewest (Table 4.2). A total of 115,497 horse races were run in 1995.

Attendance

About 39 million people visited the track in 1995 (Table 4.3), a huge (61 percent) drop from

50

TABLE 4.4

Total Pari-Mutuel Handle ($)

	Thoroughbred	Quarter Horse	Harness	Mixed	Total
Alabama	39,936,408				39,936,408
Arizona				132,863,588	132,863,588
Arkansas	152,909,671				152,909,671
California	2,155,364,806	140,146,053	55,636,308	187,311,616	2,538,458,783
Colorado				59,425,144	59,425,144
Connecticut				205,247,188	205,247,188
Delaware	100,733,752		22,042,353		122,776,105
Florida	524,189,898		76,928,299		601,118,197
Idaho				30,486,839	30,486,839
Illinois	705,161,446		496,837,846		1,201,999,292
Indiana	88,042,652		29,470,835		117,513,287
Iowa				35,018,636	35,018,636
Kansas				41,766,331	41,766,331
Kentucky	654,959,372		17,507,287		672,466,659
Louisiana	336,607,580	11,416,854			348,024,434
Maine			14,056,607	49,492,806	63,549,413
Maryland	484,028,207		111,850,364		595,878,571
Massachusetts	199,782,263		29,635,898		229,418,161
Michigan	100,790,868		208,974,623	757,654	310,522,945
Minnesota	49,037,826	467,714	2,306,481	14,768,883	66,580,904
Montana				9,707,160	9,707,160
Nebraska	116,155,074				116,155,074
Nevada	340,085,017	5,856,800	31,885,317	227,595	378,054,629
New Hampshire	131,899,874		22,054,637		153,954,511
New Jersey	261,506,299		382,231,644	577,296,136	1,221,034,079
New Mexico				110,823,297	110,823,297
New York	2,289,080,011		523,265,255		2,812,345,266
North Dakota				4,410,528	4,410,528
Ohio	228,722,951	186,781	184,016,987		412,926,719
Oklahoma	101,012,923			84,504,890	185,517,813
Oregon				61,266,175	61,266,175
Pennsylvania	702,154,958		226,848,588		929,003,546
Rhode Island				58,066,203	58,066,203
South Dakota				2,822,712	2,822,712
Texas	259,992,278	22,839,563		37,879,065	320,710,906
Vermont			797,526		797,526
Washington	132,532,709			1,582,562	134,115,271
West Virginia	102,191,464				102,191,464
Wyoming				12,066,871	12,066,871
Totals	**10,256,878,107**	**180,913,565**	**2,436,345,655**	**1,717,815,879**	**14,591,953,206**

Source: *Pari-Mutuel Racing — 1995*, Association of Racing Commissioners International, Inc., Lexington, KY, 1996

the more than 63.8 million people who attended horse racing events at the track in 1990. On-track attendance at tracks in California tumbled from 13.7 million in 1990 to 5 million in 1995. New York attendance fell from almost 7 million in 1990 to less than 4.2 million in 1995. Daily average attendance dropped from 4,610 persons per track in 1990 to 2,940 persons per track in 1995.

Horse Racing Handle

Figure 4.2 indicates the steady slide in constant dollars (which account for inflation) in horse racing handle over the past two decades. Figure 4.3 shows the growing importance of non-live betting to the industry. Pari-mutuel bettors wagered $14.6 billion on horse races in 1995 (Table 4.4). About $4.5 billion was bet at the track (which generally includes simulcasting) (Table 4.5), and $5.1 billion was bet on inter-track races (Table 4.6). Over $4.9 billion was wagered at off-track betting establishments (Table 4.7). New York ($2.8 billion), California ($2.5 billion), Illinois ($1.2 billion), and New Jersey ($1.2 billion) accounted for about half of all the money bet on horseracing (Table 4.4). Most money (70

TABLE 4.5

Pari-Mutuel Handle - Total On-Track ($)

	Thoroughbred	Quarter Horse	Harness	Mixed	Total
Alabama	5,666,161				5,666,161
Arizona				54,637,344	54,637,344
Arkansas	104,739,943				104,739,943
California	662,680,168	47,906,373	14,699,173	47,258,288	772,544,002
Colorado				6,784,487	6,784,487
Connecticut					
Delaware	27,251,269		6,969,282		34,220,551
Florida	327,881,915		45,719,347		373,601,262
Idaho				6,882,780	6,882,780
Illinois	168,278,820		107,107,256		275,386,076
Indiana	6,459,004		11,468,514		17,927,518
Iowa				4,946,271	4,946,271
Kansas				3,306,401	3,306,401
Kentucky	228,324,851		6,622,291		234,947,142
Louisiana	104,100,831	3,996,639			108,097,470
Maine			11,336,156		11,336,156
Maryland	113,252,229		32,252,764		145,504,993
Massachusetts	44,281,284		7,034,689		51,315,973
Michigan	100,790,668		208,974,623	757,654	310,522,945
Minnesota			45,968	14,768,883	14,814,851
Montana				4,290,490	4,290,490
Nebraska	25,720,893				25,720,893
Nevada				227,595	227,595
New Hampshire	27,794,009		768,901		28,562,910
New Jersey	169,375,856		263,750,505		433,126,361
New Mexico				41,831,234	41,831,234
New York	557,461,784		160,844,924		718,306,708
North Dakota				74,198	74,198
Ohio	114,119,388	186,781	166,029,429		280,335,598
Oklahoma	77,190,185			48,386,110	125,576,295
Oregon				11,626,514	11,626,514
Pennsylvania	89,965,387		35,170,557		125,135,944
Rhode Island					
South Dakota				337,157	337,157
Texas	49,219,515	13,637,415		27,343,380	90,200,310
Vermont			797,526		797,526
Washington	21,390,635			1,582,562	22,973,197
West Virginia	45,071,449				45,071,449
Wyoming				3,347,681	3,347,681
Totals	**3,071,016,244**	**65,727,208**	**1,079,591,905**	**278,389,029**	**4,494,724,386**

Source: *Pari-Mutuel Racing — 1995*, Association of Racing Commissioners International, Inc., Lexington, KY, 1996

percent) was bet on thoroughbred racing (Table 4.4). The average on-track bettor wagered $115.45.

Return to Bettors and to the Winning Horse Owners

The total pari-mutuel takeout was $3 billion or 20.93 percent of the handle. That means that an average of 79 percent of the money wagered on pari-mutuel horse races in 1995 was returned to the bettors. Owners of winning horses claimed nearly $882 million in prize money, down from the $951 million in prize money in 1990.

Government Revenues

In 1995, state and local governments received nearly $456 million from horseracing, down from $624 million in 1990. Horse racing revenue to the government peaked at $780 million in 1975. It slid downward until 1980, when it rose to $713 million. The general decline continued until 1995, when revenue rose slightly. (See Table 4.8.) Table

TABLE 4.6
Pari-Mutuel Handle - Inter-Track ($)

Thoroughbred	Quarter Horse	Harness	Mixed	Total
34,270,247				34,270,247
			10,387,994	10,387,994
48,169,728				48,169,728
883,072,524	44,888,670	19,432,393	80,096,996	1,027,490,583
Included in Off-Track Wagering				
Included in Off-Track Wagering				
73,482,483		15,073,071		88,555,554
196,307,983		31,208,952		227,516,935
			23,604,059	23,604,059
223,414,261		137,596,015		361,010,276
Included in Off-Track Wagering				
			30,072,365	30,072,365
			38,461,930	38,461,930
395,104,074		10,884,996		405,989,070
86,825,060	2,785,105			89,610,165
			18,877,296	18,877,296
306,791,156		63,258,937		370,050,093
155,500,979		22,601,209		178,102,188
49,037,826	467,714	2,260,513		51,766,053
90,434,181				90,434,181
104,105,865		21,285,736		125,391,601
77,584,187		101,718,730	472,788,649	652,091,566
			68,992,063	68,992,063
250,953,028		62,116,688		313,069,716
114,603,563		17,986,558		132,590,121
14,541,509			35,396,261	49,937,770
Included in Off-Track Wagering				
284,149,760		46,051,658		330,201,417
			58,066,203	58,066,203
210,772,763	9,202,148		10,535,685	230,510,596
6,333,478				6,333,478
57,120,015				57,120,015
3,662,574,668	57,343,637	551,475,456	847,279,501	5,118,673,261

Source: *Pari-Mutuel Racing — 1995*, Association of Racing Commissioners International, Inc., Lexington, KY, 1996

4.9 shows how much each state received from horseracing. California ($117.5 million) and New York ($128 million) got more than half of all the revenues gained by the states. State governments collected $23 million in uncashed pari-mutuel tickets, that is, winnings that were never claimed.

Marketing Horse Racing and Making It Easier to Bet

As an industry facing stiff competition from other forms of gambling, horse racing must do something to make itself more attractive and more accessible if the industry is to survive. While it might be nice to see full stands at the racetrack, the tracks may have to bring the horse races to the customer. In New Haven, the old Connecticut Teletrack has been replaced by an updated Sport Haven that offers both large screens and individual screens to bettors in a modern, comfortable environment. Other states are also trying to make off-track betting easier by permitting OTB in restaurants and bars where people are already comfortable. In today's economy, in which the

53

TABLE 4.7
Pari-Mutuel Handle - Off-Track ($)

	Thoroughbred	Quarter Horse	Harness	Mixed	Total
Alabama					
Arizona				67,838,250	67,838,250
Arkansas					
California	609,612,114	47,351,010	21,504,742	59,956,332	738,424,198
Colorado				52,640,657	52,640,657
Connecticut				205,247,188	205,247,188
Delaware					
Florida					
Idaho					
Illinois	313,468,365		252,134,575		565,602,940
Indiana	81,583,648		18,002,121		99,585,769
Iowa					
Kansas					
Kentucky	31,530,447				31,530,447
Louisiana	145,681,689	4,635,110			150,316,799
Maine			2,720,451	30,615,510	33,335,961
Maryland	63,984,822		16,338,663		80,323,485
Massachusetts					
Michigan					
Minnesota					
Montana				5,416,670	5,416,670
Nebraska					
Nevada	340,085,017	5,856,600	31,885,317		377,826,934
New Hampshire					
New Jersey	14,546,256		16,762,409	104,507,487	135,816,152
New Mexico					
New York	1,480,665,199		300,303,643		1,780,968,842
North Dakota				4,336,330	4,336,330
Ohio					
Oklahoma	9,281,229			722,519	10,003,748
Oregon				49,639,661	49,639,661
Pennsylvania	309,182,519		134,742,557		443,925,077
Rhode Island					
South Dakota				2,485,555	2,485,555
Texas					
Vermont					
Washington	104,808,598				104,808,598
West Virginia					
Wyoming				8,741,190	8,741,190
Totals	**3,504,429,903**	**57,842,720**	**794,394,478**	**592,147,349**	**4,948,814,451**

Source: *Pari-Mutuel Racing — 1995*, Association of Racing Commissioners International, Inc., Lexington, KY, 1996

consumers' needs tend to predominate, it might be necessary to bring horse racing to the bettor rather than bring the bettor to the track.

Efforts are also being made to make it easier to bet. Today, telephones are not only available at home or in the office, but in the automobile or wherever a small cellular phone can be carried. Telephone betting is legal in Connecticut, Kentucky, Maryland, Nevada, New York, Ohio, and Pennsylvania. In New York and Pennsylvania, cable television shows broadcast the latest racing information to make it easier for the bettor to phone in his bet.

Churchill Downs in Louisville, Kentucky, is experimenting with a new on-line, interactive wagering system that will allow bettors to use their cable television system to bet on horse races. This system, however, must wait for a number of changes in the law before it can be introduced. Making it easier to bet may be as simple as having readily-available runners place bets on the horses for the poker players in the card rooms at Hollywood Park in California.

TABLE 4.8
HORSE RACING
IN THE UNITED STATES

HORSE RACING REVENUE TO GOVERNMENT
1934 - 1995

1995 ... 455,764,292	1979 ... 680,919,798	1963 ... 316,570,791	1947 ... 97,926,984
1994 ... 451,546,549	1978 ... 673,063,831	1962 ... 287,930,030	1946 ... 94,035,859
1993 ... 471,735,474	1977 ... 700,239,986	1961 ... 264,853,077	1945 ... 65,265,405
1992 ... 491,259,606	1976 ... 714,629,120	1960 ... 258,039,385	1944 ... 55,971,233
1991 ... 523,249,392	1975 ... 780,081,431	1959 ... 243,388,655	1943 ... 38,194,727
1990 ... 623,839,806	1974 ... 645,980,984	1958 ... 222,049,651	1942 ... 22,005,278
1989 ... 584,888,183	1973 ... 585,201,524	1957 ... 216,747,621	1941 ... 21,128,173
1988 ... 596,202,319	1972 ... 531,404,550	1956 ... 207,456,272	1940 ... 16,145,182
1987 ... 608,351,461	1971 ... 512,838,417	1955 ... 186,989,588	1939 ... 10,369,807
1986 ... 587,357,677	1970 ... 486,403,097	1954 ... 178,015,828	1938 9,576,335
1985 ... 625,159,697	1969 ... 461,498,886	1953 ... 167,426,465	1937 8,434,792
1984 ... 650,262,852	1968 ... 426,856,448	1952 ... 142,489,696	1936 8,611,538
1983 ... 641,387,176	1967 ... 394,381,913	1951 ... 117,250,564	1935 8,386,255
1982 ... 652,888,463	1966 ... 388,452,125	1950 98,366,167	1934 6,024,193
1981 ... 680,199,584	1965 ... 369,892,036	1949 95,327,053	
1980 ... 712,727,523	1964 ... 350,095,928	1948 95,803,364	

Source: *Pari-Mutuel Racing — 1995*, Association of Racing Commissioners International, Inc., Lexington, KY, 1996

Tying More Tracks Together

The growing use of ITW can provide success for racetracks throughout the country. A racetrack up north cannot have horses racing during the winter. As a result, a huge financial investment stands idle, not earning any money. However, these racetracks can open up and have people come to the enclosed areas of the racetrack and bet on races being run in a warmer climate, such as Florida or California. Today, some northern tracks might have a have dozen different racing programs going on at the same time.

Meanwhile, racetracks in warmer climates, such as Gulfstream in southern Florida and Santa Anita in California, can have people betting on their races and adding to their revenues, even though they might be thousands of miles away. The viewing and betting on the big races all across the country benefit the originating track and all the tracks where these races are shown. For example, in 1995, the Kentucky Derby, which takes place at Churchill Downs in Louisville, Kentucky, was shown in 838 betting outlets across the country, leading to a handle of $38.6 million on a single race.

Trying to Get Organized

In 1994, in an attempt to organize and defend itself against the encroachment of other forms of gambling, the Thoroughbred Racing Agency (TRA) appointed J. Brian McGrath, an executive with a long history of marketing, as its first commissioner. McGrath was responsible for enlarging the TRA so that it could help the industry respond to the changing gambling climate by expanding the marketing of thoroughbred racing. Nonetheless, less than two years later, the track owners, unable to agree on how to best confront the future, fired McGrath and closed down the national office. This basically meant that the industry's survival would be dependent upon the success or failure of individual owners and tracks.

TABLE 4.9
Total Government Revenue ($)

Thoroughbred	Quarter Horse	Harness	Mixed	Total
1,283,034				1,283,034
			1,440,090	1,440,090
4,838,880				4,838,880
107,586,941	1,808,711	928,797	7,200,279	117,524,729
			529,490	529,490
			7,661,719	7,661,719
175,221		49,402		224,623
14,999,022		1,765,265		16,764,287
			751,269	751,269
30,898,166		21,913,362	1,340,785	54,152,313
1,922,565		687,068	295,291	2,904,924
			1,669,902	1,669,902
			1,395,388	1,395,388
9,862,982		177,061		10,040,043
9,472,073	244,063	43,320		9,759,456
		413,041	1,438,532	1,851,573
4,654,454		743,445	413,384	5,811,283
1,990,891		547,395		2,538,286
5,120,145		10,243,270	189,276	15,552,691
580,426	5,755	28,296	851,478	1,465,955
			192,778	192,778
1,062,817				1,062,817
3,455,772	57,770	335,247	2,276	3,851,065
2,904,187		446,237		3,350,424
2,681,135		3,673,864	495,435	6,850,434
			1,128,890	1,128,890
91,122,785		15,481,105	21,559,775	128,163,665
			95,280	95,280
9,875,887	14,396	7,300,136	200,384	17,390,803
2,112,071			3,121,646	5,233,717
			1,089,144	1,089,144
12,963,665		3,101,078		16,064,743
			2,946,454	2,946,454
All revenues allocated back to the racing industry				
3,215,673	282,521		1,553,040	5,051,234
		32,530		32,530
3,461,347			20,578	3,481,925
1,323,819				1,323,819
			294,634	294,634
327,563,958	**2,413,216**	**67,909,920**	**57,877,198**	**455,764,292**

Source: *Pari-Mutuel Racing — 1995*, Association of Racing Commissioners International, Inc., Lexington, KY, 1996

Expanding the Gambling Options at the Track

Many track owners are strongly considering an "if you can't beat them, join them" approach. In a number of states, tracks are introducing casino forms of gambling. Tracks that offer this combination of racing and casino gambling are called "racinos." For example, Mountaineer Park in West Virginia instituted video lottery terminals (VLTs) at the racetrack. Across the country, at Hollywood Park in California, a casino for card games has been built right next to the track. In Delaware, Dover Downs and Delaware Park introduced slot machines to their tracks. Others have considered actually integrating a complete casino with the racing facility. Currently, only Regina Exhibition Park in Regina, Saskatchewan, offers gamblers an integrated casino-racetrack facility, but this may be the wave of the future if the industry is to survive.

TABLE 4.10
HORSE RACING IN CANADA

	Live Racing Days			Number of Live Races		
	Thoroughbred	Harness	Total	Thoroughbred	Harness	Total
Alberta	200	205	405	1,647	1,965	3,612
British Columbia	150	149	299	1,341	1,537	2,878
Manitoba	67	44	131	660	374	1,034
New Brunswick		90	90		956	956
Newfoundland		18	18		120	120
Nova Scotia		193	193		1,966	1,966
Ontario	311	1,208	1,519	2,829	12,775	15,604
Prince Edward Island		124	124		1,378	1,378
Quebec		496	496		5,166	5,166
Saskatchewan	59	67	126	464	600	1,064
Totals	**807**	**2,594**	**3,401**	**6,941**	**26,837**	**33,778**

Note: Thoroughbred figures include quarter horse racing at minor circuit tracks.

Source: *Pari-Mutuel Racing — 1995*, Association of Racing Commissioners International, Inc., Lexington, KY, 1996

These options, however, are constantly imperilled by the potential opening of a casino, a riverboat, or Indian gaming nearby. To succeed, racetracks will have to make their offerings more attractive, more comfortable, and more alluring than their potential competitors. Finally, some people in the horse racing industry believe the industry has failed to effectively educate the public about how exciting horse racing can be.

Particular Problems of Harness Racing

The problems faced by the harness racing industry were highlighted in a 1993 report of the New York State Advisory Commission on Racing in the 21st Century. The report found that harness racing attendance in New York State had plunged from 9.3 million in 1970 to just 1.6 million in 1993. The on-track handle nosedived from $843.7 million in 1970 to only $231.9 million in 1993.

At the same time, revenue to the state plummeted from $86.7 million in 1970 to only $3.7 million in 1993. (None of these figures account for inflation, so the decline is even worse than it appears. For example, the $86.7 million paid to the state in 1970 would be $323 million in 1993 dollars, which would account for inflation.)

TABLE 4.11
Total Handle (C$)

	Thoroughbred	Harness	Total
Alberta	93,515,101	75,486,499	169,001,600
British Columbia	199,297,090	57,995,318	257,292,408
Manitoba	9,120,647	1,286,266	10,406,913
New Brunswick		4,131,840	4,131,840
Newfoundland		53,498	53,498
Nova Scotia		10,179,867	10,179,867
Ontario	634,853,019	587,349,776	1,222,202,795
Prince Edward Island		4,660,656	4,660,656
Quebec	69,111,741	103,252,595	172,364,336
Saskatchewan	5,535,217	1,533,860	7,069,077
Totals	**1,011,432,815**	**845,930,175**	**1,857,362,990**

Source: *Pari-Mutuel Racing — 1995*, Association of Racing Commissioners International, Inc., Lexington, KY

TABLE 4.12
GREYHOUND RACING

	Live Performances			Number of Live Races	Attendance			
	Matinees	Evenings	Total		On-Track	Average	ITW	OTW
Birmingham, AL	155	309	464	6,042	428,144	923	200,259	
Greene County, AL	302	149	451	5,863	125,225	278		
Macon County, AL	204	306	510	6,630	649,629	1,274		
Mobile County, AL	156	307	463	5,709	362,563	783		
Alabama Total	817	1,071	1,888	24,244	1,565,561	829	200,259	
Arizona	N/A	N/A	790	11,130	494,557	626		
Arkansas	71	312	383	5,031	814,154	2,128		
Colorado	N/A	N/A	720	10,933	622,969	865	567,268	
Connecticut	336	145	481	7,019	362,119	753		
Florida	1,548	2,836	4,384	60,672	6,188,050	1,412		
Idaho	102	221	323	4,258	156,314	484		
Iowa	N/A	N/A	509	7,305	N/A			
Kansas	369	455	824	11,632	1,114,546	1,353		
Massachusetts	N/A	N/A	1,068	13,428	1,510,329	1,414		
New Hampshire	480	347	827	11,592	517,100	625		
Oregon	N/A	N/A	133	1,696	N/A			
Rhode Island	281	107	388	5,044	N/A			
South Dakota	No Live Greyhound Racing Conducted							90,200
Texas	N/A	N/A	1,202	14,424	1,656,228	1,378	61,448	
West Virginia	166	613	779	11,697	1,007,355	1,293		
Wisconsin	644	767	1,411	20,915	1,574,313	1,118		
Totals	N/A	N/A	16,110	221,020	17,583,595	N/A	828,975	90,200

Note: Number of races in Greene County (Ala.), Iowa, and Rhode Island are estimated.

Source: *Pari-Mutuel Racing — 1995*, Association of Racing Commissioners International, Inc., Lexington, KY, 1996

The report recommended lower taxes on the handle, more simulcasting, less regulation, more televised races, larger purses to attract better horses, and a greater effort to increase the integrity of the sport. (In 1995, harness racing attendance in New York state fell even further to 1.3 million, and the on-track handle to $160 million. Revenue to the state was $3.9 million.)

Harness racing has had a particularly difficult time appealing to younger people. Harness racing has never really caught on in the South and the West. Harness racing occurs at night, and many gamblers have already wagered their money. Many people choose the VCR for their nighttime entertainment rather than the racetrack. In addition, because of the fear of crime, some people are afraid to go out at night.

Just as for thoroughbred racing, simulcast and inter-track wagering have helped the harness racing industry to survive. However, since harness racing is not as popular nationwide as thorough-bred racing, its market is more limited.

HORSE RACING IN CANADA

Unlike the United States, where thoroughbred racing dominates, harness racing is the most popular form of the sport in Canada. There were 3,401 racing days throughout Canada, about three-fourths at harness racing tracks. (See Table 4.10.)

The pari-mutuel handle totaled about $1.86 billion in 1995 (Table 4.11), down from nearly $2 billion in 1990. The total takeout was $437 million, or 23.5 percent. The provincial govern-

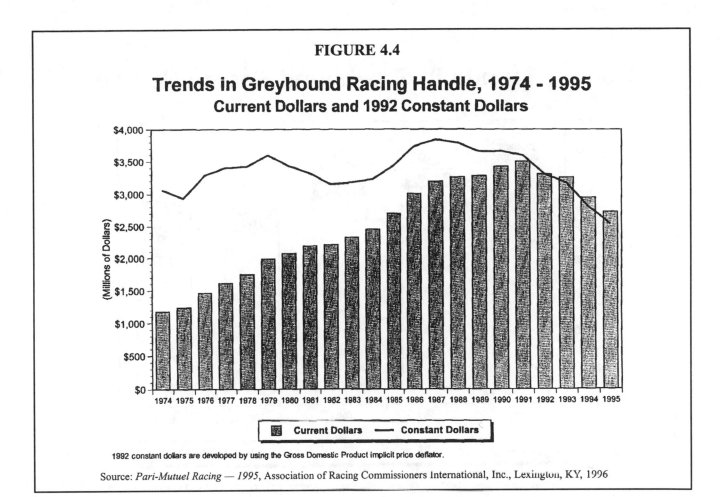

FIGURE 4.4

Trends in Greyhound Racing Handle, 1974 - 1995
Current Dollars and 1992 Constant Dollars

Current Dollars ▨ ——— Constant Dollars

1992 constant dollars are developed by using the Gross Domestic Product implicit price deflator.

Source: *Pari-Mutuel Racing — 1995*, Association of Racing Commissioners International, Inc., Lexington, KY, 1996

ments got $135 million in 1995, down from $141.7 million in 1990. The federal government received $14.8 million.

DOG RACING — THE SPORT OF QUEENS

Dog racing developed from a hunting sport called "coursing" in which a hare was released and then a pair of greyhounds was set in pursuit. The race was judged on the dogs' performance as they ran down the hare. Coursing was very popular during the reign of Queen Elizabeth I of England in the last half of the sixteenth century. For this reason, it became known as the "Sport of Queens." The modern version of dog racing developed from a coursing event in South Dakota in 1904. The sponsor of the contest, Owen Patrick Smith, loved the sport but detested the killing of the hare. Smith spent 15 years perfecting a mechanical lure, thus eliminating one of the more inhumane aspects of the sport.

Dog racing took off in Florida during the 1920s as a nighttime alternative to daytime horse racing. From there, it spread, eventually becoming legal in 19 states. Interest in dog racing peaked in the mid-1980s with a number of new race tracks being built in order to take advantage of the growing attendance. Unfortunately, the 1990s have not been as kind to the industry. The same factors that hurt horse racing and jai-alai also hit dog racing. Lotteries and casino gambling have lured bettors away. While some tracks have stayed even, many are struggling to survive, and, in fact, a number have closed.

Total Performances, Number of Races, and Attendance

During 1995, 16,110 performances took place, down from 17,520 in 1993. About one-fourth (27 percent) of all races were held in Florida. Total attendance has tumbled in just four years from

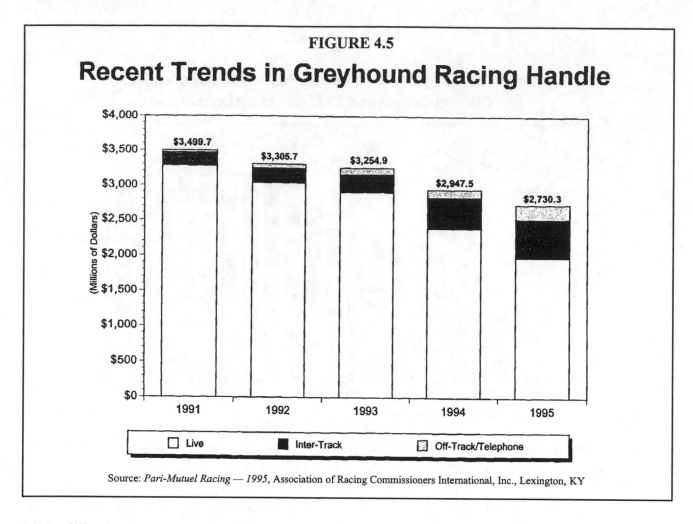

FIGURE 4.5

Recent Trends in Greyhound Racing Handle

Live ☐ Inter-Track ■ Off-Track/Telephone ▦

Source: *Pari-Mutuel Racing — 1995*, Association of Racing Commissioners International, Inc., Lexington, KY

30.5 million in 1991 to just 17.5 million in 1995. (See Table 4.12.)

The Handle, Government Revenues, and Purses to the Winning Dog Owners

Greyhound racing's serious difficulties are further reflected in the drop in virtually all financial categories during the 1990s. The amount wagered fell from $3.5 billion in 1991 to $3.0 billion in 1995. Figure 4.4 shows the decline of the greyhound racing handle. With the handle dropping, government revenues fell from $233.7 million in 1991 to $156.8 million in 1995. The purse distribution fell from $131.2 million in 1993 to $115 million in 1995.

Overall, about 82 percent of the handle is returned to the bettors, 6 percent to the government, 4 percent to purses for the winning owners, and 8 percent to the track owners for operating expenses and profit. The average bettor wagered $112.47 at the track.

Fighting to Survive

The dog racing industry is struggling to survive. The Valley Greyhound Park in Harlingen, Texas, and Greenetrack in Alabama have shut down. The Plainfield Greyhound Park has been financially devastated by the nearby Foxwoods Casino in Ledyard, Connecticut. The Coeur d'Alene Greyhound Park in Post Falls, Idaho, and the Camptown Greyhound Park in Frontenac, Kansas, have closed their doors. The Biscayne Greyhound Track in Miami Shores, Florida, the nation's second oldest track (opened in 1926), went out of business. Other recent closings include Wisconsin Dells Greyhound Park in Wisconsin, Waterloo Greyhound Park in Iowa, and Shoreline Star in Connecticut.

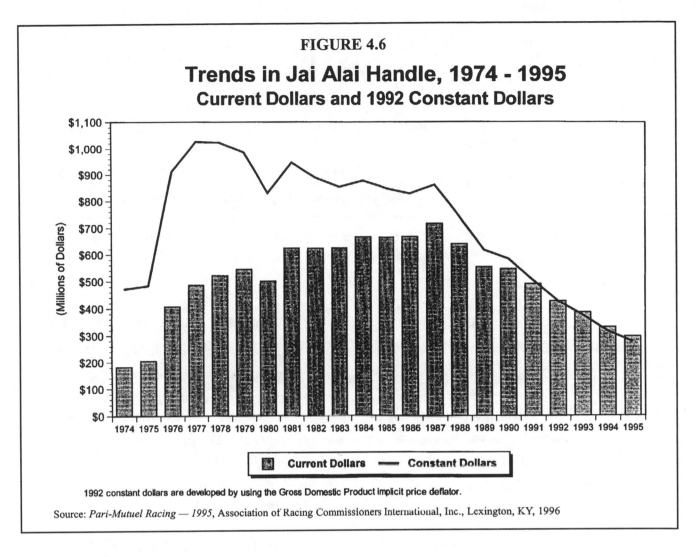

FIGURE 4.6

Trends in Jai Alai Handle, 1974 - 1995
Current Dollars and 1992 Constant Dollars

Current Dollars ▨   Constant Dollars ——

1992 constant dollars are developed by using the Gross Domestic Product implicit price deflator.

Source: *Pari-Mutuel Racing — 1995*, Association of Racing Commissioners International, Inc., Lexington, KY, 1996

As of December 31, 1996, there were 48 greyhound tracks open for live racing in 15 of the 17 states where dog racing is legal. In the last five years, 14 tracks have been closed; four of the 14 (Yuma Greyhound Park in Arizona, Coeur d'Alene in Idaho, Greenetrack in Alabama, and Camptown in Kansas) remain open for simulcasting.

Like horse tracks, dog tracks have turned to simulcasting and off-track betting. Figure 4.5 shows the increasing importance of off-site gambling to the industry. In addition to simulcasting other dog racing, most tracks are also putting on horse races. Moreover, many dog tracks have turned to casino-type games such as slot machines, video lottery terminals (VLTs), and other games. In virtually every state in which greyhound tracks operate, owners are appealing, if not begging, state legislatures to permit their tracks to operate casino games, most notably slot machines.

Without simulcasting and casino games, many dog tracks will not survive. Marketing attempts to make dog racing more attractive to younger gamblers have generally failed, and if dog tracks do not somehow incorporate the more successful forms of gambling, they will continue to suffer grave economic difficulties.

Like the owners of horse tracks, the owners of dog tracks will have to become more innovative. Lincoln Park (formerly Lincoln Greyhound Park) in Rhode Island has successfully introduced video lottery terminals (VLTs) at its facility. The income from the VLTs has attracted more customers and has allowed the track to increase the purses. The

TABLE 4.13

JAI-ALAI

	Number of Performances	Number of Games	Live Meet Attendance	Average Attendance	Live Handle ($)	Inter-Track/ Off-Track Handle ($)
Connecticut	682	9,904	577,354	847	85,369,406	10,114,319
Florida	1,910	25,159	2,251,808	1,179	168,464,333	28,488,217
Rhode Island	156	1,989	379,008	2,430	3,960,248	
Totals	2,748	37,052	3,208,170	1,167	257,793,987	38,602,536

	Total Handle ($)	Total Takeout ($)	Effective Takeout Rate	Total Government Revenue ($)	Pari- Mutuel Tax Revenue ($)	Breakage to Gov't ($)
Connecticut	95,483,725	19,177,088	20.08%	2,560,316	2,061,413	68,980
Florida	196,952,550	46,448,380	23.58%	10,219,599	8,385,731	
Rhode Island	3,960,248	811,851	20.50%	180,134	158,409	2,458
Totals	296,396,523	66,437,319	22.42%	12,960,049	10,605,553	71,438

Source: *Pari-Mutuel Racing — 1995*, Association of Racing Commissioners International, Inc., Lexington, KY, 1996

track has upgraded the facility to make it more attractive to visitors. Nonetheless, despite its success, Lincoln remains threatened by the opening of more Native American casinos in the area, which can offer more casino gambling alternatives than just the VLTs that Lincoln provides. One day the ownership of Lincoln may have to turn to the state government and ask permission to introduce other casino games, such as slot machines, so that it can compete.

Bluffs Run Greyhound Park in Council Bluffs, Iowa, has been virtually converted into a casino as a 52,000 square-foot addition offers over 1,000 slot machines to gamblers. Without this addition, it is unlikely the track would have survived.

Wonderland Greyhound Park in Boston, Massachusetts, recently began offering four-dog races on a trial basis. Called "Fast Four," each of the four races features four greyhounds, run at four different distances (3/16ths, 5/16ths, 3/8ths and 7/16ths of a mile), with four different wagering options. If the novelty races are successful, they will be offered for a longer period of time.

ANIMAL RIGHTS MOVEMENT

The dog racing industry has also run afoul of the animal rights movement. Alleged mistreatment of the dogs, including the killing of dogs that cannot win, has led to protests and the lobbying of state legislatures. Disclosures by animal rights activists of harmful treatment of the animals have led many track owners to improve the conditions for the animals and try to find more homes for the dogs who can no longer race. Many animal rights activists, however, believe the sport itself is barbaric and call for its abolition.

These activists have convinced legislators in Maine and Virginia to ban any future greyhound racing and legislators in Vermont to rescind their existing laws permitting it. Animal rights protesters often picket at dog racing tracks, and their efforts probably played a role in the closing of the Coeur D'Alene Greyhound Track in Post Falls, Idaho. However, the deteriorating financial situation was probably the major consideration as it has been for the numerous tracks that have recently shut down.

Too Little Too Late?

In November 1997, the American Greyhound Track Operators Association (AGTOA) held a "$1 Million Night of Stars" event to showcase greyhound racing and to promote greyhound adoption. Eleven tracks each hosted a live event on the program. The races were broadcast simultaneously via satellite to 150 wagering sites across the country.

Several national greyhound protection advocacy groups were angry that the adoption feature was included in an event really designed to promote the sport. According to David Wolfe, director of the National Greyhound Adoption Program, the purpose of the event was not to find homes for greyhounds, but to promote greyhound racing. The Greyhound Protection League called for demonstrations nationwide. Demonstrators protested at racetracks in Arizona, Colorado, Florida, Massachusetts, Rhode Island, and Wisconsin.

Bob Trapp, treasurer of Greyhound Pets of America, reported that a total of 32 calls were received by the toll-free adoption referral number — less than 1 percent of the expected 5,000 calls.

According to the *Racing Form*, an industry newspaper, the actual handle for the event totaled $1.2 million. An AGTOA spokesperson said

TABLE 4.14

JAI-ALAI
IN THE UNITED STATES

JAI-ALAI REVENUE TO GOVERNMENT
1978 - 1995

1995	12,960,049
1994	21,534,496
1993	26,585,724
1992	30,137,047
1991	35,031,585
1990	38,608,321
1989	38,898,706
1988	43,572,178
1987	51,377,135
1986	50,144,777
1985	50,079,524
1984	48,269,509
1983	45,398,087
1982	45,000,544
1981	44,364,100
1980	35,308,705
1979	36,036,607
1978	34,707,615

Source: *Pari-Mutuel Racing — 1995*, Association of Racing Commissioners International, Inc., Lexington, KY, 1996

previously that the total handle had to exceed $1.5 million for the event to be considered a success.

Promoting Tourism or Endorsing Racing?

In recent years, the U-Haul company has featured a racing greyhound graphic on its Kansas moving vans. According to the president of U-Haul, the design represented the Greyhound Hall of Fame and was developed after consulting a number of chambers of commerce and tourism bureaus. The graphics were not an endorsement of dog racing. In response to many complaints from individuals and groups, the graphic was changed.

Kansas U-Haul vans now sport a graphic of a steam engine locomotive.

JAI-ALAI

Jai-alai, which means "merry festival," is a fast-paced game in which the players, using a large curved basket (called a "cesta") strapped to their arms, whip a small hard ball ("pelota") made of goat skin against the three walls and floor of a huge playing court ("fronton") in much the same manner as handball or racquetball. Jai-alai was invented in the seventeenth century by the Basques, who live in northern Spain and southern France.

The game has been popular in Latin America, but is in serious trouble in the United States. Figure 4.6 shows a sharp and continuing decline since 1987, with the handle in 1995 less than half of the 1987 handle in both current and constant (which account for inflation) dollars. Pari-mutuel betting on jai-alai is available in just two states, Florida and Connecticut. (The one fronton in Rhode Island indicated for 1995 in Table 4.13 is now offering dog racing.) In 1995, seven frontons were operating in Florida and one was functioning in Connecticut. Jai-alai has never gained a following in the United States outside of southern New England and Florida.

Number of Performances, Number of Games, and Attendance

During 1995, there were 2,748 performances or events, down from 3,619 in 1990. Seventy percent of these performances took place in Florida. Florida accounted for 70 percent of total attendance — 2.25 million attendees out of 3.2 million. In 1990, 5.3 million people had attended the games. Average attendance at the games in Florida (1,179) was somewhat larger than in Connecticut (847) but smaller than in Rhode Island (2,430), which also offers greyhound racing (Table 4.13).

Handle and Government Revenue

Total pari-mutuel handle for jai-alai games in 1995 was $296 million, down from $545.5 million in 1990 and $639.2 million in 1988 (See Figure 4.6 and Table 4.13). Total takeout was $66 million and government revenue totaled nearly $13 million, barely one-fourth the $50 million the government received in 1985, 1986, and 1987 (Tables 4.13 and 4.14).

Trying to Survive

Jai-alai suffered through a painful strike from 1988 to 1991. While this hurt the game, the opening of the Foxwoods casino at Ledyard, Connecticut, has been a calamity for jai-alai in New England. The frontons in Newport, Rhode Island, and Bridgeport, Connecticut, switched to dog racing, and the Hartford fronton closed down. The fronton in Milford, Connecticut, is the only remaining jai-lai-only facility in New England.

While Florida's vote not to introduce land-based casino gambling gave jai-alai a respite from the challenge of land-based casino gambling, the future of the sport in the United States is very uncertain. Tourists in Florida can still take "cruises to nowhere" which offer casino gambling and take customers away from jai-alai. The lottery has also drawn considerable money away from the frontons. In Connecticut, the opening of more Indian gambling throughout New England will undoubtedly draw more gamblers away from the shrinking number of frontons.

Virtually every fronton has introduced simulcasting of horse races and even staggered the jai-alai games so they will not conflict with horse races. In fact, in many cases the simulcasting has become more important than the jai-alai, and the jai-alai season is becoming shorter. Jai-alai frontons often are now open with simulcast horse races on which gamblers bet, but there is no jai-alai game going on. Without simulcasting, many frontons could not make a profit. Perhaps more aggressive marketing might help the jai-alai industry, but its future is certainly in doubt.

CHAPTER V

CASINO GAMBLING

LAND-BASED CASINOS

Gambling is now bigger than baseball, more powerful than a platoon of Schwarzeneggers, Spielbergs, Madonnas, and Oprahs. More Americans went to casinos than to major league ballparks in 1993. Ninety-two million visits!
The New York Times Magazine, July 17, 1994

Technically, a casino is any room or rooms in which gaming is conducted. However, when most Americans think of casinos, they picture the gaudy hotel/casino/entertainment complexes seen on TV and movie screens. Up until the 1970s, casinos were associated exclusively with Nevada and especially Las Vegas. However, in 1977, the state of New Jersey legalized casino gambling for Atlantic City.

Over the past decade, local and state governments have increasingly turned to gambling in an effort to increase revenues. Lotteries have been the most public form of gambling, but a growing number of state and local governments have resorted to casino gambling in order to raise money without having to do the politically unpopular act of raising taxes. Economically depressed cities, such as Bridgeport, Connecticut, where the state eventually rejected a casino, or Niagara Falls, New York, which still hopes to have a facility in the future, have looked to casinos as a means to improve the local ailing economy.

Although the recent development of casinos has been most popular in the Midwest, the issue has been raised throughout the country. Not only are casinos now located in cities such as Deadwood, South Dakota, and Cripple Creek, Colorado, but casinos float up and down the Mississippi and Missouri Rivers and out into the Gulf of Mexico and the Pacific and Atlantic Oceans.

In addition, many Native American tribes have introduced casino gambling onto their reservations in an effort to raise money. These new casinos are a growing source of the total amount earned by casinos, and the management of several Las Vegas gambling casinos have shown an interest in developing the new casinos.

CASINOS IN NEVADA — A CENTURY OF GAMBLING

Nevadans adopted gambling long before the state was admitted to the Union. Casinos were located in gold mining camps and were considered a major source of entertainment, but there were few professional gamblers. By 1869, the Nevada legislature had legalized gambling in the state, and, except for a few periods of reform (gambling was made illegal in 1909 and reinstituted in 1931), casinos and Nevada have been linked ever since. Within the past 100 years, a pastime that mainly served to separate miners and cowboys from their money has become a respected state industry. Today, casino gambling is the main pillar of Nevada's economy, attracting residents and tourists alike, and, with them, so many dollars so that neither individuals nor corporations pay any state income taxes.

CASINOS IN NEW JERSEY

At the turn of the twentieth century, Atlantic City, New Jersey, was a famous seaside resort that attracted thousands of tourists to its Boardwalk on the ocean front. But, by the 1950s, its glory had faded. Cars and planes allowed East Coast residents to travel to more exotic shores, and the resort did not have an alternate economy to make up for the lost tourist dollars. In an attempt to rebuild the city's financial base, lower taxes, provide employment for its residents, and subsidize its considerable elderly population, the state of New Jersey legalized gambling in Atlantic City on June 2, 1977. All funds raised from the licensing and taxation of gambling operations were to be used for state and local social programs. As the "East Coast Vegas," Atlantic City once again became a resort — this time for gamblers and East Coast day-trippers.

AND NOW CASINOS
ARE ALMOST EVERYWHERE

During the 1980s, federal funding for state and local projects were cut, and financial demands upon state and local governments increased. Many manufacturing companies moved elsewhere in search of cheaper labor and more concessions, and areas dependent upon agriculture suffered severe economic reverses. At that time, many states and localities began to consider various forms of gambling to raise money and to provide an alternative to raising taxes. Lotteries had already gotten most state governments into the gambling business, making it easier for other methods of gambling to appear as sensible alternatives.

By the mid-1990s, cardrooms where players could gamble on card games were booming in California, Oregon, Washington, and Montana. Casinos attracted players in South Dakota and Colorado, while gamblers placed wagers on riverboats in Illinois, Iowa, Missouri, Mississippi, and Louisiana. By December 1997, 147 tribes in 24 states had approval to operate gambling establishments on their reservations (this does not include bingo). Meanwhile, many cruise lines have added or expanded casino operations in order to earn more money from existing cruises. Other cruise ships are floating casinos that sail out into the Atlantic Ocean or Gulf of Mexico so that their passengers can gamble outside United States waters.

Losing Support?

By the mid-1990s, however, the expansion of gambling had slowed. In the November 1994 elections, voters in Florida rejected a referendum that would have permitted land-based casinos. A referendum calling for limited-stakes casinos in Wyoming failed, and Colorado voters said no to expanding casino gambling. Rhode Islanders voted to limit Indian gambling to the town of Charlestown, and Iowa voters denied the city of Des Moines the right to develop riverboat gambling. Voters in Michigan rejected a proposal to permit Indian casino gambling in Port Huron. At the same time, however, Missouri voters approved an amendment permitting slot machines on the state's riverboats, while South Dakota passed a referendum legalizing video lottery terminals (VLTs). Earlier in 1994, the VLTs had been declared unconstitutional.

Gambling issues did little better in November 1995. Voters in Floyd and Clark counties in Indiana rejected a referendum calling for riverboats. Massachusetts voters said no to a casino in Springfield. Jefferson City, Missouri, residents repealed riverboat gambling, which they had approved in 1992, and voters in Washington state said no to unrestricted gambling on Indian reservations. In October and November, California voters in six of nine communities rejected attempts to introduce cardrooms.

The trend continued in the November 1996 elections. A casino proposal was defeated in Arkansas. The voters in Ohio turned down a plan to develop eight riverboat casinos, and Washington state voters rejected the idea for slot machines on Indian land. Colorado, Nebraska, and Iowa defeated limited expansions of gambling in their states. In Louisiana, video poker was ousted from 33 parishes. On the other hand, Arizona and West Virginia approved limited expansion of gambling, and voters in Michigan said yes to a casino in economically depressed Detroit.

In the past several years, no new territories have been opened up to casino gambling. The failure of several riverboats in Mississippi, corruption scandals in Louisiana, and the bankruptcy of Harrah's in New Orleans have all added to the impression that the gambling industry has lost its spark. Recent election victories by more conservative Republicans, many of whom are concerned about "family values," have often made it more difficult to get pro-casino legislation through state legislatures. Grass roots efforts by such anti-gambling organizations as the National Coalition Against Legalized Gambling have mobilized popular opposition. (See Chapter II.)

Some economic observers believe that the market may be saturated or that a natural backlash has occurred as local economies try to absorb the effects of introducing casino gambling into their areas. The improvement in the economy has made the need for additional sources of income less pressing. Other observers note that this slow period may benefit the industry so that it can consolidate its businesses. Up until recently, corporate matters have focused upon expansion. Perhaps it is time, observe some experts, that the gambling business focus upon improving the operations of existing casinos.

REGULATIONS

For many years, casino gambling in Las Vegas has been associated with organized crime. In 1959, the State of Nevada created the State Gaming Control Board, which is responsible for establishing gambling policy and suspending or revoking licenses for any cause it considers reasonable. In 1976, New Jersey formed the New Jersey Casino Control Commission (NJCCC) to be responsible for monitoring gambling activities, which are permitted only in casino rooms located within approved hotels in Atlantic City. The Control Commission strictly controls the extension of credit to gamblers and the collection of gambling funds.

States new to gambling have set up gambling control boards or commissions to regulate gambling. Many of these new states put limits on how much can be bet in order to make the new gambling operations less attractive to organized crime. However, some of these limitations were changed as competition forced some states to increase gambling limits. For example, Illinois does not limit the amount a person may bet or lose on riverboats based in that state.

On the other side of the river in Iowa, the limit was $5 per bet and $200 losses per day. The Iowa legislature reconsidered its limits since many gamblers chose to spend their money on Illinois-based riverboats. Similarly, many observers in Missouri are worried that the $500 limit will hurt gambling's growth in the state.

Because of the potential risk of stealing by gambling patrons or casino workers, all games are closely monitored. The gambling area is carefully watched and videotaped to guarantee that none of the casino employees steal from either the customers or their employers. State auditors conduct regular, unannounced audits and check the casinos' internal control systems. In every instance where money is counted and transferred from one station to another, two or more people are involved so they can check on each other, thus lessening the likelihood of "skimming" — the practice of reporting less money than is actually collected from the gamblers and stealing the difference.

CASINO GAMES

Slot Machines

Slot machines are vending-like machines into which a player drops a coin or dollar bill, pulls a lever or pushes a button, and hopes to "hit the jackpot" by releasing a large amount of money from the machine. Bettors can play for as little as 5 cents, 25 cents, or $1. High rollers can bet on the $5, $25, $100, or even $500 machines. The "pay-out" or jackpot, which is set by the casino and displayed on the machine, ranges from 78 percent

67

TABLE 5.1
Trends in Nevada and New Jersey casino win
1982 - 1996 (calendar years)
(in millions)

Game	1982 Reported win ($)	1995 Reported win ($)	1996 Reported win ($)	% change from 1982	% change from 1995	1982 market share	1996 market share	Gains (losses) in market share points 1982-1996
Blackjack	$984.8	$1,424.50	$1,414.6	43.65%	-0.69%	23.50%	12.78%	-10.72
Craps	620.9	663.4	626.9	0.98%	-5.49%	14.82%	5.66%	-9.15
Roulette	133.1	337.8	362.2	172.14%	7.23%	3.18%	3.27%	0.10
Baccarat	225.6	723.5	609.7	170.26%	-15.72%	5.38%	5.51%	0.12
Mini-Baccarat		101.9	123.1		20.84%		1.11%	1.11
Big Six	30.7	26.0	23.2	-24.35%	-10.61%	0.73%	0.21%	-0.52
Keno	138.1	128.3	118.9	-13.86%	-7.28%	3.29%	1.07%	-2.22
Bingo	3.5	0.9	-4.7	-209.10%	-506.73%	0.08%	-0.04%	-0.13
Caribbean Stud		80.6	72.5		-10.07%		0.65%	
Let It Ride		55.1	74.2		34.67%		0.67%	
Pai Gow		37.5	34		-9.39%		0.31%	0.31
Pai Gow Poker		56.9	65.3		14.79%		0.59%	0.59
Red Dog		1.0	0.8		-19.77%		0.01%	0.01
Other		115.1	154.1		33.81%	0.15%	1.39%	1.24
TOTAL GAMES	$2,142.9	$3,752.4	$3,674.8	71.49%	-2.07%	51.14%	33.20%	-17.94
Card Tables								
Poker & Panguingui	55.8	103.9	101.1	81.29%	-2.70%	1.33%	0.91%	-0.42
TOTAL TABLE GAMES	$2,198.7	$3,856.3	$3,775.9	71.73%	-2.08%	52.47%	34.12%	-18.36
Slot Machines	1,991.5	7,092.3	7,292.1	266.17%	2.82%	47.53%	65.88%	18.36
TOTAL CASINO	$4,190.1	$10,948.5	$11,068.0	164.14%	1.09%	100.00%	100.00%	

Christiansen/Cummings Associates, Inc.

Source: "The United States — 96 Gross Annual Wager," *International Gaming and Wagering Business*, New York, New York, August 1997

to 97 percent, with an average of 85 percent being returned as payoff to players, while management and the state take the rest.

Table Games

Table games include twenty-one, craps, roulette, baccarat, keno, and bingo. Not all types of games are available at all gambling establishments. The larger casinos and hotel/casino complexes generally offer the widest variety of table games.

FINANCIAL INFORMATION

All the states with casino gambling have established casino control commissions. As part of the responsibilities, these commissions issue reports (usually annually) indicating casino gambling revenues. The information in this section has been taken from these reports.

Casino Revenues

In 1996, Americans bet $438.7 billion on casino games and slot machines. Most (70 percent) of that amount was bet on table games in Nevada and New Jersey ($178.7 billion) and slot machines in Nevada and New Jersey ($126.8 billion). The total handle has increased steadily over the past few years. A growing percentage (24 percent in 1996) was bet on riverboat casinos. (See Chapter III, Table 3.4.)

The Nevada/New Jersey casinos earned $7.3 billion from slot machines and $3.8 billion from table games. Between 1982 and 1996, the win from slot machines rose 266 percent, while the win from table games rose only 72 percent.

A Shift to Slot Machines

Since 1983, casinos have earned more money from slot machines than they have earned from

68

TABLE 5.2

REVENUES AND EXPENSES FOR THE LARGER NEVADA CASINOS

Fiscal Year 1996
Statewide Casinos
With Gaming Revenue of $1,000,000 and over

AMOUNTS REPRESENT 229 LOCATION(S).

REVENUE	DOLLARS	PCT
GAMING	7,390,435,180	57.7
ROOMS	2,031,245,547	15.9
FOOD	1,538,647,478	12.0
BEVERAGE	653,150,355	5.1
OTHER	1,190,456,543	9.3
TOTAL REVENUE	12,803,935,103	100.0
COST OF SALES	1,136,180,442	8.9
GROSS MARGIN	11,667,754,661	91.1
DEPARTMENTAL EXPENSES	6,422,104,691	50.2
DEPARTMENTAL INCOME(- LOSS)	5,245,649,970	41.0
GENERAL AND ADMINISTRATIVE EXPENSES		
ADVERTISING AND PROMOTION	277,225,042	2.2
BAD DEBT EXPENSE	4,023,645	0.0
COMPLIMENTARY EXPENSE (not reported in operation departments)	155,325,552	1.2
DEPRECIATION - BUILDINGS	316,916,544	2.5
DEPRECIATION AND AMORTIZATION - OTHER	491,857,167	3.8
ENERGY EXPENSE (electricity,gas,etc.)	187,529,827	1.5
EQUIPMENT RENTAL OR LEASE	21,314,426	0.2
INTEREST EXPENSE	341,719,318	2.7
MUSIC AND ENTERTAINMENT	106,648,511	0.8
PAYROLL TAXES	77,953,057	0.6
PAYROLL - EMPLOYEE BENEFITS	159,643,569	1.2
PAYROLL - OFFICERS	50,721,219	0.4
PAYROLL - OTHER EMPLOYEES	700,910,808	5.5
RENT OF PREMISES	128,704,945	1.0
TAXES - REAL ESTATE	101,047,850	0.8
TAXES AND LICENSES - OTHER	33,745,680	0.3
UTILITIES (OTHER THAN ENERGY EXPENSE)	48,511,060	0.4
OTHER GENERAL & ADMINISTRATIVE EXPENSES	686,353,801	5.4
TOTAL GENERAL AND ADMINISTRATIVE EXPENSES	3,890,152,021	30.4
NET INCOME(- LOSS) BEFORE FEDERAL INCOME TAXES AND EXTRAORDINARY ITEMS	1,355,497,949	10.6

Source: *Nevada Gaming Abstract, 1996*, State Gaming Control Board, Carson City, Nevada, December 1996

table games. This shift to slot machines is probably the major change that has occurred on the floors of the nation's gambling casinos over the past decade. In 1982, in Nevada and New Jersey, table games produced 52 percent of all casino revenue; by 1996, these games produced just 34 percent. In 1982, blackjack accounted for 23.5 percent of winnings; by 1996, it had dropped to 13 percent. Craps dropped from 15 to 5.7 percent over the same period. Baccarat and roulette remained about

TABLE 5.3

SOURCES OR REVENUES FOR LARGER NEVADA CASINOS
CASINO DEPARTMENT

REVENUE	DOLLARS	PCT
PIT REVENUE (INCLUDES KENO AND BINGO) . . .	2,450,625,054	33.2
COIN OPERATED DEVICES	4,539,210,280	61.4
POKER AND PAN	201,026,077	2.7
RACE BOOK	105,005,850	1.4
SPORTS POOL	94,567,919	1.3
TOTAL REVENUE	7,390,435,180	100.0

Source: *Nevada Gaming Abstract, 1996*, State Gaming Control Board, Carson City, Nevada, December 1996

the same. (See Table 5.1.) Casino operators are concerned about craps, which seems to be generation-oriented, with older Americans having grown up with the game and younger people knowing little about it. Some observers believe that unless a greater effort is made to introduce this game to younger people, its decline will likely continue.

Meanwhile, the proportion produced by slot machines in Nevada and New Jersey rose from 47.5 percent in 1982 to 65.9 percent in 1996. (See Table 5.1.) For the casino, the slot machine has several advantages. A single machine costs only about $5,000, and it is not likely to complain about working hours or salary. This shift is also occurring in casinos on riverboats and Native American reservations.

This shift in gambling preferences, however, does bring a change to the feel of gambling. Table games involve the participation of the gambler, enough commitment to learn the rules of the game, some degree of thought, and, no matter how impersonal the dealer, some human contact. Playing the slot machines requires little mental commitment by the player, is solitary, and, potentially, addictive. The player continually feeds one, two, or three machines until she has lost her money, has won enough, or it is time to go home.

Slot machines are more suited than table games for the huge increase in casino gambling. A riverboat can be filled with many hundreds of slot machines. The slot machine is the perfect tool to bring gambling to the uninitiated. There is little for the new customer to learn. Furthermore, the new gambler does not have to risk embarrassment because he does not know the rules of craps. In fact, slot machines are so simple they can be placed in bars and bathrooms with no risk that the inexperienced gambler will not know how to play the game.

TABLE 5.4
LARGER NEVADA CASINOS

GAMING REVENUE PER SQUARE FOOT OF FLOOR SPACE

AREA	NO. OF CASINOS OPERATING	AVERAGE AREA IN SQUARE FEET	GAMING REVENUE PER SQUARE FOOT
PIT (INCLUDES BINGO AND KENO)	182	7,049	1,909
COIN OPERATED DEVICES	229	19,011	1,043
POKER AND PAN	69	1,175	2,422
RACE AND SPORTS	94	3,733	566
TOTAL CASINO	229	26,499	1,218

Source: *Nevada Gaming Abstract, 1996*, State Gaming Control Board, Carson City, Nevada, December 1996

TABLE 5.5
AVERAGE SALES AND REVENUES PER ROOM, LARGER NEVADA CASINOS

AVERAGE PIT REVENUE PER ROOM PER DAY	72.90	AVERAGE BEVERAGE SALES PER ROOM PER DAY	19.43
AVERAGE SLOT REVENUE PER ROOM PER DAY	135.02	AVERAGE ROOMS DEPARTMENT PAYROLL PER ROOM PER DAY	17.89
AVERAGE FOOD SALES PER ROOM PER DAY	45.77	AVERAGE ROOM RATE PER DAY	60.42

Source: *Nevada Gaming Abstract, 1996*, State Gaming Control Board, Carson City, Nevada, December 1996

GAMBLING IN NEVADA

The 229 major casinos operating in Nevada in 1996 (up from 169 locations in 1989, 182 in 1990, and 192 in 1992) produced $12.8 billion in gross revenues (up from $7.3 billion in 1989, $8 billion in 1990, and $9.1 in 1992). Net income (before federal income taxes and extraordinary items) for the year was $1.36 billion, up from $848,606,217 in 1992 and $545.9 million in 1990. Table 5.2 shows that gaming accounted for 58 percent ($7.4 billion) of total revenue. About 61 percent of gaming ("casino") revenue ($4.5 billion) came from "coin-operated devices," such as slot machines, and 33 percent ($2.5 billion) from pit revenue (blackjack, roulette, etc.) (Table 5.3). Table 5.4 shows gaming revenue per square foot of floor space.

In fiscal year 1996, 37 million rooms (up from 26 million rooms in 1992) were filled in Nevada for a 90 percent occupancy rate. Room rates in Nevada are generally inexpensive, running about $60 per day, a far lower rate than that charged by most much less luxurious hotels in other cities, although with the increase of non-gambling visitors, the prices have started to rise somewhat (see below). These low rates are meant to attract potential gamblers who, the hotel hopes, will spend a lot of money at the slot machines and gaming tables.

In fact, the average room produced $73 in revenues at the tables and $135 on the slot machines. Between the room charge, gambling revenues, and food and beverage sales, the hotels brought in an average of $335 per room per day in 1996. Table 5.5 shows where that money was earned.

The giant "Super Casinos" or mega-resorts that have developed along the Las Vegas Strip,

TABLE 5.6
REVENUE FROM DIFFERENT AREAS, LARGEST NEVADA CASINOS

AMOUNTS REPRESENT 19 LOCATION(S).

REVENUE	DOLLARS	PCT
GAMING	3,194,527,007	52.6
ROOMS	1,240,619,177	20.4
FOOD	656,570,009	10.8
BEVERAGE	277,885,298	4.6
OTHER	700,427,501	11.5
TOTAL REVENUE	6,070,028,992	100.0

Source: *Nevada Gaming Abstract, 1996*, State Gaming Control Board, Carson City, Nevada, December 1996

many in just the past few years, dominate the industry. (See below for a more detailed discussion of these hotels.) While these 19 giant hotel/resorts make up only 9 percent of the total number of hotels, they account for almost half (43 percent) of the total gambling revenue (Tables 5.6 and 5.2.).

A Time of Major Changes

Traditionally, in addition to the opportunity to gamble, famous hotel/casinos like Caesar's Palace, Circus Circus, the Dunes, the Golden Nugget, Harrah's, the Hilton, MGM Grand, and the Sahara offer a resort-type atmosphere with big name entertainment, luxurious accommodations, and lavish restaurants. Some also feature tennis, golf, swimming, boxing matches, an occasional cattle auction, and attractions for children.

side of Nevada and Atlantic City, as small as some of them might be, offer another alternative to potential gamblers who might choose to visit Dubuque, Iowa, or a nearby Native American reservation instead of flying all the way to Las Vegas.

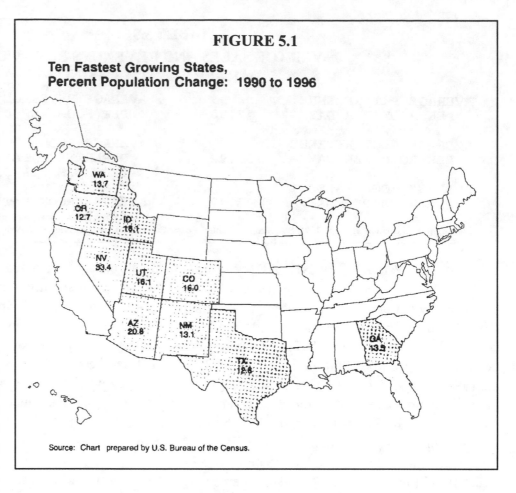

FIGURE 5.1

Ten Fastest Growing States, Percent Population Change: 1990 to 1996

Source: Chart prepared by U.S. Bureau of the Census.

The gambling industry presents itself as a business, just like selling cars, reference books, or corn flakes. While the handle in Nevada has continued to grow, there is no guarantee that demand may not slacken in the future. Casinos out-

TABLE 5.7

Ten Fastest-Growing Metropolitan Areas: 1990-1996

Rank	Area	Percent Increase
1	Las Vegas, Nev.-Ariz., MSA	40.9
2	Laredo, Texas, MSA	32.7
3	McAllen-Edinburg-Mission, Texas, MSA	29.2
4	Boise City, Idaho, MSA	25.9
5	Naples, Fla., MSA	23.7
6	Fayetteville-Springdale-Rogers, Ark., MSA	23.7
7	Austin-San Marcos, Texas, MSA	23.1
8	Phoenix-Mesa, Ariz., MSA	22.7
9	Provo-Orem, Utah, MSA	21.3
10	Brownsville-Harlingen-San Benito, Tx.,MSA	21.1

Source: *Census Bureau Release: 1996 Metropolitan Area Estimates*
(CB97-212), Bureau of the Census, Washington, DC, 1997

As a result, Las Vegas is going through one of the most interesting metamorphoses in the history of the entire gambling industry. While the 1980s were dominated by the spread of lotteries from coast to coast, gambling in the 1990s has been dominated by the growth of casino gambling on Native American Reservations (see Chapter VII) and the development of huge, mega-resort complexes in Las Vegas.

TABLE 5.8

New Las Vegas construction

1997	Estimated cost (in millions)	Rooms	Scheduled open date
Harrah's Las Vegas - Expansion	$150	1,000	2nd Quarter 1997
Desert Inn - Expansion	$114	N/A	3rd Quarter 1997
Sunset Station	$196	467	3rd Quarter 1997
Alexis Park - Expansion	N/A	100	4th Quarter 1997
Reserve	$60	225	4th Quarter 1997
Orleans	$40	N/A	4th Quarter 1997
1998			
Caesars Palace - Expansion	N/A	600	1st Quarter 1998
Bellagio	$1,350	3,000	3rd Quarter 1998
1999			
Paradise	$800	4,000	1999
Paris	$750	3,000	1999
Resort at Summerlin	N/A	300	1999
The Venetian	$1,500	6,000	1999

Christiansen/Cummings Associates, Inc.

Source: "The United States — 96 Gross Annual Wager," *International Gaming and Wagering Business*, New York, New York, August 1997

Fastest Growing Metropolitan Area in the Fastest Growing State

Between 1990 and 1996 Nevada became the fastest growing state in the nation, with a 33.4 percent increase in population (Figure 5.1). Not surprisingly, the Las Vegas metropolitan area was the fastest growing metropolitan area in the country with a 41 percent growth over only six years (Table 5.7). Reflecting the growing interest in gambling and Las Vegas, the city and gambling have played a central role in a number of recent movies including *Bugsy*, *Casino*, *Leaving Las Vegas*, *Honeymoon in Las Vega*s, and *Indecent Proposal*.

Changing the Image

The image of Las Vegas has benefited from the spread of gambling throughout American society. About three-fourths of the states now operate lotteries. Casino gambling in one form or another is legal (although not necessarily operative) in 22 states and Puerto Rico. At one time, many Americans connected Las Vegas with organized crime — after all, it was the gangster "Bugsy" Siegel who built the Flamingo, one of the first gambling casinos. The current, aggressive business interests now controlling gambling in Las Vegas have worked hard to bury this image.

Over the past decade, as gambling has become common throughout the United States and even sanctioned by government, it has tended to lose whatever criminal character may have been attached to it. In 1992, "Bugsy's" Flamingo Hotel was demolished to make way for future development. A year later, in 1993, the Dunes Hotel and Casino, once the pride of the mob, was also dynamited. Perhaps symbolically, at least in the eyes of the new gambling industry financed by Wall Street and big banks, not gangsters, these explosions blew away gambling's tie to its disreputable past.

While gambling is the basis of these giant casinos, it has become only part of the total experience. These new complexes offer opportunities for the whole family. Las Vegas is no longer a place for mother and father to go alone and gamble at the slot machines or casino tables — it is now a complete experience to which the whole family can come and enjoy themselves.

"Mega-Resorts" with "Mega" Family Entertainment

In 1989 and 1990, the huge, 3,000-room Mirage hotel and the even larger, 4,000-room Excalibur, then the biggest hotel in the world, opened in Las Vegas. Rather than billing themselves as casinos, these two new, enormous hotels were presented as resorts that happened to offer casinos as one form of entertainment.

The Mirage hotel has become a "must see" Polynesian-style attraction in the Nevada desert with a $13-million erupting volcano outside and a 20,000-gallon aquarium filled with exotic tropical fish. The Excalibur portends to take guests back to an idyllic medieval time. Medieval-costumed hosts greet arriving guests, and telephone operators tell guests to "have a royal day."

In 1993, three more gigantic hotels/casinos/tourist attractions opened. The Luxor Las Vegas is a 30-story pyramid covered by 11 acres of glass. In front of the hotel is a huge obelisk and copy of the Sphinx. A Nile River flows inside the hotel, and the atrium is the world's largest. The hotel's 2,526 rooms are done in an ancient Egyptian style. The casino covers more than 100,000 square feet. Another 1,800 rooms became available in 1996.

In keeping with its efforts to attract families with children, the hotel contains a Sega amusement arcade, and Sega has agreed to introduce all its new video products at the hotel before it markets them nationwide. In addition, Sega is operating VirtuaLand, a virtual-reality facility of 20,000 square feet. A huge child-care center allows parents to leave their children under adult supervision while they go off to play the slot machines or visit the roulette tables.

The Treasure Island Resort is loosely based on Robert Louis Stevenson's classic tale of piracy. The three 36-story towers holding 2,900 rooms face onto Buccaneer Bay, a theme park designed to look like a seaport of the 1700s. Every hour two 90-foot frigates do battle. In addition, the hotel also offers video games and other electronically simulated games.

The MGM Grand Hotel is the largest hotel (5,005 rooms in four 30-story towers) and gambling casino (as big as four football fields) in the world. In front, a seven-story lion guards the hotel. The hotel contains a 33-acre theme park with 12 major attractions plus a giant swimming complex. Circus Circus was the first to offer children-friendly entertainment, including live circus acts, a carnival midway, and a 5-acre amusement park.

At the Excalibur, children can watch Merlin the Magician battle a fire-breathing dragon. Caesar's puts on a laser light show. The 1,149-foot tower of the Stratosphere Tower and Casino is even higher than the Eiffel Tower in Paris. A 70-foot mechanical gorilla reminiscent of King Kong periodically scales the tower, while daring visitors ride the roller coaster down the side. On top of the tower is a restaurant, two observation decks, and four suites with a view for the high rollers, bettors who wager large amounts of money. The world's largest indoor/outdoor swimming pool (13,500 square feet) is located at the Tropicana Hotel and Casino.

Since 1989, when the Mirage and Excalibur opened, many of the famous old-line casinos, including the Dunes and the Riviera, have gone bankrupt. While the new casinos hope to attract the many millions of Americans who have never visited Las Vegas (MGM Grand Chief Executive Robert Maxey claims that his studies show that only 15 percent of Americans have ever been to Las Vegas), it is likely that other casinos may not survive.

On the other hand, new hotels or mega-resorts continue to be built. Two examples are the $350 million New York-New York — opened in 1997 — which recreates the Statue of Liberty, the skyscrapers of the New York skyline, and the Coney Island roller coaster. The $325 million Monte Carlo— opened in 1996 — has a Victorian theme. The Las Vegas Hilton has gone into partnership with Paramount Parks and plans to construct a 40,000-square foot *Star Trek* entertainment area. Mirage Resorts plans to build the Beau Rivage, a $900 million, 3,000-room resort surrounded by a 50-acre lake on which visitors can waterski, parasail, and windsurf. Numerous downtown hotels are being upgraded, modernized, and expanded. Table 5.8 shows projected construction scheduled through 1999 for Las Vegas.

Not surprisingly, 9 of the 10 largest hotels in the world are located in Las Vegas. The Luxor cost an estimated $390 million; the Treasure Island, $450 million; and the MGM Grand, $1.03 billion. The Bellagio, scheduled to open in 1998, and the Venetian, with a planned opening in 1999 will each cost well over $1 billion. The Holiday Inn Casino Boardwalk has been expanded to make it the largest hotel in the Holiday Inn chain. These huge investments are changing the way the gambling business is done in Las Vegas. It may no longer be enough to offer only a hotel and gambling casino. Certainly that is what the owners of many of the mega-hotels described above believe.

There is a Hard Rock Hotel, a spin-off of the Hard Rock Cafes located in most major cities in the Western world, where gamblers can enjoy over $2 million in music memorabilia and around-the-clock rock and roll music. The 27-year-old Circus Circus Hotel is adding 1,000 new rooms. Wealthy financiers are considering building a $4 billion Lake Las Vegas project 17 miles east of the city, which would include a half dozen new resorts around the edge of a man-made lake. In addition, as well as offering an alternative to the older gambling casinos, these new hotel/casinos offer an alternative to the family considering a trip to Disneyland in Anaheim, California, or Disney World in Orlando, Florida.

In downtown Las Vegas, a five-block section of Fremont Street, which intersects Las Vegas Boulevard, has been closed to traffic. This five-block-long covered pedestrian mall offers a laserlight and music show with 2.1 million lights. Street performers entertain, sidewalk cafes offer food and the opportunity to watch passersby, while merchants sell their wares in pushcarts or kiosks. Not surprisingly, with the large numbers of hotels and hotel rooms, Las Vegas has moved ahead of Chicago as the number one convention city in the United States with around 3.5 million conventioneers a year.

Bringing Malls to the Hotels

Several of the hotels are increasingly referring to themselves as "mega-resorts" in order to emphasize the changing nature of the "Las Vegas experience." These "mega-resorts" are opening retail outlets in the hotels to offer the growing number of visitors yet another opportunity to spend their money. Many of the newer tourists do not have the commitment to gambling that visitors a decade ago did. These shops give them the opportunity to purchase things they would buy on a visit to any other vacation spot, such as elegant clothing or T-shirts and sweatshirts with Las Vegas images on them.

The entrance to the MGM is part mini-mall. The expansion at Caesar's World is mainly to increase the size of its shopping mall. Even the Foxwoods Resort Casino, the gambling facility owned by the Mashantucket Pequot Indians in Ledyard, Connecticut, has incorporated retail sales spaces. Retail sales may also play a significant role in expansion plans for Atlantic City. While not all casinos are transforming gambling space into malls, the change reflects the ongoing transformation of Las Vegas.

New Image Seems to Be Working

The new image for Las Vegas appears to be successful. In 1991, 21.3 million people visited Las Vegas; by 1994, 28 million people came, and an estimated 29.6 million arrived in 1996. Despite adding 45,000 rooms in the past decade, the average room occupancy rate has been around 90

TABLE 5.9

Statistics
Casino Industry Statistics
At December 1996 and 1995

	ATLANTIC CITY HILTON(a)		BALLY'S PARK PLACE		CAESARS		CLARIDGE		HARRAH'S		RESORTS	
	1996	1995	1996	1995	1996	1995	1996	1995	1996	1995	1996	1995
TABLE GAMES:												
Blackjack	51	49	52	53	53	52	41	40	45	51	42	43
Craps	10	12	10	8	14	14	10	10	9	11	9	10
Roulette	10	10	12	12	13	13	5	5	12	12	11	11
Big Six	1	2	2	2	2	2	1	1	1	1	2	1
Baccarat	2	2	2	2	4	3	-	1	-	-	2	2
Minibacarat	4	4	2	3	3	3	1	1	2	2	2	1
Red Dog	-	-	-	-	-	-	-	-	-	-	-	-
Sic Bo	1	1	1	1	2	2	1	1	-	-	1	1
Pai Gow Poker	4	3	2	4	4	3	1	1	2	2	2	1
Pai Gow	2	1	-	-	2	1	-	-	-	-	1	-
Poker	11	14	16	22	9	7	-	-	8	-	18	18
Caribbean Stud Poker	6	4	6	6	5	5	3	3	8	6	6	8
Let It Ride Poker (c)	3	1	5	1	3	2	2	1	6	4	2	2
Mini-Craps (d)	-	-	-	-	-	-	-	-	3	-	1	-
Three Card Poker (e)	-	-	-	-	-	-	-	-	-	-	2	-
Total Table Games	105	103	110	114	114	107	65	64	96	89	101	98
KENO WINDOWS	4	4	4	6	6	6	-	-	4	4	5	5
SLOT MACHINES:												
$.05 Slot Machines	-	-	24	24	-	-	40	40	-	-	-	-
$.25 Slot Machines	1,081	1,056	1,374	1,403	1,536	1,259	1,312	1,306	1,431	1,053	1,430	1,416
$.50 Slot Machines	261	228	292	270	477	467	162	183	272	268	441	445
$1 Slot Machines	364	429	471	471	592	580	282	316	663	565	389	408
$5 Slot Machines	80	86	82	82	65	66	24	27	104	89	53	52
$25 Slot Machines	10	9	11	7	9	8	1	3	5	5	9	10
$100 Slot Machines	2	2	3	3	6	6	-	-	3	3	3	3
Other Slot Machines	31	25	74	66	102	62	-	-	29	29	25	4
Total Slot Machines	1,829	1,835	2,331	2,326	2,787	2,448	1,821	1,875	2,507	2,012	2,350	2,338
Casino Square Footage	58,124	58,124	71,380	71,380	78,470	67,470	58,705	55,624	82,023	65,511	70,000	70,000
Simulcast Square Footage	1,517	1,517	8,679	8,679	5,898	6,504	-	-	-	-	8,058	8,058
Number Of Hotel Rooms	454	509	1,268	1,258	556	638	504	504	760	760	662	668
Number of Parking Spaces (f)	1,648	1,762	2,269	2,309	2,145	2,138	1,174	398	2,395	2,337	1,483	1,475
Fixed Asset Investment ($ in Millions	428	402	821	783	508	427	47	36	447	394	229	219
Number of Employees	3,280	3,331	4,243	4,242	4,045	4,014	2,462	2,528	3,569	3,564	3,933	3,911

a) Formerly The Grand
b) Formerly TropWorld
c) Let It Ride Poker was introduced in March 1995.
d) Mini-Craps was introduced in January 1996.
e) Three Card Poker was introduced in June 1996.
f) Claridge's significant increase in parking spaces from 1995 reflects the self parking garage which opened in June 1996. Trump Plaza's additional parking spaces are due to the property expansion and inclusion of Trump World's Fair in May 1996.
g) Represents property and equipment before accumulated depreciation. Fixed asset investment for Claridge primarily only represents gaming equipment and the parking garage, since Claridge leases its hotel property and non-gaming equipment.

Continued on the following page.

percent, a very high rate for hotels. Hotel rooms and meals in Las Vegas used to be cheap because the casino owners looked on food and lodging as just part of the business of getting people to bet their money in the casinos. The money earned at the tables and slot machines subsidized the rooms and meals.

Today, many visitors coming to Las Vegas are spending less time in the casinos and, instead, are visiting the other attractions. With the increase in such visitors, more of the hotel and meal expenses have to be paid for by the tourist. As a result, hotels and meals cost more. Lodging and food in Las Vegas are now moderately priced — the $79 dollar

TABLE 5.9 (Continued)

	SANDS		SHOWBOAT		TROPICANA (b)		TRUMP CASTLE		TRUMP PLAZA		TRUMP TAJ MAHAL		INDUSTRY TOTALS	
	1996	1995	1996	1995	1996	1995	1996	1995	1996	1995	1996	1995	1996	1995
	60	60	48	47	54	51	40	43	88	54	79	81	653	624
	12	12	10	12	14	14	13	13	12	10	15	15	138	141
	12	15	13	13	13	13	9	12	15	12	19	18	144	146
	2	2	2	2	2	2	1	1	3	2	4	4	23	22
	3	5	3	3	3	3	3	3	4	4	6	6	32	34
	3	4	1	2	4	2	3	3	5	5	5	4	35	34
	-	-	-	-	-	1	-	-	-	-	1	1	1	2
	1	1	1	1	1	1	1	1	1	1	2	1	13	12
	2	4	2	1	4	2	3	2	2	2	10	5	38	30
	2	3	1	-	5	-	2	-	1	-	6	4	22	9
	16	16	6	6	50	6	6	6	-	-	64	64	204	159
	6	4	8	7	6	4	6	8	4	4	12	10	76	69
	2	-	5	-	4	2	6	-	6	3	8	3	52	19
	1	-	-	-	1	-	-	-	-	-	-	-	6	-
	-	-	-	-	-	-	-	-	-	-	-	-	2	-
	122	126	100	94	161	101	93	92	141	97	231	216	1,439	1,301
	4	4	1	1	7	6	-	-	-	-	10	10	45	46
	-	-	39	70	-	-	77	73	200	80	139	135	519	422
	1,249	1,240	2,636	2,435	1,811	1,684	1,223	1,269	2,534	1,376	2,375	2,160	19,992	17,657
	265	286	310	283	419	377	325	285	624	243	352	350	4,200	3,685
	408	413	533	430	675	662	527	514	632	522	764	642	6,300	5,952
	68	73	61	49	103	102	110	78	71	75	104	96	925	875
	6	7	2	1	8	10	15	9	7	6	13	10	96	85
	3	3	2	1	4	6	6	4	4	4	4	3	40	38
	17	-	22	7	159	107	56	37	151	6	48	-	714	343
	2,016	2,022	3,605	3,276	3,179	2,948	2,339	2,269	4,223	2,312	3,799	3,396	32,786	29,057
	53,427	53,192	76,595	76,595	99,986	92,163	73,734	71,031	139,474	73,604	126,784	120,539	988,702	875,233
	22,962	22,962	20,486	20,486	10,183	-	2,150	3,798	-	-	12,317	12,317	92,250	84,321
	532	532	800	800	1,624	1,020	728	728	1,395	732	1,250	1,250	10,533	9,399
	1,738	1,738	3,514	3,514	2,844	2,844	2,986	2,986	3,892	2,892	5,057	5,231	31,145	29,624
	317	313	439	433	678	637	519	509	666	543	1,194	909	6,293	5,605
	3,292	3,296	3,780	3,879	5,053	4,213	3,442	3,879	5,536	3,915	6,321	6,514	48,956	47,286

Source: *1996 Annual Report*, New Jersey Casino Control Commission, Trenton, NJ, n.d.

room is far nicer than a similarly-priced room in New York or San Francisco — but they are no longer the deal they once were. The famous low-priced buffets that used to cost just a few dollars may run $10, still inexpensive by any standards, but not as cheap as before.

Not all casino operators are happy with the changing situation. After all, they believe, the main point of coming to Las Vegas is to gamble, and all of the new attractions and amusements distract visitors from the casinos. On the other hand, those supporting the change note that these people could be somewhere else spending their money. Since they have come to Las Vegas, and many have never been exposed to gambling, savvy casino operators can draw them into the casinos and make gambling part of their entertainment.

Finally, the gambling industry, like all other industries, is learning to market every aspect of the business. Any business that does not take advantage of every possibility to increase revenues in the current competitive world economy is destined to fall behind and not survive.

GAMBLING IN ATLANTIC CITY

All 12 casinos operating in Atlantic City in 1996 were of the hotel/casino variety. (Table 5.9 shows statistics for the individual resorts.) Together, the casinos grossed $3.8 billion in 1996,

TABLE 5.10
THE NEW JERSEY CASINO INDUSTRY
GROSS REVENUE AND RELATED TAX
FOR THE YEARS ENDED DECEMBER 31, 1996 AND 1995

($ IN THOUSANDS)

Casino Hotel		Casino Win	Daily Average Casino Win	Adjustment for Uncollectibles	Gross Revenue	Tax
Atlantic City Hilton*	1996	250,804	685	1,014	249,790	19,983
	1995	256,348	702	1,108	255,240	20,419
Bally's Park Place	1996	351,747	961	1,113	350,634	28,051
	1995	357,525	979	1,338	356,187	28,495
Caesars	1996	391,006	1,069	1,083	389,923	31,194
	1995	371,088	1,017	3,525	367,563	29,405
Claridge	1996	162,727	445	211	162,516	13,001
	1995	169,405	464	(200)	169,605	13,568
Harrah's	1996	316,254	864	1,252	315,002	25,200
	1995	319,445	875	1,231	318,214	25,457
Resorts	1996	259,217	708	1,318	257,899	20,632
	1995	268,580	736	903	267,677	21,414
Sands	1996	243,833	666	2,100	241,733	19,339
	1995	264,977	726	2,909	262,068	20,966
Showboat	1996	343,724	939	1,314	342,410	27,393
	1995	340,891	934	1,223	339,668	27,174
Tropicana**	1996	350,702	958	2,154	348,548	27,884
	1995	313,742	860	502	313,240	25,059
Trump Castle	1996	250,652	685	1,416	249,236	19,939
	1995	278,784	764	3,191	275,593	22,047
Trump Plaza	1996	373,301	1,020	1,369	371,932	29,754
	1995	300,748	824	941	299,807	23,985
Trump Taj Mahal	1996	519,631	1,420	10,402	509,229	40,738
	1995	506,043	1,386	4,324	501,719	40,138
TOTALS	1996	3,813,598	10,420	24,746	3,788,852	303,108
	1995	3,747,576	10,267	20,995	3,726,581	298,127

* Formerly known as The Grand
** Formerly known as TropWorld

Source: *1996 Annual Report*, New Jersey Casino Control Commission, Trenton, NJ, n.d.

up from $3.2 billion in 1992. Gross revenue and related taxes for each facility are shown in Table 5.10. The State of New Jersey took in $303 million worth of taxes from the casinos. In 1996, as shown in Figure 5.2, the Taj Mahal had, by far, the largest market share of all the hotel/casinos in Atlantic City, followed by Caesar's and the Plaza.

Blackjack was the most profitable table game followed by craps and roulette. The 25-cent slot machines accounted for the largest casino win by game in 1996, followed by $1.00 and 50-cent slot machines (Figure 5.3).

The State of New Jersey Casino Control Fund

When the New Jersey legislature implemented legalized gambling in New Jersey, it established the Casino Revenue Fund to finance assistance programs for New Jersey's elderly and disabled. To finance the fund, the 12 operating casinos are taxed 8 percent of their gross revenues, or "win," each month. In 1996, the fund spent $329.9 million. To be eligible for the programs supported by the Casino Revenue Fund, a person must be at least 65 years old or receiving Social Security disability benefits. The maximum income limit is $13,650 for single persons and $16,750 for married couples. About two-thirds (66 percent) of the money went to physical and mental health — mainly to pay for medicine and medical services. (See Figure 5.4 for a breakdown on how the Casino Revenue Fund was allotted.)

Growing Competition

As noted in the 1992 *Annual Report of the New Jersey Casino Control Commission*,

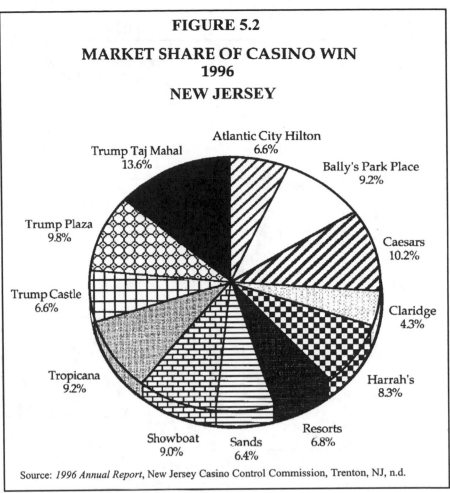

FIGURE 5.2

MARKET SHARE OF CASINO WIN 1996

NEW JERSEY

Source: *1996 Annual Report*, New Jersey Casino Control Commission, Trenton, NJ, n.d.

Despite this steady climb [in revenues], state and local officials are no longer so sanguine (optimistic) about the notion that such growth is inevitable. Atlantic City, which long had a monopoly on casino gambling in the eastern half of the United States, now faces competition for that gaming dollar. From an Indian reservation in Connecticut to riverboats on the Mississippi, gamblers now have more options. And, with the likely prospect that even more jurisdictions will legalize casino gambling in coming years, that trend will only accelerate.

The new gambling casino opened in Ledyard, Connecticut, in 1992 by the Mashantucket Pequot (see Chapter VII) has definitely cut into the number of visitors to Atlantic City. For New Englanders, it is much easier to go to Ledyard than it is to travel all the way to Atlantic City. This is particularly important because most people who

FIGURE 5.3

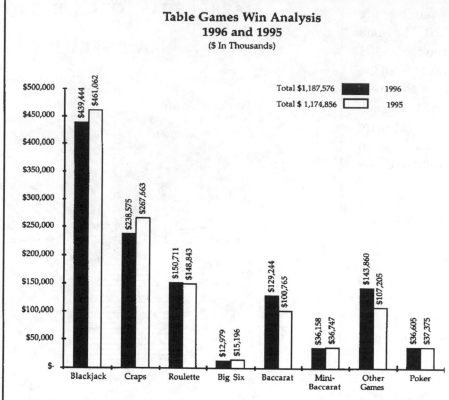

Table Games Win Analysis
1996 and 1995
($ In Thousands)

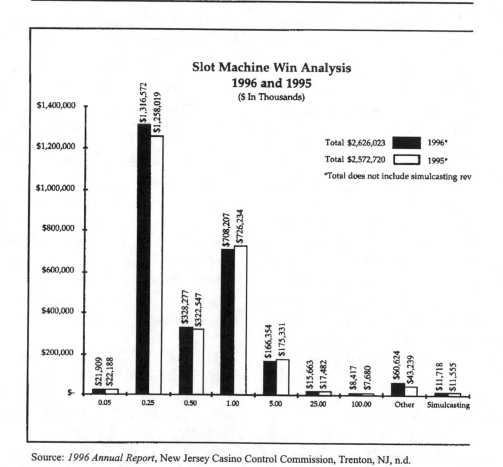

Slot Machine Win Analysis
1996 and 1995
($ In Thousands)

Source: *1996 Annual Report*, New Jersey Casino Control Commission, Trenton, NJ, n.d.

go to Atlantic City are day visitors who do not stay overnight. Saving three or four hours means more time to have fun, less time spent driving, and a chance to get home earlier. In addition, the opening of the new 90,000-square foot casino on the Oneida Reservation near Verona, New York, may draw many customers from upstate New York. A planned Oneida Casino in Sullivan County, just 60 miles north of New York City, might draw even more. The possibility of riverboats in neighboring Pennsylvania, while it never became a reality, threw an additional scare into the New Jersey Casino Control Commission and casino operators.

Nonetheless, while recognizing the drop in the number of arrivals by bus, mostly day visitors, casino managers point out that earnings from these arrivals are the least profitable. They say that future development has to court other visitors who spend more and stay longer. The occupancy rates at the Atlantic City hotels hit 97 percent in the third quarter of 1995, a good indicator that the gambling economy is becoming stronger.

Revitalizing Atlantic City

In response to these concerns, recent chairmen of the Casino Control Commission have brought a less adversarial relationship than had previously existed between the Casino Control Commission and the gambling industry in Atlantic City. They have introduced several major changes to improve the financial situation of the casinos. Gambling can now take place 24 hours a day. Additional space can be used for casinos, and more of that space can be used for more financially profitable slot machines. More and different types of games, such as poker, keno, and Caribbean Stud Poker, have been allowed. Simulcasting of horse races is now shown in the Atlantic City casinos. In addition, the New Jersey legislature further deregulated gambling, permitting one person or company to own more than three casinos (such as Trump Taj Mahal, Trump Plaza, and Trump Castle), no longer requiring Casino Control Commission approval of marketing programs, and allowing the hotels to increase the size of their casinos.

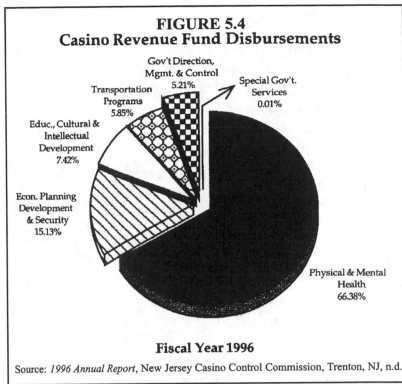

FIGURE 5.4
Casino Revenue Fund Disbursements

Gov't Direction, Mgmt. & Control 5.21%

Special Gov't. Services 0.01%

Transportation Programs 5.85%

Educ., Cultural & Intellectual Development 7.42%

Econ. Planning Development & Security 15.13%

Physical & Mental Health 66.38%

Fiscal Year 1996

Source: *1996 Annual Report*, New Jersey Casino Control Commission, Trenton, NJ, n.d.

TABLE 5.11	
AVERAGE NUMBER OF EMPLOYEES FOR THE YEAR	
CASINO DEPARTMENT	58,603
ROOMS DEPARTMENT	26,690
FOOD DEPARTMENT	45,639
BEVERAGE DEPARTMENT	12,588
G & A DEPARTMENT	33,246
OTHER DEPARTMENTS	9,337
TOTAL	186,103

Source: *Nevada Gaming Abstract, 1996*, State Gaming Control Board, Carson City, Nevada, December 1996

A new convention center, the largest between New York City and Washington, DC, has been built. The convention center will be tied to a new 500-room (non-gambling) hotel. A new airport has recently opened. A $225 million Corridor Project has widened and remade the approaches to the Boardwalk. Seven casinos invested $580 million to add another 3,000 hotel rooms. The city has even signed a new minor league baseball team.

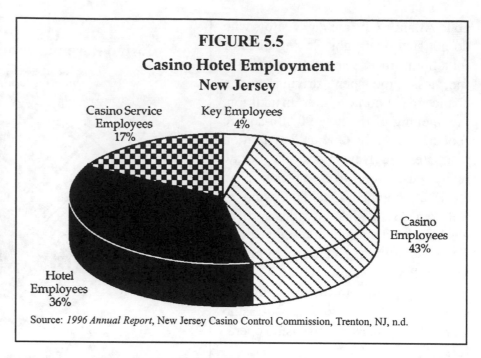

FIGURE 5.5

Casino Hotel Employment
New Jersey

Casino Service Employees 17%

Key Employees 4%

Casino Employees 43%

Hotel Employees 36%

Source: *1996 Annual Report*, New Jersey Casino Control Commission, Trenton, NJ, n.d.

In 1987, Steve Wynn, chairman of Mirage Resorts and one of the major figures in the nation's gambling industry, left Atlantic City swearing never to return. He was infuriated at a city government he considered incompetent and corrupt and a state gaming commission he considered inept and too constricting in its regulations. By 1996, his Mirage Resorts and Circus Circus had submitted a proposal for a $1 billion, two-casino complex.

While the changes in Atlantic City do not equal those occurring in Las Vegas, they are, nonetheless, significant. Furthermore, it is important to understand that Atlantic City is not Las Vegas. Las Vegas attracts visitors from all over the country and the world. Atlantic City is a regional attraction that draws visitors from the East Coast. It has gambling, a boardwalk, and a beach that can attract easterners for a vacation weekend. Few people, however, are going to fly in from Paris or San Francisco to tour Atlantic City. As a result, comparisons between the two gambling centers should be made carefully.

Increased Community Participation

Casino owners have increased their participation in the community over the past

few years. The casinos have begun to help local schools, and the Trump Castle provides food for the homeless. Casino revenues have underwritten the construction of new, subsidized housing. Atlantic City is only one deteriorating city among many in New Jersey. It had not appeared to benefit from the arrival of gambling and was often cited as an illustration that casino gambling does little, if anything, to benefit a community. While the problems confronting Atlantic City were certainly not caused by gambling, casino gambling had done little to slow the decline of the city. As casino

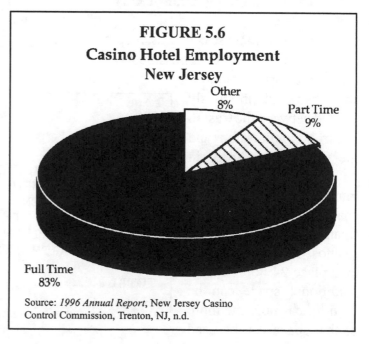

FIGURE 5.6

Casino Hotel Employment
New Jersey

Other 8%

Part Time 9%

Full Time 83%

Source: *1996 Annual Report*, New Jersey Casino Control Commission, Trenton, NJ, n.d.

gambling began to spread across the country, it became imperative for the casino companies to show that gambling could help local communities. In the past few years, Atlantic City has benefited from this.

EMPLOYMENT

The gambling industry is the major employer in Nevada, with the 229 major casinos employing an average 186,000 Nevada residents in 1996 (Table 5.11). Gamblers may tip casino employees, but all tips are pooled and divided equally among the employees to prevent any collusion between employees and customers. Many workers in the larger casinos earn more in tips than they do from their base salaries.

In New Jersey, the casino industry employed 49,500 full-time people in 1996. About one-third (36 percent) worked in the hotel section, while 43 percent worked in the casino gaming. Another 17 percent were casino service employees. (See Figure 5.5.) The majority of these employees (83 percent) worked full-time; 9 percent worked part-time (Figure 5.6).

PROMOTING GAMBLING

The largest expenditure for any casino is the cost of promoting itself. These outlays include direct advertising and promotion, as well as the junket and complimentary expenses (which can include free airline tickets, lodging, food, and drinks). Complimentary flights and rooms offered to preferred customers, the so-called "high-rollers," usually account for about 10 to 15 percent of the larger hotels' budgets.

Junkets (where a hotel/casino offers complimentary transportation, room, food, and drinks to groups of eight or more people) can be very risky for the casino, as each customer must gamble at least $2,500 in order for the hotel to cover the costs of accommodating the junketeers. Of the total expenses incurred by the major casinos in Nevada in 1996, 15 percent of room expenses, 21 percent of food expenses, and 57 percent of beverage expenses were complimentary. Both junketeers and complimentary visitors who do not gamble enough to provide the hotel with a profit are usually not invited to return.

In order to get and hold the high-rollers, or "whales," as the very top tier of gamblers is called, many casinos are introducing private luxury suites, often furnished with original artwork by such masters as Renoir, Cezanne, and Picasso. "Whales" typically bet $100,000 to $250,000 to $1,000,000 per visit. Other incentives are special programs similar to the airline mileage programs. Individuals who bet large amounts of money for at least 3 to 4 hours a day can earn complimentary benefits ranging from free rooms and meals to the best seat in the house at a show, free air travel, and, for the really high rollers, a private jet to bring them to the casinos. It all depends on how much and how long the person gambles.

RECREATING THE OLD WEST

South Dakota

As many areas of the Midwest and West began to suffer from a changing and often declining economy, some states and localities looked for alternative ways to raise money and attract tourists. The voters of South Dakota approved casino gambling in the historic town of Deadwood, where Wild Bill Hickock was killed. Almost all of the town's gambling houses are located in buildings that date to the late 1800s or early 1900s. In fact, the town of Deadwood has been designated as a National Historical Landmark.

The town has been transformed into a gambling center, but the town's citizens now debate whether gambling will have to grow in order to remain successful. Currently, there can be no more than 30 slot machines in a single building, and a single business can have no more than 90 machines. The betting limit is $5.

TABLE 5.12

SOUTH DAKOTA COMMISSION ON GAMING
RECAP OF COMMISSION ACTIVITY
11/1989 - 06/1997

GAMING ACTION	FY 95 (07/94-06/95)	FY 96 (07/95-6/96)	FY 97 (07/96-6/97)	CUMULATIVE TOTALS (11/89 - 06/97)	
TOTAL GAMING ACTION	$488,409,646.38	$482,164,324.44	$471,769,773.37	$3,156,398,093.86	
% INCREASE	13.23%	-1.28%	-3.41%		
WON BY BETTORS	$441,476,446.93	$437,582,257.64	$429,072,384.79	$2,850,706,296.57	
% OF $ WAGERED	90.39%	90.75%	90.95%	90.32%	
ADJUSTED GROSS REVENUES	$46,933,199.45	$44,582,066.80	$42,697,388.58	$305,691,797.29	
LESS: CITY SLOT REVENUES	$1,156,012.23	$1,127,119.55	$1,104,904.57	$7,118,038.56	
TAXABLE REVENUES	$45,777,187.22	$43,454,947.25	$41,592,484.01	$298,573,758.73	
% INCREASE	8.25%	-5.07%	-4.29%		
NUMBER OF LICENSED DEVICES	2256	2252	2420		
APPROXIMATE # OF ACTIVE SUPPORT AND KEY LICENSEES	1845	1634	1492		
NUMBER OF LOCATIONS (06/30)	86	89	99		
COMMISSION FUND ACTIVITY					
DEVICE TAX	$4,512,000.00	$4,504,000.00	$4,840,000.00	$31,674,000.00	51.58%
GROSS REVENUE TAX	$3,662,424.19	$3,507,707.00	$3,323,850.91	$23,829,745.54	38.81%
CITY SLOT TAX	$489,909.00	$546,091.50	$500,001.00	$3,076,776.43	5.01%
APPLICATION FEE	$222,657.57	$174,554.00	$154,035.00	$1,297,328.51	2.11%
LICENSE FEE	$99,775.20	$66,010.00	$99,370.00	$814,535.05	1.33%
DEVICE TESTING FEE	$14,439.03	$20,437.16	$13,059.74	$134,918.49	0.22%
PENALTIES	$10,305.96	$15,679.25	$18,140.00	$91,212.80	0.15%
INTEREST	$53,872.16	$59,671.03	$79,754.43	$468,603.07	0.76%
MANUAL SALES	$892.71	$1,887.90	$255.40	$15,981.56	0.03%
TOTAL	$9,066,275.82	$8,896,037.84	$9,028,466.48	$61,403,101.45	100.00%
LESS:					
SDCG OPERATING EXPENSES:	$975,858.72	$974,696.45	$984,252.39	$7,198,057.27	
% OF REVENUES	10.76%	10.96%	10.90%	11.72%	
DISTRIBUTIONS TO LOCAL GOVERNMENTS					
LAWRENCE COUNTY	$363,426.99	$354,955.23	$334,183.84	$2,308,945.76	
(10% OF 8% TAX ON AGR)	7.90%	5.38%	-8.05%		
STATE OF SOUTH DAKOTA				$5,025,549.16	
% INCREASE					
SD TOURISM **	$1,678,140.25	$1,402,961.32	$1,329,315.10	$4,410,416.67	
(40% OF 8% TAX ON AGR)	24.56%	-16.40%	-1.33%		
STATE HISTORICAL PRESERVATION **	$100,000.00	$100,000.00	$100,000.00	$300,000.00	
($100,000 ANNUALLY)					
CITY OF DEADWOOD	$6,171,551.13	$6,112,167.06	$6,321,341.44	$41,698,007.36	
(COMM FUND - OPER. COSTS)	12.81%	11.73%	2.43%		
TOTAL TO LOCAL GOVERNMENTS:	$8,313,118.37	$7,970,083.61	$8,084,840.38	$53,742,918.95	
% OF TOTAL COMM FUND REV:	91.69%	89.59%	89.55%	87.52%	

NOTE: THIS REPORT IS FOR INFORMATIONAL PURPOSES ONLY. DUE TO TIMING DEFERENCES, THERE ARE ADJUSTMENTS NECESSARY TO PROVIDE MEANINGFUL CASH FLOW STATEMENTS FOR THE COMMISSION FUND.

Source: *Annual Report, Fiscal Year 1997*, South Dakota Commission on Gambling, Pierre, SD, n.d.

Many residents prefer the quaint nature of the town, especially since much of the town's revenues from gambling have been used to restore the older, formerly rundown buildings. Gambling interests have tried to increase the number of machines permitted in each establishment, but Governor William Janklow vetoed the proposed bill. The major drive behind the proposed increases was the construction, in 1997, by actor Kevin Costner and his brother of a 635-acre, 320-room resort just outside of town. The Costner brothers already run a casino in Deadwood.

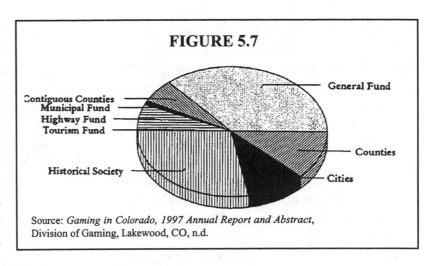

FIGURE 5.7

Source: *Gaming in Colorado, 1997 Annual Report and Abstract,* Division of Gaming, Lakewood, CO, n.d.

While promoters of casino gambling expected gamblers to bet around $4 million in Deadwood the first year, bettors wagered over $145 million in 1990. This figure more than doubled to $330 million in 1991 and has increased ever since, reaching $472 million in 1997.

Meanwhile, revenues for the South Dakota gambling casinos rose from $14.3 million in 1990 to $33 million in 1991 and $42.7 million in 1997. However, there has been a slight decrease in revenues over each of the past three years (Table 5.12). The government collected an 8 percent tax on the revenues. About 9 out of 10 dollars are produced on the slot machines, mainly the 25-cent machines. Of the $8 million distributed to local governments, the City of Deadwood got about $6.3 million, and the South Dakota Department of Tourism received about $1.3 million.

Colorado

In Colorado, the casinos in the historic mining towns of Central City, Black Hawk, and Cripple Creek have already gone through a shake out. The number of casinos peaked at 76 in September of 1992. Since then the number has dropped slowly, but steadily, reaching about 55 through 1997.

Single bets in both South Dakota and Colorado are limited to $5, but at $5 a throw, large amounts of money can still be lost rather quickly. In 1997, gamblers in the 55 Colorado casinos wagered $428 million, far more than the $244.2 million bet at 67 casinos in 1993 and the $307.6 million bet at 61 casinos in 1994. The number of gambling devices went from 10,741 in 1993 to 13,458 in 1997. In 1997, Black Hawk had 19 casinos producing $232 million in revenues, Central City

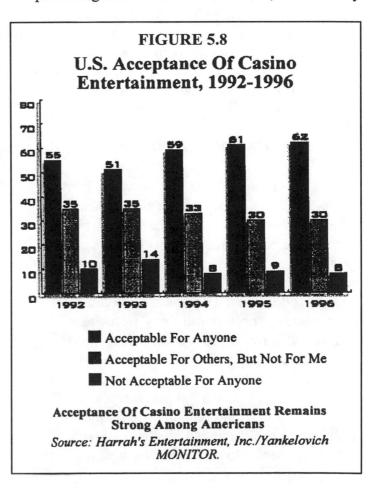

FIGURE 5.8

U.S. Acceptance Of Casino Entertainment, 1992-1996

■ Acceptable For Anyone
■ Acceptable For Others, But Not For Me
■ Not Acceptable For Anyone

Acceptance Of Casino Entertainment Remains Strong Among Americans

Source: Harrah's Entertainment, Inc./Yankelovich MONITOR.

had 12 casinos making $87.9 million in revenues, and Cripple Creek had 24 casinos earning $108 million in revenues. Fewer casinos are producing more money. Some of the money earned from the casinos is used to restore some of the dilapidated buildings in these former mining towns.

The State of Colorado taxes 2 percent of the first $2 million, 4 percent from $2 to $4 million, 14 percent from $4 to $5 million, 18 percent from $5 to $10 million, and 20 percent thereafter. In 1997, the state collected $59 million, up from only $13.5 million in 1992. One-third went to the State General Fund, one-fourth went to the State Historical Fund, and most of the rest went to the three gambling towns and the counties they were in. (See Figure 5.7.)

Some turnover has occurred in the casinos in South Dakota and Colorado. This is a rather normal occurrence, however, in any new, rapidly expanding area of business. Large numbers of entrepreneurs, many of them inexperienced, scrambled for a piece of the action, but there is little question that gambling is here to stay in the historic mining towns.

CARDROOMS

Cardrooms are small gambling parlors where individuals can play cards, usually poker and blackjack, with other people for money. The parlor usually earns its revenues by charging the players for every hour or every hand they play. Currently, cardrooms are legal, although not necessarily operative, in 14 states. Public cardrooms have been legal in California since the Gold Rush days. While card games have always been part of the state's western tradition, the passing of Proposition 13 limiting property taxes left many cities and counties in difficult financial straits. As a result, cities like Bell Gardens, Commerce, and Huntington Park legalized

FIGURE 5.9

"Casino gaming can be a fun night out."

"I would favor the introduction of casino gaming in my local community because of its benefits to the local economy."

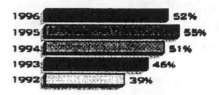

"Legalized casino gaming brings money into a local economy without hurting existing business."

"A casino can be an important part of a community's entertainment and tourism offering."

"Within reasonable limits, legalized casino gaming is a good way for cities and states to generate revenue without having to raise everybody's taxes."

Source: Harrah's Entertainment, Inc./Yankelovich MONITOR.

card clubs in an effort to raise revenue. Nonetheless, in recent voting, about half the California communities considering the introduction of cardrooms voted them down.

Eugene Martin Christiansen and Will E. Cummings, in their "The Gross Annual Wager of the United States, 1996" (*International Gaming and Wagering Business,* August, 1997), reported that betting in cardrooms has increased nearly tenfold from an estimated $1 billion in 1982 to an estimated $9.8 billion in 1996. Well over 90 percent of this amount was bet in California. Over the same period, revenues grew from $50 million to $679 million. (Figures for cardrooms are only estimates, since these rooms are privately owned and need not report their earnings.)

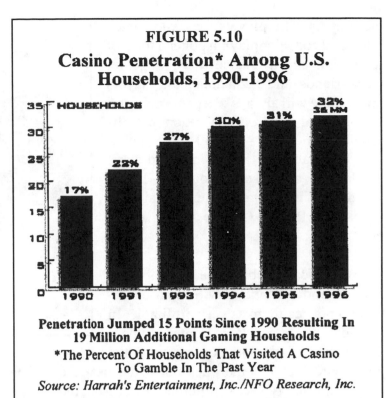

FIGURE 5.10

Casino Penetration* Among U.S. Households, 1990-1996

Penetration Jumped 15 Points Since 1990 Resulting In 19 Million Additional Gaming Households

*The Percent Of Households That Visited A Casino To Gamble In The Past Year

Source: Harrah's Entertainment, Inc./NFO Research, Inc.

Christiansen and Cummings report that at least 229 cardrooms, and perhaps as many as 330, with at least 2,164 tables, are currently operating in California. Traditionally, card clubs have been small establishments, often with only one or two tables. Only 13 clubs have 26 or more tables. Some of the more recently developed clubs, however, have been considerably larger. The largest card clubs in California are Commerce Club in Commerce with 223 tables, the Bicycle Club in Bell Gardens with 180 tables, and the Hollywood Park Casino with 140 tables. About 42 percent of all card tables are in Los Angeles County.

Card clubs in California, Las Vegas, Nevada and Atlantic City, New Jersey, got a boost from the introduction of games of Asian origin, often called the "Asian Games." Games such as Pai Gow and Super Pan Nine are much faster and, for many people, more exciting. With the introduction of these games, more people have begun visiting these cardrooms and giving the industry a real boost.

The state of Washington has more than 80 clubs and limits wagers to $10 per bet. Montana has over 50 small clubs and limits the action to $300 per pot. North Dakota has about 20 clubs, with most of the proceeds going to charity. While these small clubs provide a source of revenue for the operators, they also provide a social setting for

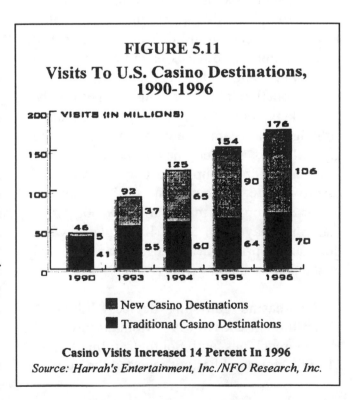

FIGURE 5.11

Visits To U.S. Casino Destinations, 1990-1996

■ New Casino Destinations
■ Traditional Casino Destinations

Casino Visits Increased 14 Percent In 1996

Source: Harrah's Entertainment, Inc./NFO Research, Inc.

the players. The players may know each other and consider playing poker a form of recreation and a chance to get together with friends and acquaintances. Players know there will always be a game going on at the local cardroom. Oregon permits "social gambling" — small-stakes poker and blackjack — in taverns and bars. Cardrooms can also be found in Deadwood, South Dakota, and in Central City, Black Hawk, and Cripple Creek, Colorado.

While card tables are available in Nevada and Atlantic City, casino operators do not see them as very profitable. In Nevada, the house take is limited to about 2.5 percent of the pot. Consequently, the per-square-foot income does not come near the output of other types of gambling. As a result, the casinos in Las Vegas have only about 300 tables and there are only about 500 tables in all of Nevada. Generally, the big casinos see card games as a method of attracting gamblers to other games.

NON-CASINO DEVICES

Eugene Christiansen and Will Cummings, in "The Gross Annual Wager of the United States, 1996," reported that in Louisiana, an estimated 16,239 gambling devices have been placed in restaurants and other retail establishments throughout the state. These video games may be poker, keno, or dozens of other possible games, although the games are often referred to generally as "video poker machines." In Louisiana, for example, to play a legal non-casino device, the bettor inserts 25-cents, $1, $5, or $10, up to a maximum of $200, with a maximum payout of $500. If the player wins, the machine prints out a ticket that can be cashed in at a nearby bar or grill.

Non-casino gambling devices did about $1.4 billion in sales in 1996. Montana has about 18,000 machines and South Carolina, about 21,600. Maryland has not reported the number

FIGURE 5.12
Share Of Household Visits To Casinos By Region, 1996

Source: Harrah's Entertainment, Inc./NFO Research, Inc.

of devices operating in the state. These machines have led to the creation of mini-casinos in Louisiana, Montana, South Carolina, and Maryland, mainly at truck stops and restaurants.

While returns have been considerable, many observers have expressed concern about the allegedly addictive nature of these machines. In Louisiana, it is also suspected that earnings from such machines have been used to influence

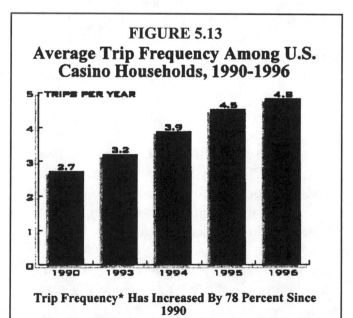

FIGURE 5.13
Average Trip Frequency Among U.S. Casino Households, 1990-1996

Trip Frequency* Has Increased By 78 Percent Since 1990

*The Average Number Of Trips Per Household Per Year
Source: Harrah's Entertainment, Inc./NFO Research, Inc.

politicians. Furthermore, a recent scandal concerning organized crime has further tainted the Louisiana devices. Members of the Gambino and Genovese crime families have been accused of conspiring with members of two suppliers of video poker games to skim profits from the devices.

GENERALLY A POPULAR ALTERNATIVE

In only a few short years, casino gambling has spread from two states to the point where it has been approved, in some form, in a total of 22 states. (This does not include gambling on Indian reservations, which is discussed in Chapter VII.) With the adoption of lotteries by the vast majority of states, the inhibitions often tied with gambling have been dropping — after all, if the state government urges that a person gamble, how bad can it be?

In addition, increasing financial demands on state and local governments, coupled with a strong voter resistance to increased taxes and, in some areas, a declining economy, have forced them to look for other alternatives for raising money. Like lotteries, casino gambling has been seen as a painless way of raising money, a "fun" or a "voluntary" form of taxation.

But Some Have Turned It Down

That does not mean that every state or locality has supported casino gambling. Floridians have periodically voted casino gambling down, but it will likely return to the ballot. Casino supporters in Arkansas saw their proposal defeated. Alaskans rejected casino gambling by a margin of almost 2 to 1, while Ohio voters also refused casino gambling by a similar

FIGURE 5.14
Top 10 Casino Feeder States, 1996

1. California	6. Texas
2. Illinois	7. New Jersey
3. Louisiana	8. Wisconsin
4. New York	9. Nevada
5. Pennsylvania	10. Minnesota

The Top Ten Feeder States Remained The Same In 1996
Source: Harrah's Entertainment, Inc./NFO Research, Inc.

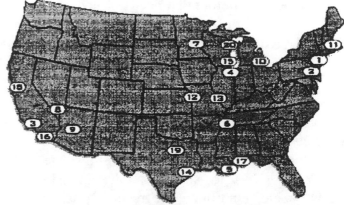

FIGURE 5.15

Top 20 Casino Feeder Markets, 1996

1. New York	9. Phoenix-	17. Mobile-
2. Philadelphia	Flagstaff	Pensacola
3. Los Angeles	10. Detroit	18. San Francisco
4. Chicago	11. Boston	19. Dallas-
5. New Orleans	12. Kansas City*	Ft. Worth*
6. Memphis	13. St. Louis	20. Green Bay-
7. Minneapolis-	14. Houston*	Appleton, WI
St. Paul	15. Milwaukee	
8. Las Vegas	16. San Diego	* Added in
		1996.

Source: Harrah's Entertainment, Inc./NFO Research, Inc.

proportion. Chicago decided against casino gambling, although riverboats from neighboring Indiana may some day fulfill some Chicagoans' desire to gamble.

Nonetheless, for many states and localities, casino gambling is considered a way to reverse economic decline and raise revenue. From an economic standpoint, the expansion of the opportunity to introduce casino gambling is seen as a growing business opportunity. Those in the gambling business believe there is a large, unmet demand for casino gambling throughout the United States. The successes of gambling in South Dakota and Colorado, of riverboat gambling on the Mississippi and other waterways, at Ledyard in Connecticut and other casinos on Native American reservations throughout the country, and the increases in casino gambling on cruise ships would seem to indicate they are right. Like any other business, gambling will continue to grow until the needs of the consumer are met. It may be some time before that need is filled.

THE HARRAH'S SURVEY OF CASINO GAMING ENTERTAINMENT

Harrah's Casino Hotels is one of the major operators of gambling casinos in the United States. Beginning in 1991, Harrah's hired the NPD Group, Inc. (formerly Home Testing Institute) (New York City) to survey public attitudes towards casino gambling. The resulting annual report, *The Harrah's Survey of U.S. Casino Gaming Entertainment* (Memphis, Tennessee), also includes findings from the *Yankelovich MONITOR Callback*, an annual national survey of attitudes and values. The NPD Group surveyed 100,000 households from which they identified 17,709 gamblers. The majority of findings in *Harrah's Survey* are based on their responses.

FIGURE 5.16

Feeder Markets Generating More Than 500,000 Household Visits To Casinos, 1996

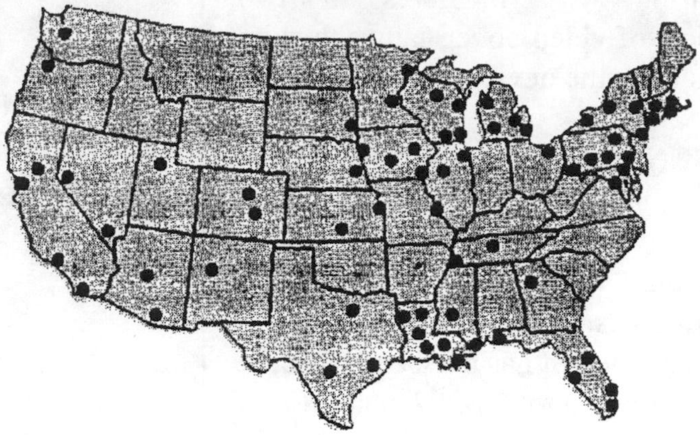

Source: *Harrah's Entertainment, Inc./NFO Research, Inc.*

General Acceptance of Casino Gambling

The *Harrah Survey* found that the public generally accepted casino gambling. About 62 percent of all those questioned thought casino gambling was "perfectly acceptable for anyone," while 30 percent believed it was "acceptable for others, but not for me." Only 8 percent thought casino gambling was "not acceptable for anyone." (See Figure 5.8.)

The general acceptance of gambling has been increasing rapidly. In 1992, 39 percent said they "would favor the introduction of casino gaming in many local communities because of its benefits to the local economy;" by 1996, 52 percent would. Well over half (59 percent) of those asked thought "legalized casino gaming brings money into a local economy without hurting existing business." A large majority (70 percent) thought "a casino can be an important part of a community's entertainment and tourism offering." Even more people (81 percent) believed "Casino gaming can be a fun night out." (See Figure 5.9.)

FIGURE 5.17

Median Household Income

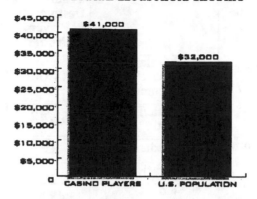

**Casino Players Have A Household Income That Is
28% Higher Than That Of The U.S. Population**

*Source: Harrah's Entertainment, Inc./NFO Research,
Inc./U.S. Census.*

Education:

Casino players

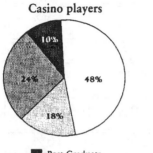

10%
24%
18%
48%

U.S. Population

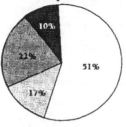

10%
22%
17%
51%

- ■ Post Graduate
- ▨ Some College
- ▨ College Graduate
- □ No College

Casino Players Are Slightly More Educated

Source: Harrah's Entertainment, Inc./U.S. Census.

Median Age

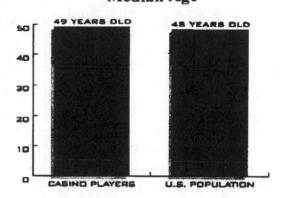

**The Median Age Of Casino Players Is Similar To
That Of The U.S. Population**

*Source: Harrah's Entertainment, Inc./NFO Research,
Inc./U.S. Census.*

Employment:

Casino players

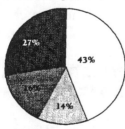

27%
16%
14%
43%

U.S. Population

28%
16%
15%
41%

- ■ Blue Collar
- ▨ Retired
- ▨ Other (Military & Homemakers)
- □ White Collar

**Casino Players Are More Likely To Be
White Collar Workers**

*Source: Harrah's Entertainment, Inc./NFO Research,
Inc./U.S. Census.*

Male/Female Ratio

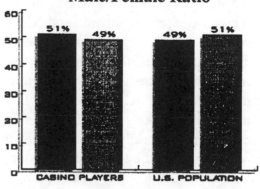

- ■ Male
- ■ Female

**There Are Slightly More Male And Slightly Fewer
Female Casino Players As Compared To The U.S.
Population**

*Source: Harrah's Entertainment, Inc./NFO Research,
Inc./U.S. Census.*

Not surprisingly, with the increased availability of casino gambling, more people have visited casinos. *Harrah's Survey* found that people from about 32 percent of the U.S. households had gambled at a casino at some time during the past year, up dramatically from 17 percent in 1990 (Figure 5.10).

These people had made an estimated 176 million trips to casinos. A lot of the increase is attributable to the new casino destinations. While 70 million trips were made to either Nevada or Atlantic City, 106 million were made to the new casino destinations. (See Figure 5.11.) With the spread of casino gambling, the visitors were pretty evenly distributed all over the country (Figure 5.12). Again, reflecting the increased availability of gambling, the number of trips to the casino made by each casino household rose from 2.7 per year in 1990 to 4.8 per year in 1996 (Figure 5.13).

Where Do the Casino Players Come From?

TABLE 5.13

	Traditional Destination Player Profile	New Destination Player Profile	United States Population
Median Household Income	$44,000	$39,000	$32,000
Male/Female Ratio	52/48	50/50	49/51
Median Age	49	47	48
Education			
No College	48%	50%	51%
Some College	23%	22%	22%
College Graduate	19%	18%	17%
Post Graduate	10%	9%	10%
Employment			
White Collar	43%	41%	41%
Blue Collar	27%	29%	28%
Retired	16%	16%	16%
Other	14%	14%	15%

Source: *Harrah's Entertainment, Inc./NFO Research, Inc./U.S. Census.*

Not surprisingly, the top 10 states which provided the most visitors were those states located either nearest to Nevada and New Jersey, states nearest to the riverboat gaming casinos, and Wisconsin and Minnesota, which have the highest number of Indian casinos. (See Figure 5.14.) Similarly, the top 10 ADIs (Areas of Dominant Influence, or TV markets around major metropolitan areas) were generally also near Nevada and Atlantic City or riverboat or Indian casinos. (See Figures 5.15 and 5.16.) Other than finding that the typical casino gambling household earned more than the general household, the profile of the gambling household did not differ much from the average household. (See Figure 5.17.) *Harrah's Survey* found virtually no differences in the characteristics between those who visited the traditional destinations of Nevada and Atlantic City with those going to the newer destinations such as riverboats and Native American casinos (Table 5.13).

THE *LODGING HOSPITALITY*/HMBA SURVEY OF CASINO VISITORS

Edward Watkins of *Lodging Hospitality* magazine and Patrick Ford of the Hotel & Motel Brokers of America (HMBA) surveyed frequent travelers to determine their interest in casinos. They found that 62 percent of those interviewed had visited a casino in the last year. In fact, 70 percent had gone at least twice, and 16 percent had

TABLE 5.14

Casino Visits: Actual & Planned

Have You Visited a Gaming Casino in the Past 12 Months?

Yes.................................62%
No..................................38%

If Yes, How Many Times in the Past 12 Months?

Once...............................30%
Twice..............................25%
3-6 Times.........................29%
More Than 6 Times ..16%

Do You Plan to Visit a Gaming Casino in the Next 12 Months?

Yes..................................64%
No...................................36%

If Yes, How Many Times in the Next 12 Months?

Once...............................30%
Twice..............................32%
3-6 Times.........................28%
More Than 6 Times ..10%

Source: Edward Watkins of *Lodging Hospitality*, and Patrick Ford of the Hotel and Motel Brokers of America, "Casino Fever Rises," *Lodging Hospitality*, May 1994

Attitudes Toward Casino Gaming

Is Casino Gaming Legal in Your State of Residence?

Yes.................................49%
No..................................51%

If No, Do You Favor Legalization of Casino Gaming in Your State?

Yes.................................57%
No..................................43%

If You Object, What Are Your Objections to Legalized Casino Gaming in Your State?

Moral Objections................31%
Fear of Crime......................30%
Fear of Overdevelopment..19%
Religious Objections 17%
Other Objections.................3%

What Could Casinos Do to Encourage You to Visit More Often?

Improve Gaming Odds......35%
Reduce Room Rates 23%
More Family Entertainment......17%
Improve Guestroom
  Accommodations 9%
Add More Table Games.......7%
Add More Slot Machines......5%
Other......................................4%

Where People Gamble

Visited in Past 12 Months		Plan to Visit in Next 12 Months
32%	Nevada	36%
31%	Indian Reservation	17%
16%	Riverboat Casino	16%
13%	Atlantic City	13%
3%	Cruise Ship	10%
3%	Caribbean Resort	6%
2%	Others	2%

Did Your Most Recent Visit Include an Overnight Stay in a Hotel?

Yes.................................66%
No..................................34%

If Yes, How Much Did You Pay For One Night's Stay?

Less than $25.......................5%
$26-$40 ....15%
$41-$60 ....23%
$61-$80 ....22%
$81-$100 ....19%
More than $100 ....16%

How Much Do You Typically Gamble on Each Visit to a Casino?

Less than $25......................12%
$26-$50 ....14%
$51-$150 ....27%
$151-$500 ....34%
More than $500 ....13%

What Was the Primary Reason for Your Most Recent Visit to a Casino?

As a Vacation......................68%
Attend a Convention 18%
Attend a Business Meeting ..10%
Part of a Tour Group.............4%

gone more than 6 times. Apparently, most of the travelers had enjoyed the experience since two-thirds (64 percent) planned to go again. (See Table 5.14.)

Most had visited either Nevada (32 percent) or an Indian Reservation (31 percent). Most visitors to Nevada, riverboats, and Atlantic City planned to return in the next 12 months, although visitors to

Indian Reservations apparently were not as satisfied. Most (68 percent) went to the casinos as part of a vacation. About two-thirds (66 percent) stayed overnight. Most gambled more than $50. (See Table 5.14.)

About half (49 percent) came from states where casino gambling was legal. Over half (57 percent) of those from states with no casino gambling favored legalizing gambling in their state. Those who objected to legalized gambling were concerned about the morality of gambling (31 percent), crime (30 percent), overdevelopment (19 percent), or violation of their religious values (17 percent). The respondents thought that the casinos could increase the number of visitors by improving the gambling odds (35 percent), reducing room rates (23 percent), or increasing family entertainment (17 percent). (See Table 5.14.)

CASINOS AROUND THE WORLD

Casino gambling is very common around the world. The casinos in Monte Carlo are probably the most famous. Although there are four casinos in Monte Carlo, the elegant Casino of Monte Carlo is probably the most well-known. There are 12 state-operated casinos in Austria and eight in Belgium. France has more than 100 casinos, many of them as beautiful as the Casino of Monte Carlo, and many are located in such exotic places as Biarritz and Cannes. Until 1996, French casinos were restricted to small towns. Starting in 1997, they may be established in tourist cities with populations over 500,000.

Almost all of Germany's 25 casinos are located in spas, probably the most famous of which is the luxurious casino at Baden-Baden. The more than 100 casinos in the United Kingdom are called "private clubs." Portugal has 6 casinos. Spain has almost 40 casinos, and several autonomous regions in Spain are beginning to act on their own authority to establish more casinos.

While the residents of Hong Kong cannot legally gamble, they can take a 75-minute hydrofoil ride to the nearby Portuguese colony of Macao where they can choose from 8 casinos. (A hydrofoil is a boat with blades attached to its hull. When the boat is travelling fast enough, the blades lift the craft above the water, enabling it to skim along rapidly.) They could also fly to Australia and try their luck in the casinos there. Casinos are planned for Cambodia and Laos in order to help promote tourism.

In the Caribbean, people may gamble at the hotel casinos of Puerto Rico or Aruba. Almost all tourists who fly to the Bahamas visit the country's four casinos. There are relatively few casinos in Latin America and South America, although Argentina has 15. Otherwise, most other Latin American and South American countries have just one or two casinos.

In October 1993, Canada opened its first casino in Montreal, Quebec, at the site of the 1967 World Exposition French Pavilion, and another casino in the Charlevoix region of Quebec is being considered. In the Province of Ontario, the government awarded a partnership of Caesar's World, Inc., Circus Enterprises, Ltd., and Hilton Hotels to build a $300 million gambling and entertainment complex in Windsor, Ontario, directly across the river from Detroit, Michigan. The casino opened in summer 1996.

Like many late twentieth century industries, the gambling business has become international. A casino opening up in Cambodia or Australia might receive financial investment from, or even be owned by, an American or European gambling corporation. A new casino opening in Great Britain might involve investment money from Singapore or Hong Kong. The leading gambling companies such as Harrah's, Caesar's (which is owned by ITT Corp.), and the Mirage are international corporations whose interests now extend far beyond America's shores.

CHAPTER VI

CASINO GAMBLING — ON THE WATER

Once baseball was considered America's favorite pastime. Nothing could beat the crack of the bat, the smell of a hot dog.... But that's changing. These days people are more into the clank of quarters dropping in slot machines and the thrill of drawing a royal flush or four-of-a-kind.
— *Knight-Ridder Newspapers,* November 20, 1994

RIVERBOAT GAMBLING

Many states that forbid casino gambling on dry land take a more liberal view of gambling on water, as if, by putting gambling on the water, it somehow separates the state from any problems that might be associated with gambling. On April 1, 1991, the State of Iowa brought back riverboat gambling to the Mississippi River. Since then, five more states (Missouri, Illinois, Indiana, Mississippi, and Louisiana) have passed laws permitting riverboat casinos. In 1996, over 80 vessels were operating in six states, producing $5.5 billion in revenues. (Indiana, which passed riverboat gambling in 1993, began operating one vessel in 1995 and added three more in 1996.)

The growth in riverboats, however, has slowed, and no additional state has introduced riverboat gambling since 1993. In fact, the industry suffered major defeats in two potentially lucrative markets, Philadelphia and Chicago. Proposals in Alabama, Kentucky, Maryland, Massachusetts, Ohio, South Carolina, Texas, Virginia, and West Virginia died. On the other hand, existing facilities are being expanded and developed to make them more attractive to visitors. The next few years are likely to be a shakeout period where weaker companies either succumb or are bought out by the larger players, many of whom have come from either Las Vegas or Atlantic City.

Often More a Barge Than a Riverboat

Most riverboats range in size from 200 to 300 feet long and 45 to 95 feet wide. The *President,* sailing out of Davenport, Iowa, is 300 feet long, has a 27,000-square foot casino, 700 slot machines, and 30 gaming tables. The smaller *Par-A-Dice* out of Peoria, Illinois, is 228 feet long, has 12,500 square feet of casino space with 478 slot machines and 40 tables. The *Casino Queen,* out of East St. Louis, offers 896 slot machines and 62 tables, while Harrah's *Vicksburg* has 525 slot machines and 38 tables.

Not all the riverboats must be seaworthy. Illinois demands that the riverboats cruise in the rivers, while Missouri and Louisiana require the ships to cruise an ill-defined "certain extent." Mississippi does not require the ships to sail and, in fact, many of the ships docked in Mississippi are not really capable of sailing — they are giant buildings constructed on barges. Mirage Resort subsidiary Golden Nugget's planned $300 million casino resort in Biloxi, Mississippi, will make few pretenses to seaworthiness. Barry Shier, president of Golden Nugget, observed, "We don't consider this to be a riverboat project. We consider this to be a major resort destination." When this project is completed in late 1998, the Beau Rivage Hotel adjoining the "riverboat" will contain 1,800 rooms, making it the largest hotel in the state.

TABLE 6.1

IOWA EXCURSION BOATS

	Admissions	Slot Drop	Coin In	Slot Revenue	Table Drop	Table Revenue	Keno Tickets Written
1991 (Apr-Dec)	2,145,810	$67,869,901	$513,096,799	$54,212,578	$25,039,112	$10,363,678	-
1992 (Jan-Dec)	2,163,637	$77,004,092	$628,594,057	$59,542,433	$26,027,874	$9,831,073	-
1993 (Jan-Dec)	1,656,634	$53,627,704	$462,174,847	$38,659,433	$18,191,143	$6,566,872	-
1994 (Jan-Dec)	3,160,836	$120,509,555	$970,625,363	$79,696,093	$102,370,058	$25,143,189	-
1995 (Jan-Dec)	6,722,396	$341,548,122	$2,422,823,693	$180,675,191	$245,968,784	$58,278,174	-
1996 (Jan-Dec)	11,424,333	$806,864,804	$4,520,060,368	$298,307,313	$454,073,425	$97,023,411	$410,208

Continued on following page.

Iowa

When Iowa introduced riverboat gambling, individual bets were limited to $5, and betting losses on the Iowa riverboats were limited to $200 per cruise. The gambler bought up to $200 worth of scrip before getting on board. When the bettor got on board, he could then change the scrip into tokens or chips for gambling. If a player took four cruises in one day, he could lose up to $800. If someone simply wanted to enjoy a brief cruise on the Mississippi and not bet money, he or she could usually buy a cruise-only ticket for $10 or less. The $200 limit, however, led many riverboat casinos to sail for more profitable shores. For example, the *Diamond Lady* and the *Emerald Lady* steamed to Mississippi, and some observers feared for the future of riverboat gambling in Iowa if the limit were maintained.

Consequently, the Iowa legislature removed betting and loss limits, restrictions on space on the riverboat devoted to gambling, and requirements that the boat actually cruise. As a result, the total revenues, which had tumbled from $69.9 million in 1992 to $45.5 million in 1993, rose sharply to $104.9 million in 1994 and reached $395 million in 1996. Most (75 percent) revenues were produced by slot machines.

Gambling revenues in Iowa are taxed on the basis of 5 percent for the first $1,000,000, 10 percent for the next $2,000,000, and 20 percent thereafter. This tax is distributed 0.5 percent each to the city and county, 1.3 percent to Gambler's Assistance (intended to help compulsive gamblers), and the remainder to the state general fund. In 1996, the State of Iowa received $70 million, while the cities and counties each got $2 million and Gambler's Assistance received $1.2 million. (See Table 6.1.) Thirteen boats were operating in Iowa in 1996.

Nonetheless, although gambling seems to have recovered in Iowa, the state's cities are being more careful this time around. Earlier, when profits did not develop because of the gambling limit, the riverboats were quick to sail off and leave many communities high and dry. This time, many of the communities are demanding that the

TABLE 6.1 (Continued)

IOWA EXCURSION BOATS

Keno Revenue	Adjusted Gross Revenue	Tax to City	Tax to County	Tax to Gambler's Treatment	Tax to General Fund (Gaming)	Admission Fee
-	$64,576,256	$322,466	$322,466	$1,972,142	$7,621,371	$672,295
-	$69,905,596*	$349,522	$349,522	$2,097,054	$10,056,902	$1,359,095
-	$45,448,294*	$231,075	$231,075	$1,386,449	$6,246,750	$1,122,822
-	$104,911,942*	$524,557	$524,557	$1,195,719	$16,327,354	$776,467
-	$239,006,059*	$1,195,031	$1,195,031	$717,018	$41,109,696	$1,408,598
$63,877	$395,394,601	$1,976,971	$1,976,971	$1,186,187	$70,091,400	$2,396,414

Source: *1996 Annual Report of the Iowa Racing and Gaming Commission*, Des Moines, IA, December 31, 1996

gambling companies develop the land around the riverboat to include hotels and restaurants. Such development would make it harder for the boat owners to lift anchor and sail away if revenues decline.

Illinois

Meanwhile, across the river in Illinois, gamblers have had the opportunity to bet without limit. Illinois believed that gamblers would come to their state instead of Iowa because of this policy. They were correct, and gamblers continued to visit the Illinois riverboats even after Iowa had lifted its limits on gambling. However, the *Silver Eagle* in East Dubuque, Iowa, closed because of the increased competition from across the river.

In 1996, 25 million people visited the state's riverboats, more than twice as many as had come in 1993. Gross receipts rose from $979.6 million in 1994 to $1.2 billion in 1995 and fell back to $1.1 billion in 1996. The casinos earned about $45 for every visitor. About $276.7 million was collected in tax revenues. The state received $194.9 million

and the local communities, $81.8 million. (See Table 6.2.) Thirteen ships were operating in 1996. Attempts to expand riverboat gambling to the Chicago area failed, with existing operators providing some of the strongest opposition.

Missouri

Missouri, located across the river from Illinois, was the fifth state to introduce riverboat gambling. By June 1996, 11 ships were operating. For the fiscal year ending June 30, 1997, adjusted gross receipts totaled $652 million and 32 million people had paid admission fees to gamble on the riverboats. The total gambling tax amounted to $130 million — $117 million was the state's portion, and $13 million remained locally. (See Table 6.3.)

Just as Iowa had earlier done and then rescinded, Missouri has set a limit to gambling losses. Bettors may lose no more than $500, a restriction that chafes the Missouri Gaming Commission, which finds that the $500 loss limit places Missouri riverboat gaming operations at a

TABLE 6.2

GAMING IN ILLINOIS

	Calendar Year Comparison					
	1991	1992	1993	1994	1995	1996
Number of Licensees in Operation	2	5	9	10	* 10	** 10
Adjusted Gross Receipts (AGR)	$14,942,909	$226,334,794	$605,684,483	$979,551,111	$1,178,311,827	$1,131,491,531
Table Games	$7,332,507	$94,306,193	$234,129,563	$334,304,445	$368,380,581	$322,007,802
Electronic Gaming Devices (EGD)	$7,610,402	$132,028,601	$371,554,920	$645,246,666	$809,931,246	$809,483,729
Patrons	N/A	N/A	N/A	N/A	14,787,836	14,075,884
AGR Per Patron	N/A	N/A	N/A	N/A	$79.68	$80.39
Admissions	308,783	4,079,819	10,679,490	20,367,119	24,835,833	25,211,329
AGR Per Admission	$48.39	$55.48	$56.71	$48.09	$47.44	$44.88
Total Tax	$3,606,147	$53,426,597	$142,495,876	$236,644,461	$285,334,031	$276,720,964
Wagering Tax	$2,988,581	$45,266,959	$121,136,896	$195,910,223	$235,662,365	$226,298,306
Admissions Tax	$617,566	$8,159,638	$21,358,980	$40,734,238	$49,671,666	$50,422,658
State Share	$2,550,219	$38,030,038	$101,532,162	$167,299,786	$201,582,607	$194,935,059
Local Share	$1,055,928	$15,396,559	$40,963,714	$69,344,675	$83,751,424	$81,785,905

* Jo Daviess Silver Eagle temporarily ceased gambling operations December 4, 1995.
** Jo Daviess Silver Eagle operation re-opens May 22, 1996.

Source: *1996 Annual Report*, Illinois Gaming Board, Springfield, IL, n.d.

competitive disadvantage as opposed to similar operations in adjoining states. The net effect appears to be a significant decrease in state revenue.

In fact, the *Missouri Gaming Commission Annual Report 1996* includes an entire section showing "The Effect of the $500 Loss Limit." Not surprisingly, the cap on the amount that may be lost limits the return. Many Missouri gamblers are willing to travel to other states to gamble in a friendlier environment. Casual surveys of license plates on cars in parking lots of riverboat casinos in Illinois show this to be true. Moreover, Missouri riverboat operators are less likely to draw out-of-state customers because of the loss limit.

Mississippi

Farther down the river, Mississippi, more than any other state, has promoted the development of riverboat gambling. While most other states have tried to closely control the expansion of casino gambling, Mississippi has opened the state up to

riverboats and let the free market decide which casinos will survive. By the end of 1997, 29 boats were operating.

Revenues from riverboat gambling have been increasing dramatically over the last few years, rising from $790 million in 1993 to $1.72 billion in 1995 and $2 billion in 1997. (See Table 6.4.) The state of Mississippi receives 8 percent of this total, or about $160 million.

Concern has developed for the Gulf Coast casinos at Biloxi. As late as July 1994, revenues from the Gulf Coast counties exceeded those from the river counties. Since then, however, the river counties have produced increasingly more revenues (Table 6.4), while several casinos on the Gulf Coast have gone bankrupt. Some believe the shakeout was to be expected with over a dozen and a half casinos competing for gamblers' attention. In addition, the development of riverboat gambling in neighboring Louisiana probably has affected attendance. Some observers believe that quality hotels should be built so that visitors have

TABLE 6.3

MISSOURI GAMING SUMMARY

LICENSEE	BOAT NAME LOCATION	LICENSE DATE	FY 1997 ADMISSIONS	ADMISSION FEES	ADMISSION FEES STATE & LOCAL PORTION	FY 1997 ADJUSTED GROSS RECEIPTS	GAMING TAX	GAMING TAX LOCAL PORTION	GAMING TAX STATE PORTION	ESTIMATED PROJECT COST**	EMPLOYEES	TABLE GAMES	SLOT MACHINES	GAMING POSITIONS
PRESIDENT RIVERBOAT CASINO MISSOURI, INC.	ADMIRAL ST. LOUIS	27-May-94	3,373,674	6,747,348	3,373,674	63,834,732	12,766,946	1,276,695	11,490,252	60,204,248	969	66	1,118	1,366
ST. CHARLES RIVERFRONT STATION, INC.	CASINO ST. CHARLES I & II ST. CHARLES	27-May-94 28-Dec-94	6,282,214	12,564,428	6,282,214	137,681,703	27,536,341	2,753,634	24,782,706	170,000,000	1,479	96	1,881	2,222
MISSOURI GAMING COMPANY	ARGOSY RIVERSIDE CASINO RIVERSIDE	22-Jun-94	3,263,423	6,526,846	3,263,423	69,902,019	13,980,404	1,398,040	12,582,363	82,597,042	849	54	972	1,170
ST. JOSEPH RIVERBOAT PARTNERS	ST. JO FRONTIER CASINO ST. JOSEPH	24-Jun-94	781,856	1,563,712	781,858	18,205,344	3,641,069	364,107	3,276,962	22,000,000	321	17	348	408
HARRAHS NORTH KANSAS CITY CORP	NORTH STAR & MARDI GRAS NORTH KANSAS CITY	22-Sep-94 15-May-96	7,323,802	14,647,604	7,323,902	163,179,336	32,635,867	3,263,567	29,372,280	165,800,000	2,152	96	1,968	2,321
AZTAR MISSOURI CORP	CASINO AZTAR CARUTHERSVILLE	27-Apr-95	736,355	1,472,710	736,355	21,961,834	4,392,367	439,237	3,953,130	56,350,000	458	27	436	542
BOYD KANSAS CITY CORP	SAMS TOWN KANSAS CITY	13-Sep-95	2,388,594	4,777,188	2,388,594	50,585,151	10,117,030	1,011,703	9,105,327	147,117,343	780	48	1,060	1,224
HILTON KANSAS CITY CORP	FLAMINGO HILTON KANSAS CITY	18-Oct-96	1,615,187	3,230,374	1,615,187	29,343,411	5,868,682	586,868	5,281,814	114,600,000	803	47	1,039	1,195
KANSAS CITY STATION CORP	RIVER KING & QUEEN KANSAS CITY	16-Jan-97	3,995,314	7,990,628	3,995,314	58,827,225	11,765,445	1,176,544	10,588,900	285,000,000	2,370	179	3,254	3,903
PLAYERS MARYLAND HEIGHTS CORP	PLAYERS ISLAND KOKOMO & GRAND CAYMEN MARYLAND HEIGHTS	11-Mar-97	1,222,855	2,445,710	1,222,855	19,534,888	3,906,938	390,694	3,516,244	140,000,000	1,036	79	1,230	1,542
HARRAHS MARYLAND HEIGHTS CORP	MARDI GRAS & EASY STREET MARYLAND HEIGHTS	11-Mar-97	1,152,418	2,304,836	1,152,418	18,940,597	3,788,119	378,812	3,409,308	169,645,000	1,659	76	1,248	1,543
GRAND TOTALS:			32,135,692	64,271,384	32,135,692	651,996,039	130,399,208	13,039,921	117,356,287	1,433,313,633	12,896	787	14,554	17,436

** Formulas used by the Licensees to arrive at total project cost vary. The figures published in this report are subject to adjustment.

Source: *Annual Summary of Riverboat Gaming Activity*, Missouri Gaming Commission, Jefferson City, MO, 1997

a place to sleep and eat and will stay more than a day.

Louisiana

Louisiana approved riverboat gambling in 1991. The law allows 15 riverboats on its 11 rivers and lakes. (As of December 1997, there were 13 riverboat casinos in the state.) While the law limits the number of riverboats per parish (county) to six, most of the riverboats sail out of New Orleans or nearby parishes. The New Orleans metropolitan area spreads out over Orleans, Jefferson, St. Tammany, and St. Bernard parishes, so it is possible that all 15 riverboats could serve the New Orleans region.

Many optimistic state political leaders and residents had hoped that riverboat gambling would turn around Louisiana's seriously ailing economy and perhaps transform New Orleans into the next Las Vegas. Unfortunately, after only two months of operation, the *Grand Palais* and *Crescent City Queen*, the two riverboats that made up the River City Complex in New Orleans, ceased operation because of poor performance in 1994 and eventually went bankrupt. This disappointment was compounded a year later by the bankruptcy of Harrah's Jazz Co., whose attempt to develop a land-based casino also foundered on poor revenues.

While the executives at Harrah's complained about inefficiency and corruption, it appears that there are just too many other things for tourists to do in New Orleans. New Orleans is one of the more unusual cities in the United States, and few visitors go there to gamble. Time is better spent walking around the French Quarter and enjoying the unique food and authentic American jazz. Finally, a recent video poker scandal involving the slot machine producer, Bally, did not benefit the image of gambling in a state with a long history of corruption.

Nonetheless, during the first half of 1996, Louisiana casinos took in $616.8 million from nearly 12.7 million gamblers, and the state collected $114.1 million in taxes. The big winners were the gambling establishments in the Texas-area markets of Shreveport, Bossier City, and Lake Charles.

OTHER PLACES TO GAMBLE WHILE ON THE WATER

Regular Cruises

A generation ago, if there was a casino on a cruise ship, the traveler had to make a determined effort to find it. Today, virtually all major cruise lines include gambling as an attraction for their passengers along with entertainment, dining, dancing, and shuffleboard. Growing competition in the cruise industry has made the money earned from casinos more important. The Carnival Cruise Lines' *Ecstasy*, a particularly large cruise ship, has 234 slots, 16 blackjack tables, 3 roulette wheels, 2 crap tables, and 3 Caribbean stud poker tables. The cruise lines emphasize that gambling is just one among many attractions. They further stress that they are a hospitality business, not a gambling business.

Virtually all cruise passengers are there to enjoy the cruise experience, not to gamble. As a result, most cruise ships have a limit of $100 to $200 in order to control losses. After all, a cruise passenger will not have had a pleasant voyage if she or he lost huge amounts of money at the gaming tables. Eugene Christiansen and Will Cummings, in their "United States Gross Annual Wager, 1996" (*International Gaming and Wagering Business*, August 1997), estimated that cruise ship companies earned an estimated $234 million in 1996 in gross gambling revenue.

The cruise business has been expanding. In addition, federally mandated safety regulations that went into effect in 1997 will lead to many older ships being moved out of the American market and into other markets where the requirements are not as strict. Therefore, in order to handle the expected passenger growth and to replace older vessels, cruise ship companies have ordered 31 ships worth about $8.5 billion over the

TABLE 6.4

MISSISSIPPI GAMING COMMISSION

Gross Revenue by Month - From the State Tax Commission (ROUNDED OFF)

DATE	Gulf Coast Counties	Mississippi River Counties	Totals
AUGUST 1992	10,616,710		
SEPTEMBER 1992	18,455,071		
OCTOBER 1992	26,987,124		
NOVEMBER 1992	32,427,490		
DECEMBER 1992	33,321,576		
1992 TOTAL	121,807,971		
JANUARY 1993	40,118,995		
FEBRUARY 1993	42,595,657		
MARCH 1993	51,243,878		
APRIL 1993	52,421,280		
MAY 1993	58,752,132		
JUNE 1993	61,396,052		
JULY 1993	74,695,230		
AUGUST 1993	78,017,868		
SEPTEMBER 1993	77,061,721		
OCTOBER 1993	80,490,318		
NOVEMBER 1993	82,836,509		
DECEMBER 1993	90,206,071		
1993 TOTAL	789,835,711		
JANUARY 1994	53,322,303	46,644,365	99,966,668
FEBRUARY 1994	58,170,877	48,207,481	106,378,358
MARCH 1994	60,329,743	59,840,790	120,170,533
APRIL 19943	64,221,627	56,862,106	121,083,733
MAY 1994	66,784,833	58,015,782	124,800,615
JUNE 1994	62,332,692	57,532,709	119,865,401
JULY 1994	72,102,662	69,809,172	141,911,834
AUGUST 1994	60,317,077	68,631,095	128,948,172
SEPTEMBER 1994	61,470,651	66,869,528	128,340,179
OCTOBER 1994	58,208,055	68,520,808	126,728,864
NOVEMBER 1994	56,904,455	65,536,548	122,441,002
DECEMBER 1994	53,161,726	68,997,562	122,159,288
1994 TOTAL	727,326,701	735,467,946	1,462,794,647
JANUARY 1995	57,169,532	76,323,990	133,493,522
FEBRUARY 1995	56,467,579	72,761,744	129,229,322
MARCH 1995	62,368,507	80,836,899	143,205,406
APRIL 1995	61,404,213	84,341,784	145,745,998
MAY 1995	59,062,693	85,671,861	144,734,554
JUNE 1995	58,613,777	80,215,783	138,829,560
JULY 1995	70,565,494	98,268,060	168,833,555
AUGUST 1995	59,724,280	84,759,463	144,483,743
SEPTEMBER 1995	60,160,593	86,232,083	146,392,676
OCTOBER 1995	55,334,961	87,242,009	142,576,970
NOVEMBER 1995	58,044,361	83,256,657	141,301,016
DECEMBER 1995	57,100,563	88,374,520	145,475,083
1995 TOTAL	716,016,553	1,008,284,853	1,724,301,405
GRAND TOTAL	911,643,682		
GRAND TOTAL	1,443,343,254	1,743,752,799	4,098,739,734

DATE	Gulf Coast Counties	Mississippi River Counties	Totals
JANUARY 1996	57,077,790	84,052,771	141,130,560
FEBRUARY 1996	60,963,023	83,633,806	144,596,830
MARCH 1996	69,349,125	104,634,960	173,984,085
APRIL 1996	62,849,810	89,805,317	152,655,127
MAY 1996	62,181,216	90,398,796	152,580,012
JUNE 1996	63,232,690	90,176,187	153,408,876
JULY 1996	70,608,566	101,051,775	171,660,342
AUGUST 1996	66,229,172	96,420,867	162,650,039
SEPTEMBER 1996	61,132,631	93,899,014	155,031,645
OCTOBER 1996	57,962,554	93,121,662	151,084,216
NOVEMBER 1996	59,505,895	94,295,404	153,801,299
DECEMBER 1996	58,226,643	91,021,846	149,248,489
1996 TOTAL	749,319,114	1,112,512,406	1,861,831,520
JANUARY 1997	59,184,097	91,805,085	150,989,182
FEBRUARY 1997	60,505,862	98,907,400	159,413,262
MARCH 1997	65,818,688	110,713,231	176,531,920
APRIL 1997	61,598,936	97,192,944	158,791,880
MAY 1997	64,419,784	107,785,860	172,205,644
JUNE 1997	64,162,328	104,944,736	169,107,065
JULY 1997	68,506,249	104,952,519	173,458,768
AUGUST 1997	70,580,030	112,360,856	182,940,886
SEPTEMBER 1997	61,789,882	97,884,789	159,674,671
OCTOBER 1997	62,697,914	100,265,065	162,962,978
NOVEMBER 1997	59,929,658	103,822,608	163,752,266
DECEMBER 1997	58,375,074	96,163,250	154,538,324
1997 TOTAL	757,568,501	1,226,798,344	1,984,366,845
GRAND TOTAL	2,950,230,869	4,083,063,549	7,944,938,099

Source: Mississippi Gaming Commission, Jackson, MS, February 3, 1998

next several years. Virtually all of these ships will offer gambling facilities. Cruise operators believe that many cruise vacationers have never been exposed to casino gambling so that there is a significant opportunity for increased revenues in this area.

Cruises to Nowhere

"Cruises to nowhere" or "day trips" are gambling opportunities offered from several coastal ports in Florida, Georgia, and Texas. In order to create a day-cruise ship, the cruise company generally purchases an older, smaller cruise ship. They strip out the cabins and replace them with dining and dancing facilities and, of course, casinos. The ship travels out three to nine miles into international waters, where neither state nor federal laws apply, and sails around for about six hours. A typical day-trip ship may make two or three trips a day. About a dozen ships operate out of Dade and Broward Counties in southern Florida.

However, these cruises, with the exception of those out of Florida, have either failed or met with limited success. In fact, all but two of the estimated 17 cruise ships operate out of Florida where day-cruise trips have proven quite profitable. In Florida, the weather is more predictable and generally pleasant year-round, and there is already a large tourist base looking for something else to do, enabling the "day-cruise" industry to succeed. Should land-based casinos ever be introduced to South Florida, the day-trip industry would probably be devastated, but Florida voters have already voted down one casino initiative, and they do not appear likely to approve a casino initiative in the near future.

Until recently, attempts at developing a "cruise to nowhere" industry in other states have failed. In 1997, a casino ship — *Liberty I* — in Brooklyn, New York, offered short, offshore, daytime gambling cruises. However, the New York City government, leery of possible ties to organized crime, opposed the gambling cruise ship. The Mayor (Rudy) Giuliani administration ordered several temporary road blocks to halt the Bay Cruise Company from operating. These included forced employee background checks, charges of violating local zoning laws, and city tax requirements. Ultimately, New York City found a loophole in federal law to force day cruises to travel 12 miles out to sea before gambling could begin. In late 1997, the Bay Cruise Company was forced to close the city's first gambling vessel.

All is not lost for New York gamblers, however. In 1998, another company, Manhattan Cruises, will begin offering overnight trips into international seas, where gambling is legal. The longer hours of the overnight cruise will allow the ship ample time to reach the 12-mile limit and still leave passengers plenty of time to gamble. The vessel is a 10-story liner, equipped with 150 slot machines and 30 table games. Up to 1,000 passengers can be accommodated on the overnight trip.

In the past three years, the day cruise gambling industry has more than doubled, growing from 10 ships to 25 vessels. In 1996, the industry generated nearly $200 million in revenues, according to *International Gaming and Wagering Business* (December 1997). In addition to Florida and New York, ships are presently operating out of Georgia, and expansion plans are underway in California and South Carolina. Such cruises not only appeal to local consumers, they permit modern casino entrepreneurs to enter the industry relatively inexpensively.

On the other hand, some state and local governments are not happy with the growth of this industry. Day-cruise casinos are unique in that they are the only form of gambling that does not need voter approval in order to operate. Some communities have fought the industry as New York City did when it used a loophole in federal law to force day cruises to travel 12 miles out to sea (above).

CHAPTER VII

CASINO GAMBLING —

NATIVE AMERICAN RESERVATIONS

As discussed in Chapter II, the Indian Gaming Regulatory Act of 1988 (PL 100-497) permits Native American tribes to introduce gambling on their reservations. Many tribes had already been holding bingo games, but the new law opened up the possibility that other forms of gambling could be played on Native American lands. It also meant that the Native American tribes could play a major role in the large expansion of gambling throughout the country.

A NEW OPPORTUNITY

As returns from bingo — the major form of gambling on reservations — were beginning to level off, many Native American tribes recognized that casino games were being offered in more places throughout the United States. (See Chapter III.) They saw this as an opportunity to bring some prosperity to their reservations.

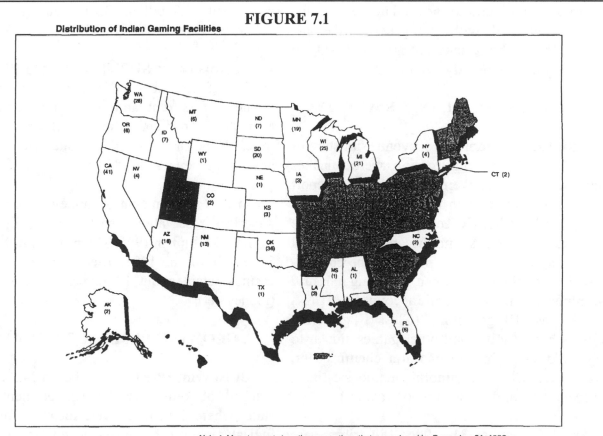

FIGURE 7.1

Distribution of Indian Gaming Facilities

Note 1: Map does not show those operations that were closed by December 31, 1996.

Note 2: This information may not agree with NIGC's records because of differences in methodologies used to identify and count facilities.

Source: *Tax Policy — A Profile of the Indian Gaming Industry*, U.S. General Accounting Office, Washington, DC, 1997

TABLE 7.1

1995 Revenues, Costs and Expenses, and Net Income for Class II and III Indian Gaming Facilities

Income statement item	Dollars in millions			Percentage of total		
	Class II (N=66)[a]	Class III (N=112)[a]	Total (N=178)[a]	Class II	Class III	Total
Revenue						
Gaming	$568	$3,979	$4,547	12%	88%	100%
Other[b]	35	306	341	10	90	100
Total	603	4,285	4,888	12	88	100
Costs and expenses	367	2,644	3,011	12	88	100
Net income	236	1,641	1,877	13	87	100

[a]The "N" represents number of facilities.

[b]Other revenues include, for example, revenues from food, beverages, hotel rooms, and interest.

Source: GAO analysis of 1995 financial statements that were filed with NIGC as of November 22, 1996.

Source: *Tax Policy — A Profile of the Indian Gaming Industry*, U.S. General Accounting Office, Washington, DC, 1997

The Indian Gaming Regulatory Act permitted the tribes to conduct any type of gambling on their reservation that was permitted in the state within which the reservation was located. The law also called for the tribe and the state to negotiate agreements or "compacts" that would allow this gambling. The states were required to bargain with the tribes in good faith. If they did not, or if a tribe was not satisfied with the process, the law permitted the tribe to take the issue to court, an option that has frequently been used.

FIRST FINANCIAL INFORMATION

Until 1997, wagering and revenue statistics for Native American gambling casinos were estimates since these facilities were not required to report their returns. However, in May 1997, at the request of Rep. Bill Archer (R-Texas), Chairman of the Committee on Ways and Means, the General Accounting Office (GAO) provided the committee with a profile of the Indian gambling industry. This report was the first public accounting of Class II and Class III gambling. (Class II gambling includes bingo, lotto, and other games similar to bingo. It does not include baccarat, chemin de fer, or blackjack. Class III gambling includes casinos, slot machines, and horse and dog racing.)

As of December 31, 1996, 184 tribes were operating 281 gaming facilities. The GAO obtained 1995 financial statements for 178 establishments operated by 126 tribes. (See Figure 7.1.) Gaming revenues (dollars bet less payouts) amounted to $4.5 billion, with eight of the largest operations accounting for 40 percent of the revenues. The gaming facilities reported earning over $300 million in revenues from sales of food, beverages, and hotel rooms. Net income (total revenues less expenses) for the 178 establishments was about $1.9 billion (38 percent of the total revenues.) (See Table 7.1 and Figure 7.2.)

Approximately $1.6 billion went to 106 tribes in 1995. (Some tribes received additional monies for taxes, fees, rent, and other reimbursements.) More than 50 percent of the $1.6 billion went to 10 tribes. None of the financial statements showed how the money was used by the tribes.

In 1996, the amount of money bet on Native American reservations reached $6.5 billion, up from $4.5 billion in 1995, $1.6 billion in 1992, and $125 million in 1985. (See Figure 7.3.) The casinos retain about 10 percent of the handle (money bet).

A GROWING NUMBER OF CASINOS

By November 1997, 147 tribes in 24 states had reached 158 compacts with the governments in the states where their lands were located. Table 7.2 indicates which tribes have reached compacts with each state. Undoubtedly the most successful Native American casino is the Mashantucket Pequot Foxwoods facility in Ledyard, in

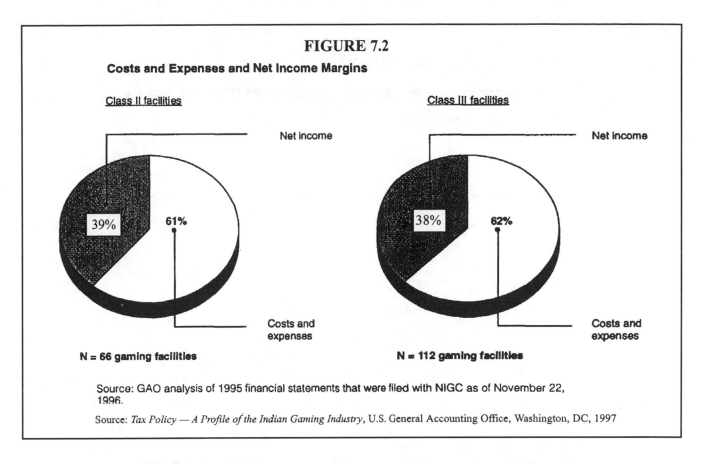

FIGURE 7.2

Costs and Expenses and Net Income Margins

Class II facilities

Net income

39%   61%

Costs and expenses

N = 66 gaming facilities

Class III facilities

Net income

38%   62%

Costs and expenses

N = 112 gaming facilities

Source: GAO analysis of 1995 financial statements that were filed with NIGC as of November 22, 1996.

Source: *Tax Policy — A Profile of the Indian Gaming Industry*, U.S. General Accounting Office, Washington, DC, 1997

southeastern Connecticut. The 79,000-square foot building offers gamblers blackjack, roulette, the big-six money wheel, baccarat, poker, and electronic video games.

The well-run, well-regulated casino has been so successful that lines form to play the games and dealers must work double shifts. Foxwoods earned an estimated $800 to $900 million in 1995. The eight largest facilities with gross gaming revenues (GGR) of at least $100 million — including Foxwoods, Mohegan Sun (in Connecticut), and the Hinckley and Mille Lacs Grand Casino operation (in Minnesota) — accounted for over 40 percent of all Class III GGR.

Foxwoods had an unusual arrangement with the State of Connecticut. The tribe agreed to pay 25 percent of the revenue from the slots or $100 million, whichever was greater, for exclusive rights to operate a casino in the state. (The arrangement has since been modified. See below.) In 1993, the Mashantucket Pequot tribe paid $113 million, and in 1997, it contributed $208 million to

the state. Undoubtedly, the success of Foxwoods has contributed to the recent investment and development down the Atlantic Coast in Atlantic City, New Jersey. Casino operators there have been very concerned about customers being drawn away from the aging casinos in Atlantic City.

Meanwhile, Foxwoods has expanded into a resort to encourage people to stay awhile and gamble longer. In addition, the tribe plans to open a new casino in the near future. The management recognizes that it will not have a monopoly on Indian gambling forever and it must try to use its early entry into the field to best advantage.

In addition to investments in the casino, the tribe has been making other investments, including buying local land for future development, a printing plant, and an historical colonial inn. It has also contributed to local schools and churches. The Special Olympics World Games, held in New Haven, received $2 million, and the tribe contributed $10 million to the Smithsonian Institute in Washington for a new American Indian

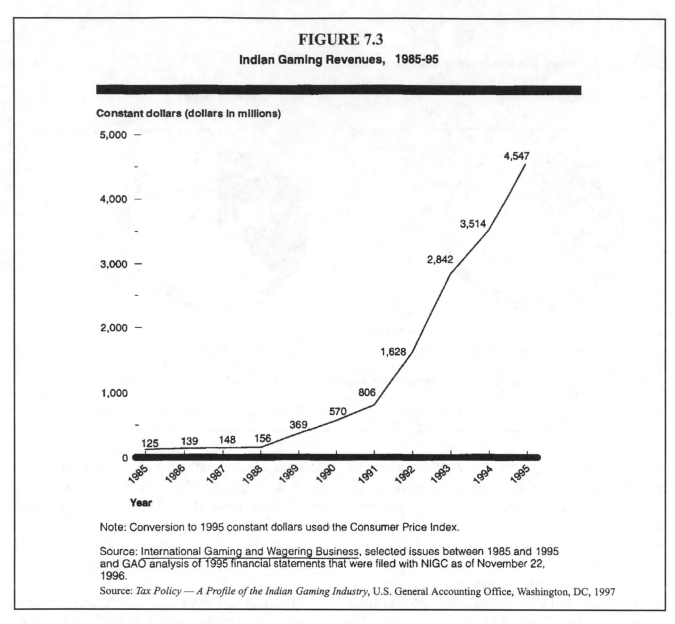

FIGURE 7.3

Indian Gaming Revenues, 1985-95

Constant dollars (dollars in millions)

Year

Note: Conversion to 1995 constant dollars used the Consumer Price Index.

Source: International Gaming and Wagering Business, selected issues between 1985 and 1995 and GAO analysis of 1995 financial statements that were filed with NIGC as of November 22, 1996.

Source: *Tax Policy — A Profile of the Indian Gaming Industry*, U.S. General Accounting Office, Washington, DC, 1997

building. The tribe even paid $500,000 to buy a stadium for the local minor league baseball team.

GROWING COMPETITION

Diversification is important; Foxwoods is no longer the only major casino in the region. In 1995, the 1,000-person Mohegan tribe, after a lengthy process of documenting its continued existence, opened a casino in Montville, Connecticut. The tribe agreed to contribute a minimum of $80 million or 25 percent of slot revenues to the state. Foxwoods, which had been given exclusive rights to slot machines in the state, agreed to a special exemption to allow the Mohegan casino to have slot machines. In return, Foxwood's minimum

contribution to the state dropped to $80 million or 25 percent of slot revenues.

In neighboring Rhode Island, the Narragansett tribe has plans for a casino in West Greenwich, only 17 miles from Ledyard. The Aquinnah Wampanoag Tribe of Gay Head, Massachusetts, would like to build a casino in New Bedford, although this project has run into serious political difficulties. In upstate New York near Verona (between Syracuse and Utica), the Oneida tribe has opened a new 90,000-square foot casino. The Oneidas are now considering opening a second casino in Sullivan County in the Catskills, just 60 miles from New York City.

TABLE 7.2
TRIBAL-STATE COMPACT LIST
TRIBAL INFORMATION FOR THOSE WITH APPROVED
TRIBAL-STATE COMPACTS AS OF NOVEMBER 19, 1997
147 TRIBES - 24 STATES - 158 COMPACTS
66 AMENDMENTS/ADDENDA

This list is maintained and updated as new compacts/amendments are published in the FEDERAL REGISTER by the Indian Gaming Management Staff, Bureau of Indian Affairs, Office of the Commissioner. (202) 219-4066.
* Tribe has compact with more than one state.
** Tribe has more than one compact for different types of games.

TABLE OF CONTENTS

Continued on following page.

CASINOS AROUND THE COUNTRY

In Minnesota, 11 tribal compacts have led to the development of 14 high-stakes casinos. The Mille Lacs band of Chippewa Indians, for example, has built a $25 million casino gambling complex near Hinckley, Minnesota. The 102,000-square foot casino contains 1,000 to 1,500 video slot machines, 60 blackjack tables, a 500-seat bingo hall, and a 100- to 150-seat keno hall. The 2,000-member Pokagon Band of Potawatomis are planning to build a $50 million facility in Dowagiac, Michigan. On the other hand, the Mohawks on the Kahnawake lands near Montreal, Quebec, voted down having a casino.

In 1995, in Philadelphia, Mississippi, the Chocktaw Indians upgraded their successful Silver Star Casino Hotel by adding 400 rooms, a swimming pool, a health spa, and a golf course to induce visitors to stay longer. Since then, the tribe has added 500 rooms and an 85,000-square foot casino. In 1998, the Silver Star Resort and Casino will add an additional 15,000 square feet. In Colorado, the Southern Utes tribe and the Mountain Utes tribe have opened casinos. In the State of Washington, the Tulalip tribe reached an agreement with the state that eventually permits 31 gaming tables with $10 and $20 bets. The $9 million 7 Cedars Casino in Blyn, Washington, built by the Jamestown S'Klallam tribe, contains an on-site art gallery.

In South Dakota, the Santee Sioux tribe offers table games and slot machines. Until recently, the complex in Flandreau, South Dakota, was popular for one-day excursions. However, by 1995, the tribe decided that it could increase its revenues and bring in more people if the casino could offer customers an entertainment facility and a convenient place to spend the night. The tribe chose to build a new casino. They spent $17.5 million on a new structure that includes a 60-room hotel, showroom/conference center and 450-seat bingo hall. The new Royal River Casino, opened in 1997, is an 82,000-square foot entertainment center that is open 24 hours a day, seven days per

week. It is the largest Las Vegas-style casino in South Dakota.

The Sault Sainte Marie tribe will be the first tribe to own and operate a casino in a major U.S. city. In 1996, Michigan voters approved casino

TABLE 7.2 (Continued)
OKLAHOMA - 7 TRIBES
CHOCTAW NATION OF OKLAHOMA
CITIZEN BAND POTAWATOMI NATION
IOWA TRIBE OF OKLAHOMA
MIAMI TRIBE OF OKLAHOMA
MIAMI-MODOC TRIBES OF OKLAHOMA
OTOE-MISSOURIA TRIBE OF OKLAHOMA
TONKAWA TRIBE OF OKLAHOMA
OREGON -9 TRIBES
BURNS-PAIUTE TRIBE
CONFEDERATED TRIBES OF COOS, LOWER UMPQUA AND SIUSLAW INDIANS
COQUILLE INDIAN TRIBE
COW CREEK BAND OF UMPQUA TRIBE OF INDIANS
CONFEDERATED TRIBES OF THE GRAND RONDE COMM.
THE KLAMATH TRIBES
THE CONFEDERATED TRIBES OF SILETZ INDIANS OF OREGON
UMATILLA INDIAN TRIBE
THE CONFEDERATED TRIBES OF THE WARM SPRINGS RESERVATION OF OREGON
RHODE ISLAND - 1 TRIBE
NARRAGANSETT INDIAN TRIBE
SOUTH DAKOTA - 9 TRIBES
CHEYENNE RIVER SIOUX TRIBE
CROW CREEK SIOUX TRIBE
FLANDREAU SANTEE SIOUX TRIBE
LOWER BRULE SIOUX TRIBE
OGLALA SIOUX TRIBE
ROSEBUD SIOUX TRIBE
SISSETON-WAHPETON SIOUX TRIBE* **
STANDING ROCK SIOUX TRIBE*
YANKTON SIOUX TRIBE OF SOUTH DAKOTA
WASHINGTON - 17 TRIBES
CONFEDERATED TRIBES OF THE CHEHALIS RESERVATION
JAMESTOWN S'KLALLAM TRIBE OF WASHINGTON
LOWER ELWHA KLALLAM TRIBE
LUMMI NATION
MUCKLESHOOT INDIAN TRIBE
NOOKSACK INDIAN TRIBE OF WASHINGTON
PORT GAMBLE S'KLALLAM
PUYALLUP TRIBE OF INDIANS
QUILEUTE TRIBAL COUNCIL
QUINAULT INDIAN NATION
SKOKOMISH INDIAN TRIBE
SQUAXIN ISLAND INDIAN TRIBE
SUQUAMISH TRIBE
SWINOMISH INDIAN TRIBAL COMMUNITY
TULALIP TRIBES OF WASHINGTON
UPPER SKAGIT INDIAN TRIBE
YAKAMA INDIAN NATION
WISCONSIN - 11 TRIBES
BAD RIVER BAND OF LAKE SUPERIOR TRIBE OF CHIPPEWA INDIANS
FOREST COUNTY POTAWATOMI COMMUNITY
LAC COURTE OREILLES BAND OF LAKE SUPERIOR CHIPPEWA
LAC DU FLAMBEAU BAND OF LAKE SUPERIOR CHIPPEWA
MENOMINEE INDIAN TRIBE OF WISCONSIN
ONEIDA TRIBE OF INDIANS OF WISCONSIN
RED CLIFF BAND OF LAKE SUPERIOR CHIPPEWA
ST. CROIX CHIPPEWA INDIANS OF WISCONSIN
SOKAOGON CHIPPEWA COMMUNITY
STOCKBRIDGE-MUNSEE COMMUNITY OF MOHICAN INDIANS OF WISCONSIN
HO-CHUNK NATION

Source: Bureau of Indian Affairs

gambling for the city of Detroit, and the Sault Sainte Marie tribe has won one of the three cites that will feature a casino in downtown Detroit. The complex will include a 1,000-room hotel with twin towers more than 40 stories tall, 100,000 square feet of gaming space, a children's center, a 1,600-seat theater, restaurants, and stores. The project will cost $519 million and will employ approximately 4,000 people. Annual casino revenues are expected to reach $400 million. The Sault Sainte Marie tribe hopes to have a temporary casino open in 1998 and the permanent casino open in 2001. The tribe currently owns and operates five casinos in Michigan's Upper Peninsula.

In Wisconsin, 11 tribes have reached agreement with the state to offer blackjack and electronic games of chance. The Winnebago tribe of Wisconsin opened a new $8.5 million casino at Black River Falls. The Mille Lacs Band of Chippewa Indians used the income from their casino to build the reservation's first schools. The Chippewa tribe has three casinos in Wisconsin. In San Diego, California, the 95-member Sycuan tribe operates a $3 million, 58,000-square foot casino offering poker, bingo, off-track betting, and lottery-type games on their reservation.

The 1,200-member Morongo Band of Mission Indians of Banning, California, have used the revenues from their successful Casino Morongo to end welfare on their reservation. In Louisiana, the Tunica-Biloxi tribe plans to build a $25 million casino, while the Coushatta tribe intends to construct a $35 million facility.

A FEW PROBLEMS

The Indian Gaming Regulatory Act of 1988 has given a growing number of Native American tribes, many of which are very poor, the opportunity to "cash in" on the gambling boom of the last several years. Like any new business venture, the budding tribal gambling establishments have run into some problems. It took three years to appoint the three members of the Indian

Gaming Commission created by the Indian gaming act. The commission was supposed to prepare the policies and procedures necessary to help develop and regulate the tribal gaming projects.

Gambling sometimes attracts disreputable individuals, and some tribal leaders have made unwise financial deals. A report prepared by the Department of the Interior noted a number of tribes had signed contracts in which the tribes had been overcharged for administrative services and gambling equipment. Several bills have already been proposed in Congress to limit the development of casino gambling on Native American reservations. (See Chapter II.)

In Minnesota, the chairman of the White Earth Band of Chippewa was charged with stealing hundreds of thousands of dollars from a casino project. In Clearlake Oaks, California, two factions of the Elem Indian Colony got into a shooting war over who should control their casino. State and local police had to be called out to end the conflict.

Many tribal leaders recognize that some tribal managers may be victimized or that some gambling operations may expand beyond their ability to handle the growth. Nonetheless, they note, these are typical business problems that often develop in any new industry, and they wonder why their growing pains are being singled out.

Politics versus Economics

In 1995, three bands of Chippewa Indians suggested turning a failing dog track into a gambling casino in Hudson, Wisconsin, on the Minnesota border. The proposal was opposed by five rival tribes already operating casinos in the region. The Bureau of Indian Affairs (BIA) in the Interior Department must issue a permit before a casino can be opened. The Minneapolis regional office of the BIA initially ruled in favor of issuing the permit. However, the ruling was overturned in Washington in July 1995 after the tribes opposing the permit contributed nearly $300,000 to the Democratic Party. Both sides had hired lobbyists to promote their cases, and the losers now accuse the winners of pressuring the White House and Interior Department to oppose the permit through the donation.

This led to allegations that the decision was political rather than economic. Interior Department officials say that the donation had nothing to do with their decision. They insist that their ruling was a result of strong local opposition from area lawmakers, the City of Hudson, Wisconsin, where the casino was to be located, and from other tribes already operating profitable gaming establishments.

Secretary of the Interior Bruce Babbitt has been accused of influencing the decision and then lying to Congress about it. Secretary Babbitt's office said that the decision to reject the request "was reached on the merits, not on the basis of any alleged political influence." However, following a Justice Department review, Attorney General Janet Reno said that there was "specific and credible evidence indicating that Secretary Babbitt may have testified falsely." In February 1998, Reno recommended that an independent counsel should investigate the matter.

The Indian tribes that lost their bid are suing the government, charging that the decision was political and that they were never told of any serious problem or given a chance to fix whatever caused their application to be denied. (See Chapter II, *Seminole Tribe of Florida v. Florida*, for explanation of why the federal government now has a major role concerning Indian gaming in the states.)

FROM DEVELOPING TO MARKETING

Eventually, there may come a time when there will be too many Native American casinos, or the growth of non-Native American casinos will create strong competition. When and if this comes, Native American casinos will have to move from effective developers of gambling casinos to effective marketers of gambling casinos in order to survive. Many tribal leaders, in fact, have approached established gambling companies to seek help to better operate and market their product. Here, too, the sovereignty issue is important, and those gambling companies that recognize that they are dealing with sovereign tribal entities will probably be most successful.

CAN REGULATION BE BENEFICIAL?

During his tenure in the early 1990s, Tony Hope, the former Chairman of the National Indian Gaming Commission (NIGC), the Native American trade organization, tried to convince tribal authorities that regulation will benefit their casinos because it will increase visitors' confidence in the integrity of their casinos. His successor, Harold Monteau, also has indicated his desire to take "a leadership role in encouraging the development of strong tribal regulatory structures." In Foxwoods, the casino works closely with the state of Connecticut to insure that the rules are followed.

Many tribal leaders are concerned about regulation because they fear it would violate their tribal sovereignty. Tim Wapato, executive director of the NIGC, is also concerned about sovereignty, but recognizes that the tribes must have some form of regulation to guarantee the integrity of the games. He suggests tribal self-regulation. He feels that a tribal-federal relationship is less violative of American Indian sovereignty than a tribal-state relationship, which he believes degrades Indian sovereignty.

Native American tribes are now getting a "piece of the action" of which they have so often been left out. The gambling has provided employment for Native Americans and for other people living near the casinos, revenues for investment for the future, and monies for investment in education, housing, health care, and other needs on reservations.

CHAPTER VIII

LOTTERIES — LEGAL AND ALLURING

DEFINITION

A lottery is a game in which people purchase numbered tickets in the hope of winning a prize. A person wins if the number on his or her ticket is the one drawn from a pool of all the tickets purchased for that particular event. In the case of instant lotteries, the bettor wins if the ticket contains a pre-determined winning number. Raffles are a form of lottery in which the prize is usually goods rather than cash. Raffles are most often conducted by churches or charitable organizations and are relatively small in size. As of 1996, lotteries were legal in 38 states, Washington, DC, the Virgin Islands, and Puerto Rico. Lotteries were also legal in the 10 provinces and two territories of Canada.

A PART OF OUR HERITAGE

Lotteries have been a part of American life since the settlement of Jamestown by the Virginia Company of London. Prior to the establishment of a regular tax system, lotteries were the most effective means of raising money to finance public works, churches, schools, and universities. Even after the American Revolution, lotteries remained the most popular form of fund-raising for public services for another generation. Some of the nation's most prestigious banks, including the Chase Manhattan Bank and First City National Bank of New York, were founded by former lottery managers who were able to make enough money to open banks.

The discovery during the 1830s of corruption and fraud among some lottery managers and public officials resulted in a flurry of reform laws. Continued opposition to lotteries was voiced by a small number of newspapers through their editorials and by the Society of Friends (Quakers). Other religious groups did not object to lotteries because they used them to finance new church construction. Most newspapers did not object to lotteries because lottery operators were big newspaper advertisers.

Eventually, however, many newspapers joined the anti-lottery crusade. By 1840, lotteries were abolished in most northern states. During the next 20 years, the number of lottery operations in the South and West also decreased, but some were revived after the Civil War to finance reconstruction efforts. Corruption and fraud continued to be a problem, however, forcing the federal government to enact a number of anti-lottery bills between 1860 and 1895, which ultimately banished lotteries (except for the Louisiana Lottery; see Chapter I) for the next 40 years.

THE MODERN LOTTERY

During the Depression Era of the 1930s, the United States was flooded with lottery tickets from the Caribbean, Latin America, and the Irish Sweepstakes, reviving interest in lottery gambling. Following hearings on organized crime before the Special Senate Committee to Investigate Organized Crime in Interstate Commerce (Kefauver Hearings, 1950), Congress approved the Revenue Act of 1951, which called for the purchase of a $50 occupational tax stamp and a 10 percent excise tax on gross receipts from wagering businesses. Although designed to tax and control other forms of gambling, the Revenue Act opened the door for the establishment of legal lottery games.*

In 1964, New Hampshire became the first state in the twentieth century to legalize lottery games. New Hampshire's funds were to be used for educational programs in local municipalities. New York followed with a state lottery in 1967, but the real revitalization of lottery games occurred in 1971. In that year, New Jersey introduced a computer-based, 50-cent weekly game and increased the size of the prize pool to 45 percent of the gross amount wagered. The New Jersey system was later adopted by New Hampshire and New York.

In 1974, the federal Commission on the Review of the National Policy Toward Gambling (referred to hereafter as the National Gambling Commission) held hearings to investigate the nineteenth century anti-lottery statutes. State lottery directors claimed that these statutes did not allow states to develop their own policies on gambling or to conduct business and raise revenues as they wished without undue federal regulation or interference. As a result of the commission's findings, the 93rd Congress passed legislation allowing states to advertise on radio and television and to send lottery information and tickets through the mail within their own states.

Lotteries did not develop nationwide until the 1980s. The federal government was transferring more financial responsibilities to the states at the same time that citizens were becoming increasingly reluctant to pay more taxes. As state and local governments became desperate for money, lotteries were seen as an easy way to raise large sums of revenues without upsetting most voters. The lotteries were often presented as a form of voluntary taxation, and most states have directed that money gained from lotteries be used for purposes with which few voters could quarrel, such as education or aid to the elderly.

The nationwide adoption and promotion of lotteries by the states have contributed to a major change in attitude towards gambling throughout the United States. Gambling has generally lost the image of sin or immorality with which it had once been connected. With the strong public acceptance of lotteries, gambling is now more likely to be seen as entertainment and fun rather than a violation of generally accepted morality. The connection it once had with corruption and fraud, for most people, has long been forgotten. This change in attitude has been a major factor in the recent boom of huge casino/hotels in Las Vegas designed to attract families to a complete entertainment experience of which gambling, while still the dominant driving engine, is only a part. (See Chapter V.)

TYPES OF LOTTERY GAMES

Instant Lottery

Instant lotteries were first introduced in Massachusetts in 1974. For $1, a player buys a ticket and immediately finds out if he or she has picked a winning number. Instant tickets have a coating which the player scratches off to uncover the number or symbol underneath that reveals whether or not the ticket is a "winning ticket." Instant lotteries are commonly the first type of lottery established by previously non-lottery states. Every state that has legalized lotteries has an instant lottery.

---

* Few local gamblers would buy the federal occupational tax stamp because it would indicate to local authorities that the person was a gambler. Paying the excise tax would also expose the gambler. Since gambling was illegal in all but one state, this law virtually made gambling a federal as well as a state crime.

Numbers — or Pick 3, Pick 4

In 1975, New Jersey was the first state to legalize numbers, a formerly illegal game (see Chapter X). In the most common form of numbers, a bettor puts money on a two- or three-digit number from 00 to 999. The winning number is determined by an arbitrary mechanism, such as numbered ping-pong balls rising in an air-filled tank. State lottery administrators have found that games must be flexible to keep pace with the interests and demands of the public, and some states have expanded to a four-digit weekly numbers game. In 1997, 29 states, the District of Columbia, and Puerto Rico offered numbers.

Lotto

Lotto was first played in the 1520s in Italy, using hand-painted game pieces and game boards carved from wood. In 1978, Massachusetts became the first state to offer lotto games. In 1997, 37 states, the District of Columbia, and Puerto Rico permitted lotto games. To play lotto, a bettor selects five to six numbers from a pool of 40 to 44 numbers and wagers between $1 and $4. Winning numbers are selected at random from a weekly drawing. If no player has the same set of numbers (in any sequence), the prize is not awarded that week, and the prize money is carried forward to the next week's drawing. Sometimes huge jackpots of many millions of dollars can develop, generating intense interest in the lottery.

Powerball

Twenty-two states, generally states with smaller populations, and the District of Colombia have combined in a Multi-State Lottery Association (MSLA) to offer their citizens *Powerball*, a lotto game that can offer huge jackpots. It is not hard for large states like California, New York, Texas, and Florida to be able to offer multi-million dollar jackpots to players. In these smaller population states, however, *Powerball* offers players the chance to win multi-million-dollar jackpots. Most of the states participating in *Powerball* believe that the multi-state lotto game benefits their state games since people often buy tickets to the state lotto games when they go in to buy a *Powerball* ticket.

Video Lottery

Many gaming industry observers see video lottery terminals (VLTs) as the future of the lottery industry. Unlike most video games played on computers, video lottery games have little to do with skill, so that winning or losing is mainly a matter of chance.

Video games are particularly attractive to young people because of their appealing graphics. Some people are concerned about the addictive nature of video lotteries, and in fact, opponents of gambling often refer to VLTs as the "crack of gambling." In addition, operators of other forms of gambling, most notably the regular lottery and pari-mutuel operations, fear that VLTs will cut into how much they earn.

Unlike most lottery games, in which only around 50 percent is paid back to the players, VLTs return about 90 percent. If VLTs paid back only around 50 percent, players would likely lose interest quickly. However, with a 90 percent return, players win often enough that, for some gamblers, it can become addictive.

For these reasons, VLTs have had a hard time getting approval in most states. VLTs have been legalized in South Dakota, West Virginia, Louisiana, Oregon, Rhode Island, and Delaware. VLTs were declared unconstitutional in South Dakota, but the issue was immediately put on the ballot, and in November 1995, the voters approved their use in the state. In 1997, in the five states that reported VLT sales separately, VLT sales represented a major proportion of all lottery sales — Delaware (89 percent), Oregon (68 percent), Rhode Island (69 percent), South Dakota (94 percent), and West Virginia (77 percent).

In West Virginia and Rhode Island, VLTs are permitted in racetracks to improve the racetracks' sagging income. Racetracks are a good place to put VLTs because there is considerable time between races during which nothing happens as horse and dog handlers prepare for the next race. During this period, many people who have come to gamble become bored. VLTs give them something to do while they are awaiting the next race. It also gives someone who came along to the races to be with a friend or a spouse, but who has no interest in racing, an opportunity to do something else. Finally, it limits the number of minors who would have access to these games, since some states ban minors from the track.

LOTTERY SALES

Lotteries are big business. According to Eugene Martin Christiansen in his annual survey for *International Gambling and Wagering Business*, sales for fiscal year (FY) 1997 totaled $42.8 billion, up 10 percent, or $3.9 billion, from FY 1996 and almost double the $21.8 billion wagered in 1992. (See Table 8.1 and Figure 8.1.) On average, the states paid back about 58 percent of sales in winnings to players. About one-third (32 percent) went into government revenues, while the rest was used to administer the lotteries.

LOTTERY REVENUES

In calendar year 1996, lotteries produced $16.2 billion in revenues, up 5 percent from the year before. (See Figure 8.1.) Lotteries keep a much higher percentage of the money bet (45.5 percent of all non-VLT bets) than any other type of gambling. (For example, horsetracks retain 20.5 percent; slot machines, 6 percent; casinos tables, 2 percent; and bingo, 24.5 percent.) Therefore, while lotteries account for only 7 percent of all monies bet on gambling, they bring in 35 percent of all revenues.

Where Do the Revenues Go?

Until recently, all state lottery revenue went into state programs. However, in 1991, New York State approved a small lottery that would benefit New York City. Proceeds from this instant lottery game would be used to help fund a crime-reduction program within the city of New York.

Most revenues from lotteries are put into the general state funds. Initially, the earnings of many of the lotteries were earmarked for beneficial state programs, most notably education. In many cases, however, instead of adding lottery revenues to their existing budgets for these programs, states cut their budgets by the amount of lottery funds received. Thus, the net benefit to the programs was zero. The most prominent example was Florida, which had introduced the lottery as a way to increase state funding for schools. However, the state then reduced educational funding by the amount of the revenues received from the lottery.

On the other hand, the neighboring state of Georgia is cited as a laudatory example of the financial possibilities of the lottery. The Helping Outstanding Pupils Educationally program (HOPE) began in 1993 and has provided free tuition to 250,000 college students. HOPE has bought new computers and satellite dishes for the state's public schools, upgraded vocational and technical schools, and introduced new preschools for children from low-income families. HOPE costs approximately $200 million per year and is financed entirely through the state lottery. As long as the Georgia governor and legislature keep their promise to use lottery returns for additional educational programs, rather than basic educational needs, the Georgia lottery will likely remain an example of how the lottery can benefit a state.

A Marketing Challenge

With lotteries directly available to about 88 percent of the nation's population, competition becomes quite keen. Lottery directors must continually develop new lottery games to maintain players' interest. To attract more players, lotteries have tied their games with the game Monopoly, the movie *Rocky*, the Winning Spirit of the Olympics, the singer Buddy Holly, and the soft drink, 7-UP.

TABLE 8.1

Fiscal 1997 Lottery Sales (unaudited results)

United States

	Instant & Pulltabs	Lotto	5-digit/ Cash Lotto	Powerball	The Big Game	Daily Millions	Daily Numbers	Keno	VLTs (1)	Other	FY1997 Total Sales	FY1996 Total Sales	Percent Change
Ariz.	$105,590,090	$62,803,000	$15,817,800	$65,365,400							$249,576,290	$258,836,100	-3.6%
Calif.	527,000,000	1,096,000,000	151,000,000				71,000,000	200,000,000		18,000,000	2,063,000,000	2,292,324,933	-10.0%
Colo.	212,200,000	125,900,000	16,900,000					5,800,000			360,800,000	331,351,344	8.9%
Conn.	396,638,552	90,560,388	47,911,085	49,381,869			188,146,507				772,638,401	706,950,208	9.3%
Del.	20,303,633	10,848,695	19,265,649				49,819,622		3,041,848,500	3,025,823	3,145,112,322	1,007,033,105	212.3%
D.C. (2)	25,000,000	7,500,000	31,000,000			6,000,000	139,000,000				208,500,000	210,620,000	-1.0%
Fla.	705,532,638	721,378,557	272,288,805				460,469,315				2,159,669,315	2,117,084,908	2.0%
Ga.	633,713,000	121,768,000	114,275,000	22,546,000	89,436,000		662,041,000	76,462,000			1,720,241,000	1,591,892,000	8.1%
Idaho	63,279,965	5,857,348	501,462	17,402,968							87,041,743	91,162,150	-4.5%
Ill.	636,155,634	295,509,137	118,885,161		92,311,506		480,672,326				1,623,533,763	1,637,408,595	-0.8%
Ind.	319,764,931	79,941,069	16,215,863	108,493,189		1,127,813	53,207,611				578,750,476	621,315,539	-6.9%
Iowa	117,030,740	10,189,620	6,386,606	32,924,898		6,136,171					190,004,182		-8.6%
Kan.	81,910,562	22,277,723		39,713,397			4,973,226	36,481,773			185,356,681	182,113,627	1.8%
Ky.	317,915,000	49,389,000	20,033,000	64,075,000			117,643,000				569,055,000	542,845,000	4.8%
La.	113,626,650	40,416,900	13,139,000	67,288,300		4,439,302	41,743,600				280,653,730	289,223,025	-3.0%
Maine	104,414,845	28,840,168	4,977,466	8,026,515							146,258,994	148,689,711	-1.6%
Md.	161,529,835	60,280,531	36,001,558		38,176,590		505,977,449	233,765,411			1,035,731,374	1,114,422,209	-7.1%
Mass.	2,077,763,000	176,852,000	66,641,000		55,862,000		377,544,000				3,029,700,000		5.2%
Mich. (2)	573,830,245	208,508,543	36,637,976		126,844,349		680,742,549	14,103,427			1,640,667,089	1,423,649,000	15.3%
Minn.	272,486,589	31,905,099	19,726,304	53,133,760			9,575,032			986,993	368,516,684	375,650,142	-1.9%
Mo.	251,083,508	22,783,598		76,145,527			48,364,325				439,857,089	422,530,945	4.1%
Mont.	6,063,023	4,715,222	5,290,564	11,759,857		368,694					28,197,360	31,761,414	-11.2%
Neb. State	41,316,756	7,528,523		24,479,158			3,295,288				76,619,725	81,829,662	-6.4%
Neb. City/County								160,521,574			160,521,574	179,430,240	-10.5%
N.H.	111,021,139	18,256,453	8,678,752	29,293,628		1,366,301	8,034,284				176,650,557	162,816,770	8.5%
N.J.	383,265,987	340,337,686	110,450,915				722,025,820				1,556,080,408	1,588,028,875	-2.0%
N.M.	56,761,000			22,783,000		2,747,000					82,291,000	28,435,000	189.4%
N.Y.	1,056,633,000	874,321,000	341,282,000				1,095,398,000	618,746,000		5,934,000	3,992,314,000	3,610,638,000	10.6%
Ohio	1,195,451,770	410,590,967	78,754,033				552,167,603			63,446,666	2,300,411,039	2,380,207,093	-3.4%
Ore.	150,485,034	38,658,051	30,381,335	3,150,498			101,519,358		3,636,670,650	8,866,037	3,969,740,963	3,629,304,969	9.4%
Pa.	409,249,770	291,225,382	150,902,298				858,636,472				1,710,013,922	1,673,751,534	2.2%
R.I.	27,356,236		1,112,026	5,051,443			29,405,124	41,801,453	406,108,530	37,881,052	548,715,864	455,297,841	20.5%
S.D.	15,200,000	2,000,000	1,200,000	7,400,000			1,900,200		505,200,000		532,900,000	519,761,138	2.5%
Texas	2,357,649,081	906,345,847	322,858,261				158,549,125				3,745,402,314	3,432,309,408	9.1%
Vt.	62,638,051	10,544,883	2,137,505	2,002,875							77,323,314	74,740,669	3.5%
Va.	300,290,000	162,330,000	35,710,000		53,750,000		353,280,000			15,470,000	920,830,000	924,320,468	-0.4%
Wash.	206,377,696	121,878,908	49,715,108				17,459,595	12,770,083			408,201,390	389,880,814	4.7%
W.Va.	80,302,642	30,325,133		16,009,819			16,977,467		944,111,911		1,106,894,464	719,455,049	53.9%
Wis.	273,341,654	47,453,119	37,642,807	30,383,419		11,955,423	30,383,419				431,101,555	482,123,961	-10.6%
Total U.S.	$14,450,172,256	$6,417,528,892	$2,181,814,086	$896,185,853	$456,380,445	$67,995,003	$7,748,791,852	$1,950,812,546	$8,533,939,991	$115,729,519	$42,819,350,448	$38,948,899,648	

Notes:
(1) Video lottery figures for Delaware, Oregon and West Virginia are total amounts played (cash & credit); sales indicated for Rhode Island and South Dakota are cash-in figures only.
(2) District of Columbia and Michigan figures are lottery estimates for the fiscal year ending 9/30/97.

Continued on following page.

TABLE 8.1 (Continued)

Canada

	Instant & Pulltabs	Lotto	Spiel	3-digit	4-digit	Sports Lottery	Passive	Keno	VLTs (1)	Other	FY1997 Total Sales	FY1996 Total Sales	Percent Change
Alberta	$73,489,800	$181,450,354	$42,035,092	$5,293,888		$35,111,950	$1,507,624				$338,888,708	$359,986,656	-5.9%
BC	320,758,721	380,416,423	60,959,263	5,174,991		21,468,057	4,521,740	$70,728,716			864,027,911	792,787,000	9.0%
Manitoba	33,034,684	68,828,063	15,433,160	2,519,325		15,051,606	394,426				135,261,264	130,786,740	3.4%
New Bruns.	45,760,915	45,880,074	10,103,081		$958,485	2,660,179	388,320	2,332,146	$116,274,282	$1,603,385	225,960,867	210,290,400	7.5%
Newf.	99,665,711	34,751,104	7,366,545		546,526	1,988,218	163,740	2,242,073	60,793,641	788,920	208,306,478	203,781,500	2.2%
North Terr.	2,251,780	2,819,416	551,624	83,585			893,536	34,041		63,170	6,697,152	6,717,719	-0.3%
NS	77,436,660	69,107,206	11,605,585		1,317,509	4,409,036	2,484,820	4,283,272	106,006,636	2,049,145	278,699,869	263,800,200	5.6%
Ontario	623,742,000	986,810,000	128,539,000	44,404,000		202,207,000	5,076,000	73,830,000			2,064,608,000	2,118,000,000	-2.5%
PEI	10,610,188	10,432,667	1,572,602		180,641	975,358	43,880	466,982	16,872,953	233,125	41,388,396	39,934,900	3.6%
Quebec	404,541,000	734,088,000	132,342,000	24,319,000		50,001,000	98,427,000	126,335,000	466,286,000		2,036,339,000	1,884,739,000	8.0%
Sask.	32,278,785	56,089,681	16,348,956	1,319,488		8,322,643	440,541	706,486		834,772	116,341,352	114,202,443	1.9%
Yukon	1,237,891	2,472,195	532,195	84,355		485,666	28,288				4,840,590	4,652,945	4.0%
Total Canada	**$1,724,808,135**	**$2,573,145,183**	**$427,389,103**	**$83,198,632**	**$3,003,161**	**$343,574,249**	**$113,510,420**	**$280,924,675**	**$766,233,512**	**$5,572,517**	**$6,321,359,587**	**$6,129,679,503**	

All figures are in Canadian dollars.
(1) All video lottery figures in Canada represent net machine income only. VLT revenues for Alberta, Manitoba and Saskatchewan were not available at press time. For comparative purposes, VLT revenues for these provinces have been removed from FY1996 sales.

Source: "North American Lottery Sales Report," *International Gaming and Wagering Business*, New York, New York, October 1997

The Search for Younger Players

Most lottery players are currently older than 40 years of age. Marketers for the state lotteries have to figure out ways to attract younger players to ensure the future growth of the game. Younger players seem to be attached to games of skill or games in which they think skills are involved — games that involve more than scratching a single space.

Some marketers believe the best chance to attract younger players (at least male players) is to tie the lottery to sports. At the same time, the lotteries do not want to alienate older players. Finally, a program to attract younger players must not appear to be aimed at attracting people under 18 years. Any marketing campaign that appeared to be designed to attract children to gambling would likely cause a negative public reaction.

THE PLAYERS

The *International Gaming and Wagering Business* magazine surveyed lottery directors in 1985 to determine a profile of lottery players. In New Jersey, they found that about 38 percent of the players with incomes below $15,000 claimed they had no interest or very little interest in lottery games. Most persons in this category said they could not afford to play and therefore did not (although this does not explain why they were playing at the time they were surveyed). As a group, poor people played lottery games less frequently than middle- and high-income groups. Middle-income persons who had discretionary (spare) money generally considered betting on lotteries harmless fun that offered them a chance for luck to change their lives.

In 1986, several lottery market research groups developed a profile of the "typical" lottery player in Colorado and Washington. They found the average player usually played the game with the hope of winning money. Males and females in both states were equally interested in playing, but there were differences between the states in terms of age and income levels. In Colorado, most players were between 18 and 54 years and earned an average of $15,000 to $20,000 yearly. In Washington, the average player was 42 years old, with an annual income of $28,900. In both states, about 63 percent of the players had some college background or technical school experience beyond high school. Most players believed the lottery was a good way to raise money for state expenses.

In a Maine study, lottery directors found that different game formats appealed to different

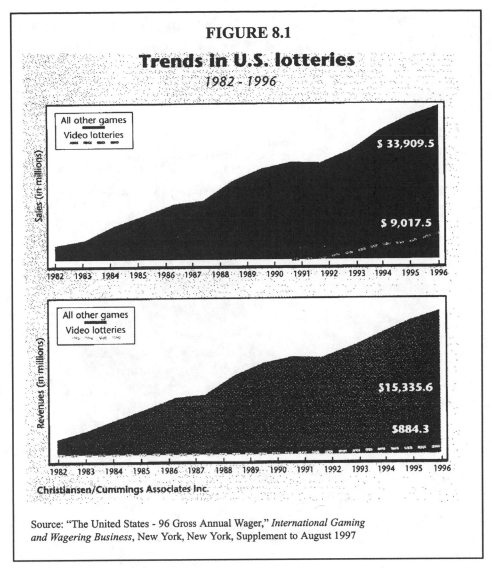

FIGURE 8.1

Trends in U.S. lotteries

1982 - 1996

All other games
Video lotteries

$ 33,909.5

$ 9,017.5

1982 1983 1984 1985 1986 1987 1988 1989 1990 1991 1992 1993 1994 1995 1996

All other games
Video lotteries

$15,335.6

$884.3

1982 1983 1984 1985 1986 1987 1988 1989 1990 1991 1992 1993 1994 1995 1996

Christiansen/Cummings Associates Inc.

Source: "The United States - 96 Gross Annual Wager," *International Gaming and Wagering Business*, New York, New York, Supplement to August 1997

and older. They also found that most Minnesotans played the game rather regularly. About 31 percent bought tickets once a week or more, 23 percent bet on the lottery two or three times a month, and 46 percent wagered once a month or less. Most Minnesotans (58 percent) felt positive about the lottery, while 36 percent were negative about it. (Six percent had no opinion.)

A NATIONAL LOTTERY

Thomas Jefferson, author of the Declaration of Independence and third president of the United States, thought "the lottery is a wonderful thing; it lays taxation only on the willing." Recent successes in state lotteries have inspired several congressmen to introduce national lottery bills, but to date, none has succeeded.

Some of the major arguments in support of a national lottery are:

- It would be a voluntary method of raising money;

- Revenues, estimated at between $6 and $50 billion a year, could help reduce the national debt, bolster the nation's Social Security system, or supplement education and child-welfare programs;

- A lottery is no more regressive (in which a larger portion of revenue is taken from the poor than

groups of people. One game, named Tri-State Megabucks, was played to fulfill a fantasy, but Instant Games were played in the hope of winning money. Pick 3 and Pick 4, which are daily numbers games, were played by people who thought they had a lucky number. The state of Maine developed advertising campaigns to promote specific lottery games based on the information obtained in these marketing studies.

In 1991, National Analysts interviewed 1,021 Minnesotans for Carmichael Lynch, the advertising agency for the Minnesota Lottery. They found that younger people were most likely to play the lottery. About 71 percent of those ages 18 to 34 had played the lottery, compared to 60 percent of those age 35 to 64 and 44 percent of those 65 years

117

from middle- and upper-income groups) than sales taxes, which affect everyone equally, regardless of income;

• Studies indicate that state-operated lotteries decrease activity in illegal numbers games.

Some of the major arguments against a national lottery are:

• Better methods of balancing the federal budget should be used;

• It is not a productive revenue-raiser and would make only a small dent in the total national debt;

• It is immoral, creating an environment where the "chance ethic" is more important than the "work ethic;"

• It promotes compulsive gambling;

• It is a regressive form of taxation;

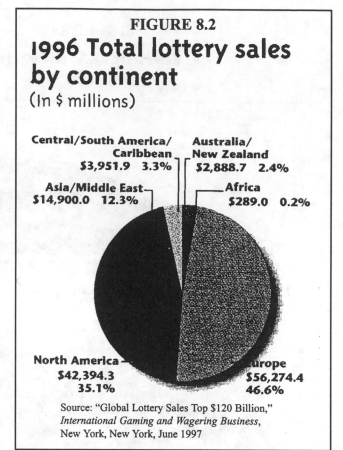

FIGURE 8.2
1996 Total lottery sales by continent
(In $ millions)

Central/South America/Caribbean $3,951.9 3.3%

Australia/New Zealand $2,888.7 2.4%

Asia/Middle East $14,900.0 12.3%

Africa $289.0 0.2%

North America $42,394.3 35.1%

Europe $56,274.4 46.6%

Source: "Global Lottery Sales Top $120 Billion," *International Gaming and Wagering Business*, New York, New York, June 1997

TABLE 8.2
Countries ranked by total 1996 lottery sales

1.	UNITED STATES	$36.4 BILLION
2.	SPAIN	$10.3 BILLION
3.	GERMANY	$9.7 BILLION
4.	UNITED KINGDOM	$9.6 BILLION
5.	JAPAN	$7.6 BILLION
6.	FRANCE	$6.6 BILLION
7.	ITALY	$6.4 BILLION
8.	CANADA	$5.1 BILLION
9.	MALAYSIA	$2.5 BILLION
10.	AUSTRALIA	$2.5 BILLION

World's top ten lottery organizations by 1996 sales

1.	THE NATIONAL LOTTERY	UK	$8.1 BILLION
2.	DAI-ICHI KANGYO BANK LOTTERY	JAPAN	$7.6 BILLION
3.	ORGANISMO NACIONAL DE LOTERIAS Y APUESTAS	SPAIN	$7.2 BILLION
4.	LA FRANÇAISE DES JEUX	FRANCE	$6.6 BILLION
5.	AMMINISTRAZIONE AUTONOMA DEI MONOPOLI DI STATO (APPROX. 1995 SALES)	ITALY	$4.2 BILLION
6.	NEW YORK STATE LOTTERY	U.S.	$3.6 BILLION
7.	TEXAS STATE LOTTERY	U.S.	$3.4 BILLION
8.	ORGANIZACION NACIONAL DE CIEGOS DE ESPANA	SPAIN	$3.0 BILLION
9.	MASSACHUSETTS STATE LOTTERY	U.S.	$3.0 BILLION
10.	OHIO STATE LOTTERY	U.S.	$2.4 BILLION

Source: "Global Lottery Sales Top $120 Billion," *International Gaming and Wagering Business*, New York, New York, June 1997

- It contributes to organized crime;

- A national lottery would become a direct competitor to state lotteries.

Politically Unlikely

Probably the most important reason that a national lottery is unlikely is that it would draw money away from the state lotteries. The North American Association of State and Provincial Lotteries, a trade organization that represents the state and provincial lotteries in North America, strongly opposes a federal lottery and has vowed to fight it. They feel that it will be easy for state lottery officials to convince the representatives and senators from their states that a national lottery would have a devastating impact on their state incomes. This would be especially true for small states whose jackpots could never compete with that of a national lottery. Furthermore, it is easier to convince voters that lottery money should help out at the state and local level, rather than be sent to Washington, DC.

LOTTERIES — A WORLDWIDE PASSION

Lotteries are as popular in other parts of the world as they are in the United States. There are lottery games in countries on every continent. In 1996, a lottery in the United Kingdom with a jackpot of $65 million resulted in the sale of $100 million in tickets. The lottery administrators reported that tickets were selling at the rate of 5,000 per minute and an estimated 90 percent of all adults in the United Kingdom had purchased a ticket. According to *International Gaming and Wagering Business,* worldwide lottery sales (including the United States) in 1996 reached over $120 billion, almost double the $64.4 billion in 1990. Europe had the most lottery sales ($56.3 billion), followed by North America ($42.4 billion), Asia and the Middle East ($14.9 billion), Central and South America ($4 billion), Australia and New Zealand ($2.9 billion), and Africa ($289 million). (See Figure 8.2.)

By country, the United States sold the most lottery tickets ($36.4 billion), followed by Spain ($10.3 billion), Germany ($9.7 billion), the United Kingdom ($9.6 billion), Japan (7.6 billion), and France ($6.6 billion). (See Table 8.2.)

The largest lotteries in volume sales in 1996 were the United Kingdom's National Lottery ($8.1 billion), Japan's Dai-Ichi Kangyo Bank Lottery ($7.6 billion), the Spanish National Lottery ($7.2 billion), the French Lottery ($6.6 billion), and the Italian National Lottery ($4.2 billion in 1995). (See Table 8.2.)

CHAPTER IX

BINGO AND OTHER CHARITABLE GAMES

HOW MUCH MONEY IS BET ON CHARITY GAMING?

Since 1986, the National Association of Fundraising Ticket Manufacturers (NAFTM, Minneapolis, MN) has annually surveyed states permitting charitable activities to determine how much money is raised at charity gaming throughout the United States. The 1996 survey did not include California, Hawaii, Maine, Maryland, Montana, Nevada, Tennessee, or Utah because these states either had no gambling or did not have any reporting requirements for charity gambling. Alabama, Arkansas, and Delaware could not provide any of the information requested, and Vermont did not reply.

According to the 1996 World Gambling Abstract, charitable gambling constitutes 5.5 percent ($2.1 billion) of the total amount wagered

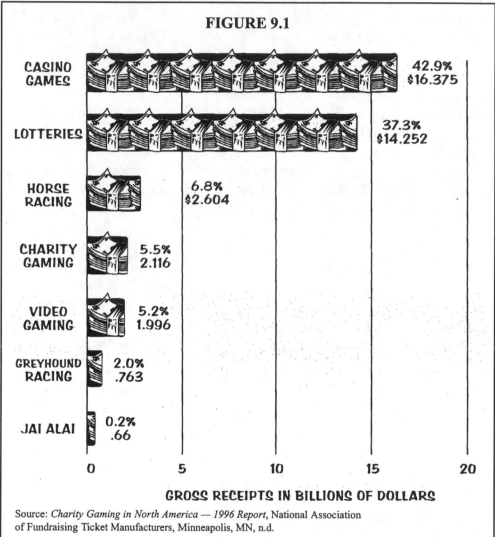

FIGURE 9.1

CASINO GAMES — 42.9% $16.375

LOTTERIES — 37.3% $14.252

HORSE RACING — 6.8% $2.604

CHARITY GAMING — 5.5% 2.116

VIDEO GAMING — 5.2% 1.996

GREYHOUND RACING — 2.0% .763

JAI ALAI — 0.2% .66

0   5   10   15   20

GROSS RECEIPTS IN BILLIONS OF DOLLARS

Source: *Charity Gaming in North America — 1996 Report*, National Association of Fundraising Ticket Manufacturers, Minneapolis, MN, n.d.

for legalized gambling in the United States. (See Figure 9.1.) In 1991, charity gaming made up 3.7 percent of the total amount bet. On the other hand, Eugene Martin Christiansen and Will E. Cummings, in their "1996 Annual Gross Annual Wager" presented in the *International Gaming and Wagering Business* (August 1997) estimated gross

TABLE 9.1

TOTAL AMOUNT OF MONEY WAGERED ON CHARITABLE GAMING

STATE or PROVINCE	GROSS RECEIPTS	POPULATION*	DOLLARS WAGERED PER CAPITA
Alaska	$ 210,373,000	607,000	$ 346.58
Arizona	$ 41,982,000	4,228,000	$ 9.93
Colorado	$ 220,601,000	3,823,000	$ 57.70
Connecticut	$ 58,902,000	3,274,000	$ 17.99
Florida[1]	$ 66,182,000	14,400,000	$ 4.60
Georgia[2]	$ 34,826,000	7,353,000	$ 4.74
Idaho[2]	$ 6,997,000	1,189,000	$ 5.88
Illinois	$ 286,659,000	11,847,000	$ 24.20
Indiana	$ 457,093,000	5,841,000	$ 78.26
Iowa	$ 51,103,000	2,852,000	$ 17.92
Kansas[2]	$ 44,422,000	2,572,000	$ 17.27
Kentucky	$ 471,079,000	3,884,000	$ 121.29
Louisiana	$ 230,151,000	4,351,000	$ 52.90
Massachusetts	$ 211,680,000	6,092,000	$ 34.75
Michigan	$ 326,390,000	9,594,000	$ 34.02
Minnesota	$ 1,392,296,000	4,658,000	$ 298.90
Mississippi	$ 134,705,000	2,716,000	$ 49.60
Nebraska	$ 321,092,000	1,652,000	$ 194.37
New Hampshire	$ 82,231,000	1,162,000	$ 70.77
New Jersey	$ 83,480,000	7,988,000	$ 10.45
New Mexico	$ 55,412,000	1,713,000	$ 32.35
New York[2]	$ 183,558,000	18,185,000	$ 10.09
North Carolina	$ 34,688,000	7,323,000	$ 4.74
North Dakota	$ 288,088,000	644,000	$ 447.34
Ohio	$ 745,372,000	11,173,000	$ 66.71
Oklahoma	$ 52,509,000	3,301,000	$ 15.91
Oregon	$ 83,506,000	3,204,000	$ 26.06
Rhode Island	$ 16,545,000	990,000	$ 16.71
South Carolina	$ 79,236,000	3,699,000	$ 21.42
Texas	$ 605,380,000	19,128,000	$ 31.65
Virginia	$ 205,608,000	6,675,000	$ 30.80
Washington	$ 742,790,000	5,533,000	$ 134.25
West Virginia	$ 79,044,000	1,826,000	$ 43.29
Wisconsin	$ 67,449,000	5,160,000	$ 13.07
Alberta[3]	$ 693,536,000	2,546,000	$ 272.40
Manitoba[3]	$ 111,500,000	1,114,000	$ 100.09
Newfoundland[3]	$ 76,075,000	552,000	$ 137.82
Ontario[3]	$ 2,270,000,000	10,085,000	$ 225.09
Prince Edward[3]	$ 13,300,000	135,000	$ 98.52
Saskatchewan[3]	$ 213,903,000	989,000	$ 216.28

[1]Pari-mutual races only. Other charitable gambling is regulated by the state.
[2]IGWB data.
[3]Canadian currency.

Source: *Charity Gaming in North America — 1996 Report*, National Association of Fundraising Ticket Manufacturers, Minneapolis, MN, n.d.

wagering for total charitable gaming at $9.7 billion with nearly half ($4.25 billion) coming from charitable bingo.

Charity gaming is permitted in all states except Arkansas, Hawaii, Tennessee, and Utah. According to NAFTM, charity gambling is intended:

to fund activities in local communities ... to fund activities that no longer enjoy the benefit of state or federal support ... to add value to the lives of members of the local community by providing services and programs which might otherwise be neglected for lack of funds.

TABLE 9.2
TOTAL AMOUNT RAISED FOR CHARITY AS A PERCENTAGE OF TOTAL GROSS RECEIPTS

STATE or PROVINCE	GROSS RECEIPTS (GR)	NET PROCEEDS (NP)	NP AS % OF GR	TOTAL TAXES/FEES	TAXES/FEES AS % OF GR	GAMES INCL. IN GR*
Alaska[1]	$ 210,373,000	$ 20,040,000	10%	$ 1,755,000	0.83%	B,P,R
Arizona	$ 41,982,000	$ 6,806,000	16%	$ 719,000	1.71%	B
Colorado	$ 220,601,000	$ 30,800,000	14%	$ 825,000	0.37%	B,P,R
Connecticut	$ 58,902,000	$ 19,010,000	32%	$ 1,604,000	2.72%	B,P,R,O
Florida	$ 66,182,000	$ 3,999,000	6%	$ 250,000	0.38%	O
Georgia[2]	$ 34,826,000	$ 980,000	3%	N/A	N/A	B
Idaho[2]	$ 6,997,000	$ 2,164,000	31%	$ 19,000	0.27%	B,R
Illinois	$ 286,659,000	N/A	N/A	$15,700,000	5.48%	B,P
Indiana	$ 457,093,000	$ 54,885,000	12%	$ 6,154,000	1.35%	B,P,R,O
Iowa	$ 51,103,000	$ 14,122,000[3]	28%	$ 2,357,000	4.61%	B,R
Kansas[2]	$ 44,422,000	N/A	N/A	$ 1,053,000	2.37%	B,P
Kentucky	$ 471,079,000	N/A	N/A	$ 2,355,000	0.50%	B,P,R,O
Louisiana	$ 230,151,000	$ 27,249,000	12%	$ 1,025,000	0.45%	B,P,R,O
Massachusetts	$ 211,680,000	$ 31,619,000	15%	$13,723,000	6.48%	B,P,R,O
Michigan	$ 326,390,000	$ 62,181,000	19%	$ 628,000	0.19%	B,P,R,O
Minnesota	$ 1,392,296,000	$ 92,383,000	7%	$64,928,000	4.66%	B,P,R,O
Mississippi	$ 134,705,000	$ 13,719,000	10%	$ 1,072,000	0.80%	B,P,R
Nebraska	$ 321,092,000	$ 34,571,000	11%	$ 8,290,000	2.58%	B,P,R,O
New Hampshire	$ 82,231,000	$ 10,288,000	13%	$ 1,819,000	2.21%	B,P
New Jersey	$ 83,480,000	$ 25,678,000	31%	$ 810,000	0.97%	B
New Mexico	$ 55,412,000	$ 5,731,000	10%	$ 238,000	0.43%	B,P,R,O
New York[2]	$ 183,558,000	N/A	N/A	$ 1,595,000	0.87%	B,P,R
North Carolina	$ 34,688,000	$ 4,134,000	12%	$ 32,000	0.09%	B
North Dakota	$ 288,088,000	$ 16,765,000	6%	$11,545,000	4.01%	B,P,R,O
Ohio	$ 745,372,000	$ 92,356,000	12%	N/A	N/A	B,P
Oklahoma	$ 52,509,000	$ 1,967,000	4%	$ 701,000[7]	1.33%	B,P
Oregon	$ 83,506,000	$ 9,206,000	11%	$ 737,000	0.88%	B,P
Rhode Island	$ 16,296,000	$ 3,867,000	24%	$ 6,730	0.04%	B,P
South Carolina	$ 79,236,000	$ 511,000	1%	$ 9,223,000	11.64%	B
Texas	$ 605,380,000	$ 40,937,000	7%	$28,106,000	4.64%	B,P
Virginia	$ 205,608,000	$ 22,560,000	11%	$ 1,219,000[4]	0.59%	B,P
Washington	$ 742,790,000[5]	$ 69,706,000	9%	$ 9,666,000	1.30%	B,P,R,O
West Virginia	$ 79,044,000	$ 12,239,000	15%	$ 1,214,000	1.54%	B,P,R
Wisconsin	$ 67,449,000	$ 28,111,000	42%	$ 954,600	1.42%	B,R
Alberta[6]	$ 693,536,000	$ 90,181,000	13%	$ 4,228,000	0.61%	B,P,R
Manitoba[6]	$ 111,500,000	$ 15,600,000	14%	$14,000,000	12.56%	B,P,R,O
Newfoundland[6]	$ 76,075,000	$ 12,132,000	16%	$ 539,000	0.71%	B,P,R,O
Ontario[6]	$ 2,270,000,000	$311,000,000	14%	$25,000,000	1.10%	B,P,R
Prince Edward[6]	$ 13,300,000	$ 2,040,000	15%	$ 242,000	1.82%	B
Saskatchewan[6]	$ 213,903,000	$140,851,000	66%	$ 132,000	0.06%	B,P,R

[1] Preliminary data.
[2] International Gaming & Wagering Business, Vol. 18, No. 7 July, 1997
[3] Net proceeds are estimated.
[4] Does not include a full year of fees.
[5] Includes commercial activity.
[6] Canadian currency.
[7] Data represents approx. 52% of licensees reporting.

*B = Bingo, P = Pulltabs, R = Raffles, O = Other

Source: *Charity Gaming in North America — 1996 Report*, National Association of Fundraising Ticket Manufacturers, Minneapolis, MN, n.d.

Charity gaming activities are conducted by and for charitable non-profit organizations and include bingo, charity game tickets, pulltabs, jar tickets, breakopens, instant bingo, Lucky 7's, pickle cards, raffles, casino nights, and various other games of chance. The NAFTM survey does not include statistics for gaming conducted on Native American reservations. (For information on gambling on Native American reservations, see Chapter III.)

The NAFTM estimates* that nearly $8 billion was wagered in 1996 in the 34 states that reported receipts from charity gaming. Minnesota ($1.4

* The National Association of Fundraising Ticket Manufacturers (NAFTM) estimate of the total amount of money wagered is based on the information provided by only the states that responded to their survey. Within those states, the type and amount of information gathered may vary. As a result, NAFTM advises that figures in its report are low estimates and that "it is important to realize that actual charity gaming amounts are considerably higher than the figures reported." The NAFTM refers to the total amount wagered as annual gross receipts as noted, for example, in Table 9.1. The amount earned by the charitable game is referred to as "net proceeds" as noted in Table 9.2.

billion) was, by far, the leading charity game state, followed by Ohio ($745 million), Washington State ($743 million) and Texas ($605 million). Canadians wagered approximately $3.4 billion — up significantly from the year before — most of it in Ontario ($2 billion) and Alberta ($693 million). (See Table 9.1.)

Since Eugene Christiansen and Will Cummings, in their annual report in *International Gaming and Wagering Business,* estimate the total handle for the whole country, their estimate will be higher than the NAFTM estimates, which cover only responding states.

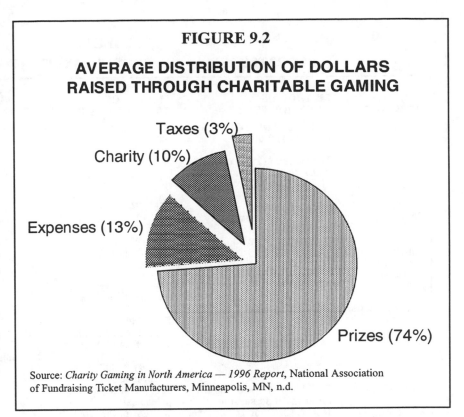

FIGURE 9.2

AVERAGE DISTRIBUTION OF DOLLARS RAISED THROUGH CHARITABLE GAMING

Taxes (3%)
Charity (10%)
Expenses (13%)
Prizes (74%)

Source: *Charity Gaming in North America — 1996 Report,* National Association of Fundraising Ticket Manufacturers, Minneapolis, MN, n.d.

How Much Went to Charity?

NAFTM reported that in the 30 states that reported net proceeds, $758.5 million was raised for charitable organizations in 1996. Charities received the most money from charitable gambling in Minnesota and Ohio ($92 million each), Washington ($70 million), and Michigan ($62 million). In Canada, about $572 million was raised for charity. Most of the money went to charities in Ontario ($311 million) and Saskatchewan ($141 million). (See Table 9.2 and Figure 9.2.)

How Much Went to Tax Revenue?

According to the NAFTM, charitable gaming in 35 states, through taxes and license fees, contributed almost $197 million in 1996 to the various states. State and local treasuries in Minnesota ($64 million), Texas ($23 million), and Illinois ($15 million) benefitted the most. (See Table 9.3.)

WHO PLAYS WHAT?

All the states that permit charitable gambling allow bingo. The other most commonly permitted charitable games are raffles (32 states and DC), charity game tickets (such as pulltabs, breakopen, jar tickets, or pickle tabs in which the player takes off the tops of the tabs to see if a winner is behind it) (40 states and DC), and Las Vegas nights (casino nights) (17 states). (See Table 9.4.)

BINGO — FROM UNKNOWN ORIGINS TO A UNIQUELY AMERICAN GAME

Historians are unsure of the origin of bingo. Experts attribute it to the English, the Dutch, or the Swedes. Others believe bingo developed either from the sixteenth century Italian game of lotto, or from the popular lottery game of keno, first played in New Orleans during the 1840s. In the 1920s, bingo was played at local movie theaters. Operated as a "raffle" to avoid state laws against certain forms of gambling, the movie theater games were the first to make bingo a form of public entertainment. The winner of the "raffle" drawing would shout "Bingo" and claim the prize.

Modern-day bingo, also known as beano, is a simple game. It is based entirely on chance and played until a participant wins. Players purchase a bingo card, which is made of cardboard or paper

TABLE 9.3
TAX RATES/FEES — METHODS OF TAXATION FOR CHARITIES

STATE or PROVINCE	BINGO- METHOD OF TAXATION FEES	PULLTABS- METHOD OF TAXATION/FEES	RAFFLES- METHOD OF TAXATION/FEES	TOTAL TAXES OR FEES
Alaska	TAX: 1% of NR if GR exceeds $20,000	TAX: 3% of Ideal Net. If GR exceeds $20,000, 1% of combined GR	1% of NR if Gross exceeds 1%	N/A
Arizona	TAX: Class A(2.5% of adjusted gross) Class B (1.5% of gross) Class C (2% of gross)	N/A		$ 694,000
Colorado	FEE: .3% of GR	FEE: .3% of GR	FEE: .3% of GR	$ 661,803
Connecticut	FEE: 5% of GR less prizes paid	FEE: 10% of retail value	N/A	$ 1,524,000
Indiana	Included in licensing fees	TAX: 10%		$ 1,008,000
Illinois	TAX: 5% of GR	TAX: 5% of GR		$ 14,543,000
Iowa	TAX: 5% of GR			$ 2,167,000
Kentucky	FEE: .5% of GR	FEE: .5% of GR	FEE: .5% of GR	$ 2,536,000
Louisiana	FEE: charity pays 5% on bingo supplies to supplier	FEE: charity pays 3% of ideal net to supplier	N/A	$ 698,000
Massachusetts	TAX: 5% of GR	TAX: 10% of retail value	TAX: 5% of GR	$ 13,692,000
Michigan	N/A	50% of ideal net less supplier commission	N/A	$ 11,405,000
Minnesota	TAX: 10% of adjusted GR	TAX: 2% of ideal gross + (2% of gross over $500,000, 4% over $700,000, 6% over $900,000)	TAX:10% of adjusted GR	$ 64,368,000
Mississippi	FEE: 1% or 1/2% of the GR for each bingo session.	FEE: 5% of the NR of pulltab sales		$ 1,182,246
Missouri	TAX: 2/10th's of 1¢ per face.	TAX: 2% of the retail sales value		$ 4,392,000
Nebraska	TAX: 6% on GR	TAX: 10% of NR	2% of GR	$ 7,861,000
New Hampshire	TAX: 7% paid on all games	FEE: $15.00 per deal		$ 1,819,000
New Mexico	TAX: adjusted GR minus expenses x .03	See bingo	same	$ 213,000
North Dakota	TAX: Formula determined on all games	TAX: 4 1/2% of GR	See Bingo	$ 11,447,000
Oklahoma	TAX: .015 cents on each bingo face	TAX: 10% on the GR		$ 13,462,000
Oregon	FEE: GR x .95%		FEE: GR x .5%	$ 705,000
Rhode Island	No Tax	No Tax	No Tax	
South Carolina	TAX: .05 cents per $1.00 plus prorated admission tax			$ 9,023,000
Texas	TAX: 5% of prizes paid	TAX: 5% of prizes paid	TAX: 5% of prizes paid	$ 22,834,000
Virginia	FEE: 2% of GR	FEE: 2% of GR	FEE: 2% of GR	$ 1,099,000
Washington	TAX:10% of NR to local city/county	TAX: 5% of GR to local city/county	TAX:10% of NR to local city/county	$ 7,887,000
West Virginia	N/A	FEE: 20% of retail value, some charities are exempt from fee.	FEE: 20% of retail value, some charities are exempt.	$ 866,000
Wisconsin	TAX: 2% of GR paid semi-annually			$ 566,000

GR = Gross Receipts
NR = Net Receipts

Source: *Charity Gaming in North America — 1996 Report*, National Association of Fundraising Ticket Manufacturers, Minneapolis, MN, n.d.

and contains five rows of five squares each. (At the end of the session, the cards are returned to the game manager to be used again.) One letter of the word BINGO appears above each of the vertical columns. All of the squares contain a number from 1 to 75, except the "free" center square.

In a typical game, an announcer calls a letter/number combination, such as "B-15." As a combination is called, players who have that combination on their card place "beans" or other markers on the correct square. When a player has covered five squares in a vertical, horizontal, or diagonal column, he or she shouts "Bingo." The announcer then checks the player's card against a master card, and if the cards match, the player receives a prize and a new game begins.

TABLE 9.4

STATES CONDUCTING CHARITY GAMING — WHAT IS BEING PLAYED

STATE or PROVINCE	BINGO	PULLTABS	RAFFLES	CASINO NIGHTS	OTHER
Alabama	X				
Alaska	X	X	X	X	X
Arizona	X				
California	X	X	X		
Colorado	X	X	X		
Connecticut	X	X	X	X	X
Delaware	X	X	X	X	
DC	X	X	X		
Florida	X				X
Georgia	X	X[1]			
Idaho	X	X[1]	X		
Illinois	X	X[1]	X	X	
Indiana	X	X[1]	X	X	X
Iowa	X	X[1]	X	X	
Kansas	X	X	X		
Kentucky	X	X	X	X	X
Louisiana	X	X	X	X	
Maine	X	X	X	X	
Maryland	X	X	X	X	
Massachusetts	X	X[1]	X	X	
Michigan	X	X[1]	X	X	
Minnesota	X	X	X		X
Mississippi	X	X			X
Missouri	X	X			
Montana	X	X			
Nebraska	X	X	X		X
Nevada	X				
New Hampshire	X	X			
New Jersey	X	X	X		X
New Mexico	X	X	X		
New York	X	X	X		
North Carolina	X				
North Dakota	X	X	X	X	X
Ohio	X	X	X	X	
Oklahoma	X	X			
Oregon	X	X	X	X	
Pennsylvania	X	X			
Rhode Island	X	X[1]	X		
South Carolina	X				X
South Dakota	X	X	X		
Texas	X	X			
Vermont	X	X	X	X	
Virginia	X	X	X		
Washington	X	X	X	X	X
West Virginia	X	X	X		
Wisconsin	X	X[1]	X		
Wyoming	X	X	X		
Alberta	X	X	X		X
British Columbia	X	X	X	X	X
Manitoba	X	X	X	X	X
New Brunswuck	X				
Newfoundland	X	X	X	X	X
Northwest Territory	X				
Nova Scotia	X	X	X		
Ontario	X	X	X	X	
Prince Edward	X		X		
Quebec	X	X	X	X	X
Saskatchewan	X	X	X		X

[1]Pulltabs are part of the state lottery.

Source: *Charity Gaming in North America — 1996 Report*, National Association of Fundraising Ticket Manufacturers, Minneapolis, MN, n.d.

Bingo — The "Innocent" Gambling Game

Bingo is unique among the various forms of gambling. Many Americans learned to play the game as children and do not consider it to be gambling. Bingo sessions are a common form of fundraising by charitable organizations, such as churches, synagogues, or service clubs, so many people view the game as socially and morally acceptable. It is also a relatively inexpensive way

TABLE 9.5
BINGO

STATE or PROVINCE	BINGO GROSS RECEIPTS (96)	'96 NET PROCEEDS	PAYOUT %	BINGO GROSS RECEIPTS (95)	POPULATION	GROSS PER CAPITA
Arizona	$ 41,982,000	$ 6,806,000	77%	$ 43,301,000	4,428,000	$ 9.48
Colorado	$ 66,499,000	$ 8,223,000	78%	$ 68,224,000	3,823,000	$ 17.39
Connecticut	$ 32,691,000	$ 6,444,000	73%	$ 32,534,000	3,274,000	$ 9.99
Georgia[1]	$ 34,826,000	$ 980,000	63%	N/A	7,353,000	$ 4.74
Idaho[1]	$ 5,223,000	$ 1,194,000	58%	$ 6,275,000	1,189,000	$ 4.39
Illinois	$ 142,489,000	N/A	N/A	$ 145,883,000	11,847,000	$ 12.03
Iowa	$ 43,330,000	$ 11,760,000	68%	$ 44,920,000	2,852,000	$ 15.19
Kansas[1]	$ 30,419,000	N/A	N/A	N/A	2,572,150	$ 11.83
Kentucky	$ 105,380,000	N/A	N/A	$ 98,485,000	3,884,000	$ 27.13
Louisiana	$ 129,784,000	$ 10,936,000	80%	$ 132,099,000	4,351,000	$ 29.83
Massachusetts	$ 128,987,000	$ 3,942,000	81%	$ 136,562,000	6,092,000	$ 21.17
Michigan	$ 184,524,000	$ 27,746,000	73%	$ 194,040,000	9,594,000	$ 19.23
Minnesota	$ 80,659,000	$ 5,543,000[2]	76%	$ 80,503,000	4,658,000	$ 17.32
Mississippi	$ 102,067,000	$ 10,426,000[2]	77%	N/A	2,716,000	$ 37.58
Nebraska	$ 21,103,000	$ 291,000	78%	$ 21,937,000	1,652,000	$ 12.77
New Hampshire	$ 37,057,000	$ 121,200	83%	$ 40,963,000	1,162,000	$ 31.89
New Jersey	$ 83,480,000	$ 25,678,000	66%	N/A	7,988,000	$ 10.45
New Mexico	$ 36,459,000	$ 2,350,000	78%	$ 41,507,000	1,713,000	$ 21.28
New York[1]	$ 179,483,000	N/A	N/A	$ 166,293,000	18,185,000	$ 9.87
North Carolina	$ 34,688,000	$ 4,134,000	N/A	$ 35,171,000	7,323,00	$ 4.74
North Dakota	$ 54,934,000	$ 3,353,000[2]	83%	$ 53,041,000	644,000	$ 85.30
Ohio	$ 227,030,000	$ 26,783,000[2]	N/A	N/A	11,173,000	$ 20.32
Oklahoma	$ 47,697,000	$ 1,790,000[2]	74%	$ 28,264,000	3,301,000	$ 14.45
Oregon	$ 79,698,000	$ 6,934,000	79%	$ 84,582,000	3,204,000	$ 24.87
Rhode Island	$ 11,960,000	$ 1,591,000	N/A	$ 12,478,000	990,000	$ 12.08
South Carolina	$ 79,236,000	$ 511,000	71%	$ 89,719,000	3,699,000	$ 21.42
Texas	$ 484,668,000	$ 30,293,000[2]	77%	$ 496,660,000	19,128,000	$ 25.34
Virginia	$ 104,595,000	$ 11,505,000[2]	79%	N/A	6,675,000	$ 15.67
Washington	$ 183,482,000	$ 12,852,000	75%	$ 197,417,000	5,533,000	$ 33.16
West Virginia	$ 34,398,000	$ 4,175,000	79%	$ 32,259,000	1,826,000	$ 18.84
Wisconsin	$ 28,312,000	$ 6,269,000	78%	$ 28,321,000	5,160,000	$ 5.49
Alberta[3]	$ 301,334,000	$434,774,000	69%	$ 317,270,000	2,546,000	$ 118.36
Manitoba[3]	$ 81,600,000	$ 9,500,000	77%	$ 82,900,000	1,114,000	$ 73.25
Newfoundland[3]	$ 36,999,000	$ 2,118,000	78%	$ 41,019,000	552,000	$ 67.03
Prince Edward[3]	$ 13,300,000	$ 2,040,000	72%	$ 13,322,000	135,000	$ 98.52
Saskatchewan[3]	$ 130,822,000	$ 26,020,000	66%	$ 128,045,000	989,000	$ 132.28

[1] IGWB data.
[2] Net proceeds estimated.
[3] Canadian currency.

Source: *Charity Gaming in North America — 1996 Report*, National Association of Fundraising Ticket Manufacturers, Minneapolis, MN, n.d.

for people to do something together socially. Players can sit out a game or two and talk with their friends. All these factors give bingo a respectability that, until recently, was not enjoyed by most other forms of gambling. Even commercial bingo (see below) is viewed favorably by many people.

Charitable Bingo Games Run by Commercial Bingo Operations

In most states, bingo games are legal only when they are operated as "charitable gaming activities," that is, at least part of the money bet must go to a charitable (or non-profit religious, educational, etc.) organization. Some charitable organizations run their own bingo games, but many turn to commercial operators to run the games for them. These commercial operators may set up permanent bingo parlors where players can find a game going at almost any time of the day or night.

For their services, commercial bingo operators charge a commission on the proceeds of every game. Their commission is deducted from the "donations" to the charitable organization, thereby reducing the charitable organization's revenue. But because professional operators have the time and money to invest in large-scale operations, charitable organizations generally realize more revenue than if they tried to operate the games themselves.

Almost Anyone Can Play

Only Arkansas, Hawaii, Tennessee, and Utah, which permit no charitable gambling of any type, do not allow bingo. The National Association of

Fundraising Ticket Manufacturers (NAFTM) estimated the gross receipts for bingo in 1996 at about $2.86 billion from 31 states in the United States and $564 million from 5 provinces in Canada (Table 9.5). Eugene Martin Christiansen and Will E. Cummings, in their "1996 Annual Gross Annual Wager" presented in the *International Gaming and Wagering Business* (August 1997), estimated charitable bingo wagering in the United States at $4 billion in 1996, considerably higher than the NAFTM estimate.

According to the NAFTM, Texas ($485 million), Ohio ($227 million), Michigan ($185 million), and Washington ($183 million) had the greatest handle in the United States, while Alberta ($301 million) and Saskatchewan ($131 million) had the largest handles in Canada. Prize payouts averaged 75 percent in 1996, ranging from 83 percent in New Hampshire and North Dakota to 58 percent in Idaho. (See Table 9.5.) Similarly, *International Gaming and Wagering Business* estimated the amount of the handle retained was 24 percent, meaning that about 76 percent was paid out in prizes. The charities received about 6 percent of the total money bet, while the company administering the bingo game earned the rest.

Eugene Martin Christiansen, writing in *International Gaming and Wagering Business* believes that bingo is a mature sector of the gambling industry. This means that the public's demand for bingo has been met, and as a result revenues from bingo have leveled off and are unlikely to grow significantly in the future. (See Figure 9.3.) Christiansen also thinks the spread of casino gambling may likely hurt bingo's future as bingo players find another way to spend their money.

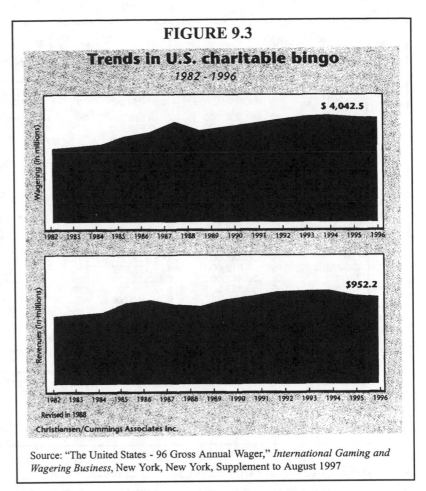

FIGURE 9.3

Trends in U.S. charitable bingo
1982 - 1996

$ 4,042.5

$952.2

Revised in 1988

Christiansen/Cummings Associates Inc.

Source: "The United States - 96 Gross Annual Wager," *International Gaming and Wagering Business*, New York, New York, Supplement to August 1997

Bingo on Native American Reservations

These figures do not, however, include bingo on Native American reservations, which has grown dramatically and has been cutting into non-reservation bingo games. The handle on bingo played on Native American reservations rose from almost nothing a decade ago to about $2 billion in 1996. Meanwhile, revenues earned from bingo reached $627.5 million in 1996. (These are figures for Class II gambling on Indian Reservations, almost all of which is bingo.)

Bingo revenues on Native American reservations have leveled off. Just as non-reservation bingo has been affected by the expansion of casino gambling, so has Native American bingo. In fact, with 147 tribes in 24 states having signed compacts to open casinos, the leveling off of revenues from bingo, rather than a sharp decline, would seem to attest that bingo has a firm base of

TABLE 9.6
PULLTABS — TOTAL RECEIPTS IN NORTH AMERICA

STATE or PROVINCE	PULLTABS GROSS RECEIPTS (96)	'96 NET PROCEEDS	PAYOUT %	PULLTABS GROSS RECEIPTS (95)	POPULATION	GROSS PER CAPITA
Colorado	$ 147,237,000	$ 18,289,000	79%	$ 122,363,000	3,823,000	$ 38.51
Connecticut	$ 10,854,000	$ 2,838,000	64%	$ 13,124,000	3,274,000	$ 3.32
Illinois[1]	$ 144,170,000	N/A	N/A	$ 135,949,000	11,847,000	$ 12.17
Kansas[1]	$ 14,003,000	N/A	N/A	N/A	2,572,150	$ 5.44
Kentucky	$ 353,302,000	N/A	N/A	$ 303,056,000	3,884,000	$ 90.96
Louisiana	$ 82,913,000	$ 9,209,000	77%	$ 87,857,000	4,351,000	$ 19.06
Massachusetts	$ 62,183,000	$ 18,655,000	60%	$ 64,389,000	6,092,000	$ 10.21
Michigan	$ 89,811,000	$ 11,620,000	74%	$ 74,761,000	9,594,000	$ 9.36
Minnesota	$1,266,585,000	$ 84,069,000[2]	81%	$1,262,347,000	4,658,000	$271.92
Mississippi	$ 10,986,000	$ 1,096,000	78%	N/A	2,697,000	$ 4.07
Nebraska	$ 130,295,000	$ 15,805,000	75%	$ 158,705,000	1,652,000	$ 78.87
New Hampshire	$ 45,174,000	$ 10,167,000	72%	$ 51,249,000	1,148,000	$ 39.35
New Mexico	$ 18,564,000	$ 3,202,000	74%	$ 22,809,000	1,713,000	$ 10.84
North Dakota	$ 191,592,000	$ 11,065,000[2]	79%	$ 187,745,000	644,000	$297.50
Ohio	$ 518,342,000	$ 65,572,000[2]	75%	N/A	11,173,000	$ 46.39
Oklahoma	$ 4,812,000	$ 177,000[2]	74%	$ 2,752,000	3,301,000	$ 1.46
Texas	$ 120,712,000	$ 10,643,000[2]	68%	$ 139,272,000	19,128,000	$ 6.31
Virginia	$ 53,653,000	$ 6,091,000[2]	67%	N/A	6,675,000	$ 8.04
Washington	$ 510,284,000[3]	$ 45,389,000	67%	$ 509,007,000	5,533,000	$ 92.23
West Virginia	$ 44,646,000	$ 8,064,000	73%	$ 38,858,000	1,826,000	$ 24.45
Alberta[4]	$ 38,986,000	$ 7,790,000	74%	$ 61,510,000	2,546,000	$ 15.31
Manitoba[4]	$ 17,400,000	$ 3,000,000	70%	$ 20,700,000	1,114,000	$ 15.62
Newfoundland[4]	$ 27,478,000	$ 5,304,000	73%	$ 33,566,000	552,000	$ 49.78
Saskatchewan[4]	$ 60,720,000	$ 11,867,000	74%	$ 73,902,000	989,000	$ 61.40

[1] IGWB data.
[2] Net proceeds estimated.
[3] 78.5% of Gross Receipts is commercial activity.
[4] Canadian currency.

Source: *Charity Gaming in North America — 1996 Report*, National Association of Fundraising Ticket Manufacturers, Minneapolis, MN, n.d.

support. Of course, whether the customer chooses to visit the bingo hall or the casino, in many cases, the money will go into the same tribal coffers.

CHARITY GAME TICKETS

In 1996, charity game tickets were permitted for use by non-profit organizations in 34 states and 9 provinces. Charity game tickets are also known as pulltabs, jar tickets, breakopens, instant bingo, and pickle cards. According to the NAFTM, far more money was wagered on charitable game tickets in the United States than on bingo ($3.8 billion — with just 20 states reporting — compared to $2.86 billion), while about $144.5 million was bet on charity games in Canada, with only 4 provinces — Alberta, Manitoba, Newfoundland, and Saskatchewan — reporting. Minnesota ($1.3 billion) had, by far, the greatest amount of money wagered on charity games, followed by Ohio ($518 million), and Washington ($510 million). In Canada, Saskatchewan ($61 million) and Alberta ($39 million) had the largest handles. Typical payouts were around 73 percent,

ranging from 81 percent in Minnesota to 60 percent in Massachusetts. (See Table 9.6.)

RAFFLES

Many states that permit raffles do not require organizations that operate them to report them to the state. As a result, the NAFTM notes that the gross proceeds figure is only a fraction of the actual amount bet. Eighteen states reported raffle wagering of about $241 million, while five Canadian provinces reported $174 million. The payout on raffles is generally very low. (See Table 9.7.)

CHARITABLE GAMBLING STILL GROWING

Eugene Christiansen, in *International Gaming and Wagering Business,* estimated that about $5.7 billion was wagered on non-bingo charitable games in 1996, producing about $1.5 billion in revenues for a retained amount of 26 percent, or a payout of around 74 percent. Unlike bingo

128

TABLE 9.7
RAFFLES — TOTAL RECEIPTS IN NORTH AMERICA

STATE or PROVINCE	'96 RAFFLES GROSS RECEIPTS	96 NET PROCEEDS	% PAYOUT	'95 RAFFLES GROSS RECEIPTS	POPULATION'	GROSS PER CAPITA
Colorado	$ 6,865,000	$ 4,461,000	32%	$ 6,209,000	3,823,000	$ 1.80
Connecticut	$ 14,213,000	$ 8,973,000	N/A	$ 12,461,000	3,274,000	$ 4.34
Idaho	$ 1,774,000	$ 970,000	37%	N/A	1,189,000	$ 1.49
Indiana	$ 10,164,000	$ 1,225,000	N/A	N/A	5,841,000	$ 1.74
Iowa	$ 7,773,000	$ 2,362,000'	57%	$ 6,460,000	2,842,000	$ 2.74
Kentucky	$ 5,207,000	N/A	N/A	$ 5,265,000	3,884,000	$ 1.34
Louisiana	$ 7,304,000	$ 4,754,000	24%	$ 7,128,000	4,351,000	$ 1.68
Massachusetts	$ 18,627,000	$ 8,382,000	N/A	$ 18,414,000	6,092,000	$ 3.06
Michigan	$ 37,503,000	$ 16,514,000	46%	$ 35,795,000	9,594,000	$ 3.91
Minnesota	$ 26,613,000	$ 1,848,000'	36%	$ 4,456,000	4,658,000	$ 5.71
Nebraska	$ 3,289,000	$ 1,685,000	41%	$ 3,241,000	1,652,000	$ 1.99
New Mexico	$ 409,000	$ 77,000	47%	$ 236,000	1,713,000	$ 0.24
North Dakota	$ 1,806,000	$ 722,000'	40%	$ 1,716,000	644,000	$ 2.80
Oregon	$ 3,808,000	$ 2,272,000	34%	$ 3,397,000	3,204,000	$ 1.19
Rhode Island	$ 4,336,000	$ 2,276,000	N/A	N/A	990,000	$ 4.38
Virginia	$ 47,360,000	$ 4,963,000'	80%	N/A	6,675,000	$ 7.10
Washington	$ 5,261,000	$ 2,673,000	37%	$ 4,917,000	5,533,000	$ 0.95
Wisconsin	$ 39,137,000	$ 21,841,660	44%	$ 36,670,000	5,123,000	$ 7.64
Alberta[2]	$ 58,585,000	$ 21,403,000	44.5%	$ 54,041,000	2,546,000	$ 23.01
Manitoba[2]	$ 12,300,000	$ 5,700,000	37%	$ 11,500,000	1,114,000	$ 11.04
Newfoundland[2]	$ 10,756,000	$ 4,277,000	48%	$ 86,282,000	552,000	$ 19.49
Ontario[2]	$ 70,000,000	$ 11,000,000	34%	$ 70,000,000	10,085,000	$ 6.94
Saskatchewan[2]	$ 22,361,000	$ 8,967,000	44%	$ 20,529,000	989,000	$ 22.61

[1]Net proceeds are estimated.
[2]Canadian currency.
Source: *Charity Gaming in North America — 1996 Report*, National Association of Fundraising Ticket Manufacturers, Minneapolis, MN, n.d.

wagering, which has been leveling off, the betting on non-bingo charitable gaming has been growing. (See Figure 9.4.) Nonetheless, Christiansen still wonders how well charitable gambling will withstand the spread of casino gambling.

Charitable gambling has several advantages over commercial gambling. The players often feel they are doing something good for their community, especially for their more immediate community, such as the church, synagogue, fraternal, or veterans group. Charitable gambling also offers an opportunity for a social gathering. The gambling is only one part of having a good time with friends and acquaintances.

On the other hand, charitable gambling cannot offer the professional embellishments such as the bright lights and fancy interiors. Winnings are usually limited so that charitable gaming cannot always offer the excitement and payoff some gamblers require. Nonetheless, charitable gambling has been able to maintain its niche in the gambling industry.

REGULATION AND ENFORCEMENT

Despite the popularity of bingo and other forms of charity gambling as fund-raisers and their reputation as harmless pastimes, they are as susceptible to abuses as any other forms of gambling. While Americans might conceive of charitable gambling as just the bingo game at the corner church, the Las Vegas New Year's party at the local synagogue, or the slot machines at the American Legion Hall down the street, charitable gambling is big business. Eugene Christiansen and Will Cummings, of Christiansen/Cummings Associates, Inc., estimate the gross receipts from charity gambling at about $2.4 billion. This is far more than the on-track revenues from horse racing ($1.1 billion) and not too far behind the $3.1 billion taken from all types of legal betting on horses.

Although the revenues are comparable, the administration of horse racing and charitable gambling are not. Horse racing is run by professionals with many years of experience. If the management of a horse racing track is sloppy or inattentive, the track will lose money and the manager his or her job. Charitable gambling is run by volunteers who have often never managed any type of gambling operation. Since the administrative positions are usually voluntary, they turn over frequently so the volunteers develop little experience. If they do not do a good job, they probably will not be asked to do it again the next year.

Because they have little experience, charitable groups frequently hire outside administrators to manage the program. Often a considerable amount of money is involved and there is little oversight by the charitable organization. As a result, dishonest agents may take advantage of the situation. Racketeers are suspected of controlling some commercial bingo operations; however, when commercial bingo games are held under the sponsorship of a charitable organization, questions are seldom asked.

Skimming — the practice of under-reporting income from games and pocketing the difference — is thought to be the biggest problem facing officials who enforce bingo regulations. As with other forms of gambling, it is required that the revenues from bingo operations be reported to the government. The government considers skimmed money as not just stolen money, but also as untaxed money. Therefore, both charitable groups and the government, through the loss of tax revenue, lose money when it is skimmed by dishonest bingo operators.

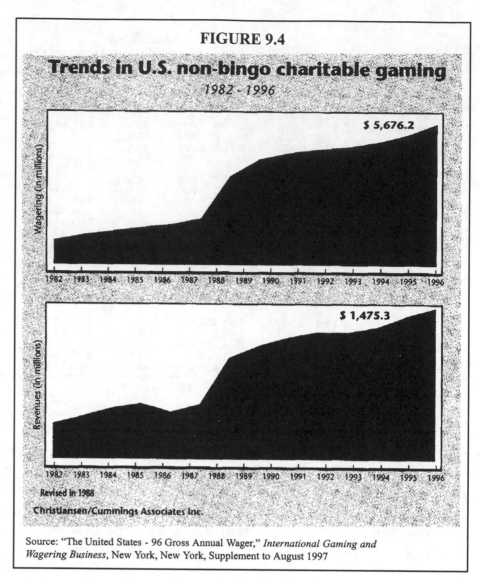

FIGURE 9.4

Trends in U.S. non-bingo charitable gaming
1982 - 1996

$ 5,676.2

$ 1,475.3

Revised in 1988

Christiansen/Cummings Associates Inc.

Source: "The United States - 96 Gross Annual Wager," *International Gaming and Wagering Business*, New York, New York, Supplement to August 1997

All states require bingo licenses (Table 9.8), but few have license control boards. Law enforcement officials generally ignore illegal or dishonest bingo or charitable games because their efforts to regulate them are resisted by the general public. Few municipal or state budgets have funds for bingo investigation. In addition, many police officers believe bingo is a "victimless" crime, too insignificant to merit substantial enforcement time and effort. As a result, bingo and other forms of charitable gambling continue to have the potential for large revenues with little regulation by government or law enforcement agencies.

Several states have brought charitable gambling under state regulation, and many others are planning to. While government regulation is

TABLE 9.8
METHODS OF LICENSING FOR CHARITIES

STATE or PROVINCE	BINGO: METHOD OF LICENSING	PULLTABS: METHOD OF LICENSING	RAFFLES: METHOD OF LICENSING	TOTAL # OF LICENSEES	TOTAL $ FROM FEES
Arizona	Class A($10) Class B($50) Class C($200)			761	$ 23,000
Colorado	$62.50 annual license	Additional license not required	Additional license not required	1564	$ 97,750
Connecticut	Class A($75) Class B($5) Class C($50)	Varies from $5 to $75	Varies from $10 to $100	2108	$ 80,000
Idaho	$100-$300 depending on gross revenue		$100-$300 depending on gross revenue		$ 18,700
Indiana	$25 to $25,000	Included in Bingo License fee	$25 to $25,000	2315	$ 5,146,000
Illinois	$200 for a weekly license, $50 for limited bingo	$500 for regular license, $50 for limited bingo		3104	$ 1,157,000
Iowa	$150 for a 2 year license	$150 for a 2 year license			$ 190,000
Kentucky	$100-$300 based on annual gross receipts	See bingo	See bingo	821	
Louisiana	$50 per license and $25 per modification	See bingo	See bingo	1007	$ 327,000
Massachusetts	$50 per year	Additional license not required	N/A		$ 31,000
Michigan	$10-$150 licensing fee	All bingo licensee may sell pulltabs	$15-$50 licensing fee	10961	
Minnesota	Premise permits vary from $25-$400. $200 gambling manager license	See bingo	See bingo	3082	$ 560,000
Mississippi	$50 licensee fee paid annually by charity	Additional license not required		132	$ 140,600
Missouri	$50 for regular license, $25 of special license	Additional license not required			$ 52,375
Nebraska	Class I($15) Class II($50)	Class I($100) Class II($150)	$15 license	1072	$ 428,000
New Hampshire	$25 license fee paid per night	$10.00 license fee per month		N/A	N/A
New Mexico	$30 fee per event	See bingo	See bingo	257	$ 26,000
New Jersey	$10 per occasion	$500 for annual license	See bingo	11483	N/A
North Carolina	$100 per year license fee			320	$ 32,000
North Dakota	All Games:$150 per license			656	$ 98,000
Ohio	$100 per organization	Additional license not required			$ 130,000
Oklahoma	$100 per organization	Additional license not required		230	$ 23,000
Oregon	Class A($100) Class B($50) Class C+D($20)	Class A($50) Class B($20)		766	$ 31,000
Rhode Island	$5.00 annual application fee per charity		$5.00 application fee per charity per raffle	1306	$ 6,730
South Carolina	$1,000 per organization annually (prorated)				$ 200,000
Texas	$100-$2,500 per license	See bingo	See bingo	1626	$ 3,874,000
Virginia	$200 per organization	See bingo	See bingo	600	$ 120,000
Washington	Varies by class ($52-$12,000)	Varies by class ($527-$9,880)	Varies by class ($52-$1,300)	1494	$ 1,779,000
West Virginia	$200 or $500 annually depending on Gross Receipts	See bingo	See bingo	417	$ 349,000
Wisconsin	$10 per occasion		$25 for annual license	7,685	$ 388,400
Alberta	FEE: If gross is less than $150,000 per year, fee is $30 per event.	FEE: 1.5% gross revenue paid by charity	FEE: 1.5% gross revenue paid by charity	5199	$ 4,228,000
Manitoba	1.5% of gross	See bingo	See bingo	1422	$ 1,400,000
Newfoundland	1% of prize payout	See bingo	See bingo		$ 539,000
Ontario	Up to 3% of total prize board	See bingo	See bingo	2246	$ 25,000,000
Prince Edward	2% of prizes awarded paid by charity		2% of all prizes awarded		$ 242,000
Saskatchewan	$50 per charity	$20 per charity	$20 per charity/$5 with prizes less than $1,000		

Source: *Charity Gaming in North America — 1996 Report*, National Association of Fundraising Ticket Manufacturers, Minneapolis, MN, n.d.

usually considered an interference, it also can provide legitimacy to charitable groups and provide them with guidelines that will help make their charitable gambling operations less susceptible to dishonest administrators.

CHAPTER X

ILLEGAL GAMBLING IN AMERICA

Illegal gambling, like legal gambling, is deeply rooted in American society. Despite innumerable federal and state laws and competition from state-supported legal gambling, illegal wagering remains a part of American life.

TYPES OF ILLEGAL GAMBLING

The four principal forms of illegal gambling are:

- The numbers,

- Horse books (betting on horses),

- Sports books (betting on sporting events), and

- Sports cards.

The Numbers Game

The forerunner of modern numbers gambling was a game called "policy." Policy was often a sideline game of the lotteries. Originally, lotteries were used to raise money for civic or charitable causes, while policy was played to earn money for the lottery company, since policy can be played more quickly than a lottery. It is commonly believed that the game of policy gave rise to gambling syndicates, which raised the large sums of money required to operate a policy shop.

Policy gambling radically changed when "numbers" was introduced as a separate and rival game. (See below how the games are played.) During the 1920s, African-Americans migrated from the rural South into northern cities where more opportunities existed. Policy and numbers appealed to members of poor African-American communities and political organizations. During the 1930s, ex-bootleggers fought for control of Black policy and numbers operations.

Using their political connections and money gained from bootlegging, White mobsters forced African-American policy and numbers operators to join with them or risk being put out of business — or worse. This conflict usually ended in a partnership, with the original African-American owners staying on as managers and operators and the White mobsters providing such services as "protection," financial backing, regulation of competition, and legal representation in court when required.

How the Numbers Game Is Played

To be successful, numbers games require the participation of many people. The bettor places his or her bet for any desired amount on a number from 000 to 999 and receives a receipt indicating the chosen number and the amount wagered. One-digit numbers have an 8-to-1 payoff ($8 is won for every $1 wagered), two-digit numbers have a 60-70 to 1 payoff, and three-digit numbers pay 550-600 to 1.

The wager money is left with a "collector" (who often operates a numbers game as a sideline to a restaurant, candy store, drugstore, gas station, or other business that involves a lot of public contact). A "pickup man" collects the wagers from the collector and delivers them to the "bank," which is a central headquarters or processing center where the winning numbers are determined and payoffs are made, usually based on the results at a local racetrack or a stock market closing.

Usually, the collector does not know what bank the pickup man works for, so if a collector is arrested, the entire operation will not be jeopardized. Gross profit for the bank may be as high as 40 percent of the total amount wagered, but the administrative costs are also high. The net profit for numbers games is usually about 1 percent and rarely exceeds 10 percent.

One of the Most Popular Forms of Illegal Gambling

Although illegal, most numbers operations take place openly while law enforcement officers may be paid to look the other way. In fact, numbers is often cited as a primary source of police corruption. When the occasional police raid does occur, numbers operators and their customers view them as a minor nuisance.

The game still thrives in New York City, especially in economically depressed neighborhoods, and is probably the most lucrative form of illegal gambling in the city. Some politicians and observers believe that the numbers racket is so deeply entrenched in the culture of poor neighborhoods that it has become part of the local economy. Recent immigrants and many poor people may not even know that the game is illegal and that it often supports organized crime. Various types of lottery games are easily available in states where they are legal, giving bettors an option to play lottery games that they never had before.

Horse Books — How a "Bookie" Operates

The bookmaker or "bookie" was first identified with the gambling business during the 1870s, when racetracks licensed them to accept bets at the tracks. For that privilege, bookies paid the racetrack operators a daily fee, usually around $100 (a very large sum in those days). Once established, bookies branched out into (illegal) off-track betting parlors in the cities to provide services to bettors who could not attend races.

When placing a bet with a bookie, the bettor makes his or her choice from a scratch sheet that contains information on post (starting) times, post positions, a horse's lineage and past performance, expected odds, and handicappers' picks. The bookie pays off the same amount as the track, keeping the 15 percent normally charged by the track for himself. After expenses, the bookie normally makes a 10 to 11 percent net profit.

To have enough financial support to cover bets, bookies generally form syndicates. The syndicate gives each bookie the latest information about jockey changes, betting odds, and racetrack conditions.

Sports Books — The Most Popular Form of Illegal Gambling

While many forms of gambling in the United States have been legalized, gambling on sporting events continues to be illegal in all but four states (Montana, Nevada, North Dakota, and Oregon) and is legal statewide only in Nevada. Some sources estimate that professional football alone attracts $50 billion in wagers per season or possibly as much as $10 million per football weekend in major cities. This figure does not include wagers on college football games. According to Eugene M. Christensen of *International Gaming and Wagering Business*, sports betting is the fastest growing type of illegal gambling. This is especially true since gamblers can now bet legally in many states on the numbers-like lotteries.

The "Point Spread"

A sports bookie is literally playing both ends against the middle (trying to balance the bets), hoping to come out on top. The line, or "point spread," is manipulated to try to keep the betting

133

on both teams even. A bookie must be careful not to change the spread too much or he might end up paying off both sides. Lines vary among bookmakers, and some bettors shop around for the spread that is most acceptable.

During the football season, the "early line" is posted every Tuesday in the legal sports books in Nevada. For example, in a game in which the Washington Redskins are playing the Dallas Cowboys, the line might start at Dallas +6. This means that, for the Cowboys supporter, Dallas must win by 7 points for the bettor to win because 6 points will be subtracted from the Cowboys' final score.

Both the legal line in Las Vegas and the illegal line created by the bookies fluctuate during the week, usually because of the bettor's interpretation of everything from changes in the weather to the condition of the players' health. Competent bookies, however, will move the line only in response to how much money is being bet on each team, not conjecture about players and the weather.

A good bookie does not care who wins. He or she moves the point spread up or down in order to keep the betting even. If the line goes from Dallas +6 to Dallas +8, it is because that is what is needed to get more people to bet on Washington instead of Dallas. Normally, by the end of the week as the game approaches, the legal and illegal point spread will usually be very close, if not the same.

The point spread is not the only thing the gambler may bet on. In the over/under (O/U) bets, the gambler wagers on how many points will be scored by both teams. On big games, such as the National Football Conference or American Football Conference championship games or the Super Bowl, odds and lines are posted so that gamblers can bet on any number of aspects of the game. Some of these may include total touchdown passes, the first player to score, total number of running or passing touchdowns, the total number of fumbles lost by both teams, which team will

score the most points in the first quarter or first half, or whatever the gambler can convince a bookie to accept.

Today, most bookmaking operations are partnerships that employ several workers to record bets and compute the day's business. The bookmakers decide how to shift the point spread, when to lay off bets (get help from other bookies in covering bets), what limits to set for bets, and how much credit to extend to customers. Just as in most other types of businesses, the computer has helped the illegal gambler organize his business and make it more efficient.

As with numbers games, illegal sports betting sometimes requires that law enforcement officials be unobservant. In order to avoid confrontations with the law, bookies use various methods to conceal their operations, such as frequently moving, using answering services, and changing telephone numbers.

Sports Cards

Sports cards are very popular for the $1 to $10 sports bettor. Sports cards list a particular week's sporting events, along with the point spreads. The cards are distributed no later than Tuesday for games which will take place the coming weekend. The bettor selects the team(s) he or she thinks will win, tears off the card stub, and submits it to the bookie before the game takes place.

PROFESSIONAL AND COLLEGE SPORTS GAMBLING

College officials nationwide are expressing alarm at the phenomenal increase in betting on college sports. Many people think betting poses a threat to the integrity of sports. "Point shaving" scandals (paying a player to deliberately score fewer points than he or she might have during a particular game) still occasionally surface. Basketball is considered the easiest game to "fix" because it is so easy to purposely miss shots without appearing to be doing so. A player on a team that is winning might easily rationalize missing a basket here and there in order to stay within the point spread — his team will win anyway and so, he thinks, neither team nor fans get hurt. A missed shot, however, can be very important to someone betting on a specific point spread.

The issue of point spread sometimes comes up at the end of a football game when a team does something that appears to make little sense; for instance, the losing team goes for a field goal when the game is far out of reach and the almost-certain three points mean little, or a team that is leading by a wide margin goes for an extra touchdown. So far, however, there has never been any proof of point shaving in college or professional football.

Illegal Gambling on Campus

In early 1998, a 20-year-old student at Columbia University in New York City and a 27-year-old Columbia alumnus and law student at New York University were arrested for accepting bets on sporting event from other students. The wagers, usually between $40 and $200, were telephoned in to a gambling ring based in Queens, New York, operated by people with links to organized crime.

School officials were concerned that Columbia's athletes had bet on their own games and even tried to affect the results. Following the arrests, school administrators and the National Collegiate Athletic Association (NCAA) began an investigation and urged any athlete who had bet illegally on professional or college games to come forward. A number of current and former Columbia athletes interviewed after the arrests said that they knew athletes who had made illegal bets. They also claimed that it was easy to find illegal gambling on and around the campus. The NCAA believes that there are student bookies on every campus in America.

The problem of illegal gambling on college campuses has troubled schools for 50 years.

Between 1947 and 1950, 32 players at seven schools were implicated in a plot to fix games. In the past decade alone, there have been sports scandals at more than 10 schools, including Arizona State University, where two basketball players pleaded guilty to federal charges that they had helped shave points in four games in 1994.

In 1996, 13 football players at Boston College were suspended for gambling on games; two players bet against their own team. In 1995, five athletes, including the quarterback of the football team at the University of Maryland, were suspended for gambling on sports. At Northwestern, in 1994, a football starter and a basketball starter were suspended for betting on college games. In 1992, five basketball players at Bryant College were suspended. They had amassed a $54,000 gambling debt. A former player and a student were arrested and charged with bookmaking.

A nationwide survey conducted in 1996 by the University of Cincinnati (Ohio) involving Division I (large schools) basketball and football players found that one-fourth of the players had gambled on other college sports, and nearly 4 percent said that they had gambled on a game in which they participated. Three athletes admitted that they had been paid by a gambler for not playing well in a game. An athlete gambling on his or her own team is serious, because the athlete may have the opportunity to help himself with his bet.

LIVING WITH GAMBLING

Gambling represents a quandary for the National Football League. While it is absolutely necessary that fans believe in the integrity of the game, a good proportion of those watching (an estimated 20 to 30 percent) are watching because they have money bet on the game. In fact, these gamblers may be more committed viewers than those who do not have bets on the game. A game in which the Oakland Raiders are beating the Philadelphia Eagles by a score of 31-15 may be considered a lost cause to an Eagles fan, who may change the channel. On the other hand, a bettor who has the Raiders +10 is only a touchdown away from winning. He or she is more likely to stay tuned and watch more of the commercials that pay for the overhead of the NFL.

Radio, television, and newspapers, the major media that promote football and other sports, also contribute to the huge amount of betting on sporting events. Most local newspapers make the point spreads readily available to the general public, and it is not unusual for sportswriters and sportscasters to predict the outcome of a game and include the "point spread" in their predictions. The "point spread" is very much a part of the hype that increases the interest in upcoming games and helps ensure that many millions of fans will watch the games and the commercials that support the league.

Many bettors consider the advice of these professional sportswriters and sportscasters before they call their bookies to make bets. Since sports betting is legal in only a few states, the media is quite aware that some people will be using these point spreads and the advice given by sports commentators to make illegal bets.

While the NFL reports who is injured and not likely to play for the information of fans, it is also reported for gamblers. The information that as important a player as Emmett Smith of the Cowboys or Jerry Rice of the San Francisco 49ers had been injured would certainly help determine whether to bet on the Cowboys or 49ers. The NFL is concerned that if such information were not reported and a gambler found out about it, this knowledge would give the gambler an "edge" — an advantage.

Many gamblers would do a lot to get such an edge, including offering players money to report who is unable to play. Once the player had been compromised by giving such information, the gamblers could put greater pressure on the athlete to do other things, including throwing a game. Consequently, the NFL feels it is better to voluntarily give out information that gamblers want to know rather than create a situation that could threaten the integrity of the game.

HOW MUCH MONEY IS BET ILLEGALLY?

It is virtually impossible to accurately estimate how much money is bet illegally in the United States. The last complete survey of American gambling behavior was done in 1975 for the Federal Commission on the Review of the National Policy Towards Gambling. Because it is 20 years old, this study is of little value in the 1990s. The U.S. Treasury estimated the amount of illegal gambling from 1973-1981 (released in 1983), but gave up on a 1990 attempt to update their findings. The U.S. Treasury concluded that there was simply not enough reliable data available to make even a broad estimate.

Until their 1989 survey of gambling in America, *International Gaming and Wagering Business* included an estimate of illegal gambling, but in 1990 dropped their estimate because

No one — not the FBI, not Treasury, not Internal Revenue, or your local police department and certainly not your local newspaper — *knows* how much illegal gambling there is in the United States.

The absence of reliable statistics cannot be made up from the annual accumulation of anecdotal records: media reports of gambling arrests, more or less informed investigations by law enforcement and legislative agencies, telephone calls, conversations with more or less knowledgeable persons with an interest in the subject.

... Therefore, estimates of illegal gambling have been deleted from the 1991 installment of this series — not because illegal gambling does not exist, it does, but because there is no basis for making estimates. And there the matter will have to rest, unless and until new data become available (Eugene M. Christiansen, "U.S. Gaming Handle up 14% in '90," *International Gaming and Wagering Business*, July 15, 1991, and August 14, 1991).

Based on earlier estimates and their own intuition, *International Gaming and Wagering Business* had estimated in 1989 that Americans had illegally bet $43 billion — $8.1 billion on horse books, $27.4 billion on sports betting, $2.1 billion on sports cards, and $5.5 billion on numbers. Of the total $43 billion, *International Gaming and Wagering Business* estimated that the house, either organized crime or individual bookies, kept about $6.7 billion — $2.8 billion from numbers, $1.4 billion from horse books, $1.2 billion from sports books, and $1.3 billion from sports cards. *Forbes Magazine* has estimated illegal sports betting at $100 billion. These figures, however, represent little more than educated guesses. In 1996, the Council on Compulsive Gambling estimated that over $125 billion was bet illegally in the United States in the previous year. Of that amount, $88 billion (or 70 percent) was wagered on sports events.

Still A Major Factor

In conclusion, Eugene Christiansen believes that, based on all accounts, "illegal gambling is flourishing in this country. There is no reason to suppose the illegal games, except, perhaps, illegal numbers games that have to compete with well-run, extensively advertised state lottery numbers games, have suffered measurable declines — but there is no way to know."

So much has happened in gambling over the past decade that it is hard to know exactly how illegal betting has been affected. The easy availability of legal lotteries has undoubtedly hurt the numbers game. In addition, the growth of the drug trade in poorer urban areas has attracted some people to drug dealing who, in an earlier time, might have been running numbers operations.

Although off-track betting is more available than ever, many bettors still prefer an illegal bookie. Sometimes it is more convenient to deal with a bookie who is located nearby. More importantly, if bettors win big, and most hope that they will, the Internal Revenue Service (IRS) will not become involved. When bettors win big at the racetrack, the IRS either takes a percentage immediately, or the track reports the winnings so that the bettor will have to pay taxes. When bettors wager with an illegal bookie, they never have to worry that the IRS will be informed.

With the increased acceptance of state-sanctioned legal gambling, it is not surprising that Americans are less concerned about gambling. High school students bet on weekly basketball and football games. For many people, it is a tradition to have some money bet on the Super Bowl or the World Series. With all that parents worry about with their children, discovering that a son or daughter bet on the World Series does not compare with their concern that they might be using drugs, drinking alcohol, or engaging in sex. Finally, a generation ago, crime and the criminal underworld were often associated with gambling. Today, they are overwhelmingly associated with drugs.

With the continued growth of amateur and professional sports and the unlikelihood that legal sports gambling will extend beyond the states in which it is currently legal in some form, illegal sports betting will likely continue to grow and be the most important part of illegal gambling. (See Chapter II — Professional and Amateur Sports Protection Act of 1992.) Americans consider betting on major sporting events as American as apple pie, and there will likely always be an illegal bookie available to take a bet.

ILLEGAL OFFSHORE GAMBLING

Wagering on sports is illegal everywhere in the United States, except for Montana, Nevada, North Dakota, and Oregon. However, in recent years, a number of American bookmakers have relocated to West Indies countries, such as Antigua, where sports gambling is legal. Local governments license these operations, which use advanced technology to communicate, set odds on games, and record wagers. To receive a license, applicants must pay the government $75,000 for telephone gambling operations and $100,000 for on-line enterprises. The industry has created hundreds of jobs for local residents and built an offshore sports book business that analysts say is taking in 1 to 5 percent of the estimated $100 billion that is bet illegally on sports each year in the United States.

Approximately 60 offshore sports books operate throughout the Caribbean and Central America. Of those, 25 are based in Antigua, where local officials created a free trade zone in 1994. This permits bookies to operate without paying corporate taxes.

Many of the sports books also operate on-line casinos, which allow customers to bet on interactive games, like slot machines, blackjack, and poker. The sudden popularity of these off-shore gambling operations has called attention to the Wire Act of 1961 (PL 87-216), a federal law that prohibits using telephone lines for gambling. Gambling opponents are calling for new laws banning Internet casinos and offshore sports books from doing business in the United States. Foes of offshore gambling are more concerned with the on-line casinos. They claim it is too difficult to regulate the fairness of interactive casino games, which will pose a greater threat to consumers.

The Money

Many offshore bookmakers use the World Wide Web to take bets. Customers set up an account by transferring money through a wire, cashier's check, or credit card debit. The customer receives a toll-free number to call, a personal identification number, and an on-line password.

Until recently, offshore companies have used Western Union as one of their preferred means of receiving wagers and sending winnings. However,

Florida's attorney general and Western Union have agreed that Western Union will no longer wire money for the offshore companies. The offshore bookies will now have to depend on bank wires, cashier's checks, and overnight mail.

Government Action

In 1997, Senator John Kyl (R-AZ) introduced legislation to expand the current gambling laws to include Internet wagering and to implement fines and jail terms for bookies and their customers. The bill, S 474, was voted out of the Senate Judiciary Committee and is expected to be heard by the full Senate in 1998. (The House Judiciary Committee is also scheduled to hear a similar bill, HR 2380, in 1998.)

Several states have attempted to halt offshore gambling, claiming that while it may be legal to gamble in the country where the bookies are located, it is not legal in the states where the bets are being placed. (See Chapter III.) However, according to the Justice Department, the offense has not taken place on U.S. soil, and the government has no jurisdiction in these offshore locations.

The bookmakers have started their own lobbying effort in Washington. They are currently searching for a sponsor of legislation that would legalize and regulate their industry. The bookies claim that they would be willing to pay taxes and "do everything by the book" if the government would allow them to. They point out that the government will not receive any tax revenue as long as bookmaking operations are kept offshore. (Offshore bookmakers are not under any obligation to report winners' earnings to the Internal Revenue Service.)

Today, illegal sports betting is an estimated $100 billion business. Currently, prospects for legalization are not bright. However, in hard economic times, some legislators may decide the taxes from such gambling could benefit the nation.

GAMBLING ARRESTS

In 1982, police arrested 41,200 people for illegal gambling. In 1987, they arrested 23,000. In 1990, police arrested only 19,300; in 1992, 17,100; and in 1994, 18,500. This huge drop in the number of people arrested for gambling occurred during a time when the overall number of arrests was increasing. The 16,040 people arrested for gambling in 1996 made up 0.16 percent (one sixth of one percent) of all those arrested.

More than eight times as many people were arrested for curfew violations (132,747), and nearly five times as many were arrested for forgery and counterfeiting (79,477). With the increase in violent crime and drug-related crimes and the growth and general acceptance of legal gambling, illegal gambling has become a low priority for both the nation's citizens and their police.

CHAPTER XI

PUBLIC OPINION ABOUT GAMBLING

In 1996, the Gallup Poll surveyed Americans to determine their attitudes towards gambling and the huge increase in legal gambling over the past few years. In 1989, when the Gallup researchers surveyed the country on gambling, 29 states and the District of Columbia had introduced lotteries. Seven years later, 37 states were offering their citizens the chance to win the lottery. Meanwhile, along the Mississippi River, in the states of Illinois, Indiana, Iowa, Louisiana, Mississippi, and Missouri, riverboat gambling had become legal. Today, casinos in Colorado and South Dakota attract hundreds of thousands of patrons, and gambling casinos located on Native American reservations across the country draw many more hundreds of thousands.

A LITTLE MORE SUPPORT
FOR GAMBLING

In 1996, people generally gambled more than they had in 1992. In 1992, the Gallup survey found what seemed to be a "cooling off" in the nation's enthusiasm toward gambling when compared to 1989. However, that may have been a reaction to the state of the America's economy, which was less healthy in 1992 than it was in either 1989 or 1996.

The Gallup researchers asked those surveyed whether they approved or disapproved of various forms of gambling. About 77 percent said they approved of bingo for cash prizes, almost unchanged from 75 percent in 1989, but significantly higher than the 68 percent who

approved in 1975. More than two-thirds (68 percent) supported casino gambling at resort areas, up from 54 percent in 1989, and far more than the 40 percent in 1975. (See Table 11.1.)

More than half (55 percent) approved of gambling in major cities such as New Orleans, up from 40 percent in 1992. Americans also supported casino gambling on riverboats (63 percent). (See Table 11.1.)

Support for the lotteries remained nearly the same (77 percent) in 1996 as it had been (75 percent) in 1992, but was well above the 61 percent who supported lotteries in 1975. Support for off-track betting on horses rose from 49 percent in 1992 to 55 percent in 1996.

Americans definitely felt more uncomfortable with betting on professional sports, such as baseball, basketball, and football. In 1982, about half (51 percent) of those interviewed approved of such gambling. However, by the end of the decade, support had dropped to 42 percent and, in 1992, only one-third (33 percent) of Americans thought betting on sports was a good idea. In 1996, 40 percent of the respondents supported professional sports betting.

In 1996, support for gambling on Indian reservations (57 percent) was significantly greater than it had been in 1992 (42 percent). Support for video poker games remained the same (37 to 38 percent) for both years (Table 11.1).

ARGUMENTS SUPPORTING GAMBLING

Americans generally agree with the arguments supporting gambling, many of which are economic. In 1996, most Americans agreed that gambling "creates jobs and helps stimulate the local economy" (65 percent). Fewer people (51 percent) felt that gambling "provides much-needed revenue for programs such as education and senior citizens," down somewhat from 57 percent in 1992. (See Table 11.2.)

In 1996, about 3 out of 5 people (62 percent) thought "people will gamble anyhow, so the state might as well make it legal and get some of the revenue." On the other hand, only one-third (33 percent) believed that "if the state sponsors gambling, organized crime can be kept out," down from 37 percent in 1992 (Table 11.2).

ARGUMENTS OPPOSING GAMBLING

At the same time that most Americans agreed with the arguments supporting gambling, a ma-

---

TABLE 11.1

Thinking now about gambling... As you may know, some states legalize betting so that the state can raise revenues. Please tell me whether you would approve or disapprove of each of the following types of betting as a way to help *your state* raise revenue. First, would you approve or disapprove of... (If respondent says already legal, asked "Do you approve or disapprove of its being legal.") Next, how about... (RANDOM ORDER)

Types of Gambling Activities – Trend**

	Approve	Disapprove	No opinion
Bingo for cash prizes			
1996 Jun 27-30	77%	20	3
1992	72%	25	3
1989	75%	23	2
1982	74%	–	–
1975	68%	–	–
Lotteries for cash prizes			
1996 Jun 27-30	77%	22	1
1992	75%	24	1
1989	78%	21	1
1982	72%	–	–
1975	61%	–	–
Casino gambling at resort areas			
1996 Jun 27-30	68%	30	2
1992	51%	47	2
1989	54%	42	4
1982	51%	–	–
1975	40%	–	–
Casino gambling on so-called "river boats"			
1996 Jun 27-30	63%	34	3
1992	60%	38	2
Casino gambling on Indian reservations			
1996 Jun 27-30	57%	37	6
1992	42%	51	7
Casino gambling in a major city			
1996 Jun 27-30	55%	41	4
1992	40%	47	3
Off-track betting on horse races			
1996 Jun 27-30	55%	41	4
1992	49%	47	4
1989	54%	42	4
1982	54%	–	–
Betting on professional sports such as baseball, basketball, or football			
1996 Jun 27-30	40%	58	2
1992	33%	65	2
1989	42%	55	3
1982	51%	–	–
1975	31%	–	–
Video poker machines at local establishments			
1996 Jun 27-30	37%	59	4
1992*	38%	52	10

* Wording: "Video poker."

** Sources of trend data:
1992, 1989 – The Gallup Poll
1982 – Gallup, for *Gaming Business Magazine*
1975 – University of Michigan

Source: *The Gallup Poll Monthly*, The Gallup Organization, Princeton, NJ, July 1996

jority also agreed with many of the arguments opposing gambling. More than 2 out of every 3 Americans (67 percent) thought that gambling "encourages people who can least afford it to squander their money." (See Table 11.2.) Sixty-one percent believed it "open[ed] the door for organized crime," and another 61 percent thought gambling "can make compulsive gamblers out of people who would never participate in *illegal* gambling." One-fourth (27 percent) believed gambling was immoral.

HOW AMERICANS GAMBLE

The 1996 Gallup Poll found participation in some forms of gambling was up, while the rate for others was down. The proportion of those who played bingo within the last year remained the same as in 1992 — 9 percent. The percentage who bet on horse races dropped from 14 percent in 1989 to 12 percent in 1992 to 6 percent in 1996, indicating the serious problems facing the pari-mutuel industry. (See Table 11.3.)

TABLE 11.2

Next, we'd like to know whether you agree or disagree with each of the following arguments *in favor of* legalized state-sponsored gambling. First, do you agree or disagree that [item].. Next, that [item].. (RANDOM ORDER)

Pro-gambling Positions – Trend

	Agree	Disagree	No opinion
It creates jobs and helps stimulate the local economy			
1996 Jun 27-30	65%	32	3
1992	64%	33	3
People will gamble anyway so the state might as well make it legal and get some of the revenue			
1996 Jun 27-30	62%	37	1
1992	61%	38	1
It provides much-needed revenue for programs such as education and senior citizens			
1996 Jun 27-30	51%	42	7
1992	57%	41	2
If the state sponsors gambling, organized crime can be kept out			
1996 Jun 27-30	33%	63	4
1992	37%	59	4

Now we'd like to know whether you agree or disagree with each of the following arguments *against* legalized gambling. First, do you agree or disagree that [item]... Next, that [item]... (RANDOM ORDER)

Anti-gambling Positions – Trend

	Agree	Disagree	No opinion
It encourages people who can least afford it to squander their money			
1996 Jun 27-30	67%	31	2
1992	64%	34	2
It opens the door for organized crime			
1996 Jun 27-30	61%	35	4
1992	62%	33	5
It can make compulsive gamblers out of people who would never participate in illegal gambling			
1996 Jun 27-30	61%	36	3
1992	58%	40	2
It is immoral			
1996 Jun 27-30	27%	70	3
1992	32%	65	3

Source: *The Gallup Poll Monthly*, The Gallup Organization, Princeton, NJ, July 1996

Betting on sporting events was uneven. The percentage betting on professional sports slipped from 22 percent in 1989 and 12 percent in 1992 to 10 percent in 1996. While the proportion betting on college sports fell from 14 percent in 1989 to 6 percent in 1992, it remained the same (7 percent) in 1996. However, wagers on boxing were down from 8 percent in 1989 to 6 percent in 1992 to 3 percent in 1996.

More people visited casinos in 1996 — 27 percent compared to 22 percent in 1992. Video poker was more popular with 17 percent playing in 1996, up from 11 percent in 1992. Since lotteries have become an accepted part of American life, over half of the nation has participated. (Table 11.3).

In 1996, 22 percent said they played the lottery every week, 20 percent played monthly, and 15 percent said they bought tickets less often. This is about the same as in 1992, when 19 percent purchased tickets every week, 20 percent played the lottery monthly, and 16 percent participated less frequently (Table 11.4).

TABLE 11.3

Please tell me whether or not you have done any of the following things in the past 12 months. First, how about: played bingo for money; visited a casino; bet on a horse race; bought a state lottery ticket; bet on a professional sports event such as baseball, basketball, or football; bet on a *college* sports event such as basketball or football; bet on a boxing match; participated in an office pool on the World Series, Superbowl or other game; gambled for money on the Internet; played a video poker machine; done any other kind of gambling not mentioned here.

Types of Gambling in Last Year – Trend
(those saying "yes")

Lottery ticket	
1996 Jun 27-30	57%
1992	56
1989	54
1982†	18
Visited casino	
1996 Jun 27-30	27%
1992	22
1989	21
1984	18
1982†	12
Office pool	
1996 Jun 27-30	23%
Video poker	
1996 Jun 27-30	17%
1992	11
Pro sports	
1996 Jun 27-30	10%
1992	12
1989	22
1984	17
1982†	15
Played bingo	
1996 Jun 27-30	9%
1992	9
1989	13
1982†	9
1950	12
College sports	
1996 Jun 27-30	7%
1992	6
1989	14
Horse race	
1996 Jun 27-30	6%
1992	12
1989	14
1984	11
1982†	9
1950	4
1938	10
Boxing match	
1996 Jun 27-30	3%
1992	6
1989	8
Gambled on Internet	
1996 Jun 27-30	1%
Other	
1996 Jun 27-30	10%

† Gallup for *Gaming Business Magazine*

Source: *The Gallup Poll Monthly*, The Gallup Organization, Princeton, NJ, July 1996

TABLE 11.4

(Asked of respondent for each gambling activity done in last 12 months) How often do you [item] – Once a week or more often, two to three times a month, once a month, once every few months, or less often? (RANDOM ORDER)

Number of Times in Past Year – Trend

	Weekly or more	Monthly	Less often	No opinion	(% of total respondents)
Lottery ticket					
1996 Jun 27-30	22%	20	15	•	(57%)
1992 Nov	19%	20	16	1	(56%)
1989 Apr	23%	16	14	1	(54%)
Pro football					
1996 Jun 27-30	3%	2	4	•	(10%)
1992 Nov	5	3	4	•	(12%)
1989 Apr	6	5	11	•	(22%)
Visit casino					
1996 Jun 27-30	•	2	24	•	(27%)
1992 Nov	1	2	19	0	(22%)
1989 Apr	1	1	18	1	(21%)
Horse race					
1996 Jun 27-30	•	•	5	•	(5%)
1992 Nov	1	2	8	1	(12%)
1989 Apr	1	3	10	1	(14%)

• Less than 0.5%

Source: *The Gallup Poll Monthly*, The Gallup Organization, Princeton, NJ , July 1996

TABLE 11.5

(Asked of those who buy lottery tickets, 581 respondents, ±5%) How much money do you usually spend each month on lottery tickets?

Monthly Spending on Lottery – Trend

	Apr 1989	Nov 1992	Jun 1996
$30 or more	12%	9%	7%
$20-$29	11	11	10
$10-$19	18	19	22
$5-$9	24	17	23
$1-$4	22	28	26
Less than $1	11	14	11
No opinion	2	2	1
	100%	100%	100%

Source: *The Gallup Poll Monthly*, The Gallup Organization, Princeton, NJ, July 1996,

---

TABLE 11.6

Have you *ever* visited a casino?

Yes	**66%**
in last 12 months	27
not in last 12 months	39
No	**34**
No opinion	•
	100%

• Less than 0.5%

Source: *The Gallup Poll Monthly*, The Gallup Organization, Princeton, NJ, July 1996

Meanwhile, the number of people who spent $30 or more monthly on the lottery dropped from 12 percent in 1989 and 9 percent in 1992 to 7 percent in 1996. The percentage of those who spent between $20 and $29 dollars monthly remained fairly constant. The proportion who spent $10 to $19 was up from 18 percent in 1989 to 22 percent in 1996. (See Table 11.5.)

The percentages who bet on pro football games and visit the track have been dropping significantly. Most people who visit casinos, do so less than monthly (Table 11.4). Many people schedule a periodic visit to a distant casino as a big event. Two-thirds (66 percent) of those polled said that they had visited a casino at some time; 27 percent had visited within the last year (Table 11.6). (For additional surveys on casino gambling, see Chapter V.)

DOES GAMBLING CAUSE PROBLEMS?

The Gallup researchers asked the respondents, "Do you sometimes gamble more than you think you should?" About 7 percent, down somewhat from the 9 percent of 1992, thought they gambled too much. (See Table 11.7.) When asked whether "gambling [has] ever been a source of problems within your family?", 5 percent indicated that it had, unchanged from 1992. (See Table 11.8.)

THE COUNCIL ON COMPULSIVE GAMBLING OF NEW JERSEY SURVEY

The Council on Compulsive Gambling of New Jersey, Inc. is aware that, for some people, gambling can cause grave problems. The Council asked the Gallup Organization (the Gallup Poll) of Princeton, NJ, to study the "New Jersey residents' behavior and attitudes related to gambling." The Gallup Organization surveyed 1,016 adults to produce *New Jersey Residents' Attitudes and Behavior Regarding Gambling* (Trenton, New Jersey, 1993).

This is the most recent poll that the Council has commissioned. This survey is particularly valuable because it is in a state in which a major gambling center is located.

The survey found that almost all (96 percent) New Jersey residents had gambled at some time during their lives. Most had played the lottery (82 percent), played slot machines (75 percent), or gambled in a casino (74 percent). This should not be surprising in a state that has a lottery and a major gambling center.

About half (50 percent) had bet on the horses or dogs, and significant percentages had played cards for money (44 percent), bingo for money (34

TABLE 11.7

Do you sometimes gamble more than you think you should?

Gamble too Much? – Trend

	Apr 1989	Nov 1992	Jun 1996
Yes	10%	9%	7%
No/doesn't apply (vol.)	90	91	93
No opinion	0	0	•
	100%	100%	100%

• Less than 0.5%

TABLE 11.8

Has gambling ever been a source of problems within your family?

Create Family Problems? – Trend

	Apr 1989	Nov 1992	Jun 1996
Yes	4	5	5
No/doesn't apply (vol.)	96	94	95
No opinion	•	1	•
	100%	100%	100%

• Less than 0.5%

Source of both tables: *The Gallup Poll Monthly*, The Gallup Organization, Princeton, NJ, July 1996

percent), and the numbers (31 percent). (See Table 11.9.)

Among those who gambled, 40 percent played the lottery at least once a week, 31 percent played the numbers at least once a week, 19 percent bowled, shot pool, or played golf for money at least once a week, and 11 percent played cards for money at least once a week. (See Table 11.10.)

The Largest Amount Ever Gambled

The Gallup surveyors asked what was the largest amount the respondent had ever gambled. The average largest amount ever gambled averaged $403, although most (53 percent) had never gambled more than $100. About 8 percent claimed they had gambled $1,000 or more at one time. (See Table 11.11.)

145

Getting Hooked

When asked how often they went back to win lost money, 80 percent said they never did. However, 16 percent said they did some of the time, 3 percent most of the time, and 1 percent every time. (See Table 11.12.) When asked, "Have you ever gambled more than you intended to?", 77 percent said no, and 23 percent said yes.

Men (28 percent) were more likely to have gambled more than they intended than women (18 percent). Younger people were more likely to gamble more than they intended than were older people.

About 5 percent said they would like to stop gambling, but could not. Eight percent of men, compared to 2 percent of women, would have liked to have stopped gambling, but could not. About 3 percent of those interviewed saw gambling as a way to escape their problems.

Do You Know Anyone with a Gambling Problem?

When asked if they knew anyone who now had, or did have, a gambling problem, three-quarters (76 percent) did not know anyone. Fourteen percent knew a friend, and 13 percent knew a relative. The fathers of 3 percent and the spouses of 2 percent had a problem. (See Table 11.13.) About 4 percent said that gambling, either by the respondent or a member of the family, had made his or her home life unhappy. When asked whether they knew anyone who gambled too much (but did not necessarily have a gambling "problem"), 28 percent said they knew someone with such a problem.

Who Should Provide Assistance to Compulsive Gamblers?

Most New Jerseyites believed that the state and the legal gambling companies should contribute to educate state residents about

TABLE 11.9

TYPES OF GAMBLING EVER DONE

	Total %	Gender Male %	Gender Female %	Age 18-34 %	Age 35-49 %	Age 50-64 %	Age 65+ %
Played the lottery	82	85	80	82	88	84	70
Played slot machines, poker machines or other gambling machines	75	79	72	72	81	78	72
Gambled in a casino (legal or otherwise)	74	79	70	67	82	81	69
Bet on horses, dogs or other animals (at OTB, the track or with a bookie)	50	57	43	44	55	58	43
Played cards for money	44	59	31	48	46	42	37
Played bingo for money	34	28	40	25	39	37	39
Played the numbers	31	35	28	30	32	28	35
Played scratch off games other than lotteries	31	34	28	38	27	30	23
Bet on sports (parlay cards, with a bookie, or at Jai Alai)	26	41	13	34	26	24	13
Bowled, shot pool, played golf or some other game of skill for money	25	38	12	32	22	25	12
Played the stock, options and/or commodities market	24	30	20	21	29	30	17
Played dice games (including craps, over and under or other dice games) for money	19	30	8	20	18	20	15

Source: *New Jersey Residents' Attitudes and Behavior Regarding Gambling*, prepared by the Gallup Organization, Inc., for The Council on Compulsive Gambling of New Jersey, Inc., Princeton, NJ, 1993

TABLE 11.10

FREQUENCY OF PLAYING WITHIN PAST 12 MONTHS

(Based on those who have ever gambled)

	Once a Week Or More %	Less Than Once A Week %	Not At All/DK %
Played the lottery	40	45	15
Played slot machines, poker machines or other gambling machines	4	45	51
Gambled in a casino (legal or otherwise)	4	51	45
Bet on horses, dogs or other animals at OTB, the track or with a bookie	5	29	66
Played cards for money	11	33	56
Played bingo for money	8	24	68
Played the numbers	31	32	37
Scratch off games other than lotteries	11	48	41
Bet on sports (parlay cards, with a bookie, or at Jai Alai)	15	49	36
Bowled, shot pool, played golf or some other game of skill for money	19	37	44
Played the stock, options and/or commodities market	18	42	40
Played dice games (including craps, over and under or other dice games) for money	5	40	55

Source of both tables: *New Jersey Residents' Attitudes and Behavior Regarding Gambling*, prepared by the Gallup Organization, Inc., for The Council on Compulsive Gambling of New Jersey, Inc., Princeton, NJ, 1993

TABLE 11.11

LARGEST AMOUNT EVER GAMBLED

	Total %	Men %	Women %
Under $10	14	11	17
$10-49	26	20	32
$50-99	13	12	13
$100-149	15	15	16
$150-199	1	2	1
$200-249	8	11	5
$250-299	*	*	*
$300-399	3	3	2
$400-499	2	2	1
$500-599	4	6	3
$600-999	1	1	*
$1,000 or more	8	13	4
Don't know	5	4	6
Total	100	100	100
MEAN	$403	$594	$219
Number of Interviews	(976)	(504)	(472)

*Less than one-half of one percent.

gambling and help treat compulsive gamblers. A large majority (78 percent) thought the state should provide education programs to students. A smaller majority (58 percent) believed the state should provide funding for treatment of compulsive gamblers. Almost three-fourths (72 percent) agreed that gambling companies should provide financial support for gambling programs.

Attitudes towards Legal Gambling

The New Jersey study found that while most residents did not think gambling was illegal, most did believe that gambling entailed risks to society. Only 22 percent of those interviewed believed that gambling was immoral. Those over age 65 (30 percent) and those earning less than $25,000 (28 percent) were most likely to believe gambling was immoral. (See Table 11.14.)

However, 66 percent thought gambling "encourag[ed] people who can least afford it

TABLE 11.12

FREQUENCY OF GOING BACK TO WIN LOST MONEY

| | | Gender | | Household Income | | |
	Total %	Male %	Female %	<$25K %	$25K-$39.9 %	$40K+ %
Never	80	75	85	76	77	83
Some of the time	16	20	13	18	19	14
Most of the time	3	3	1	4	2	2
Every time	1	2	1	2	2	1
Don't know/Refused	*	*	0	0	0	*
Total	100	100	100	100	100	100
Number of Interviews	(976)	(504)	(472)	(290)	(208)	(398)

*Less than one-half of one percent.

TABLE 11.13

PEOPLE IN LIFE WHO HAVE GAMBLING PROBLEM

| | | Gender | |
	Total %	Male %	Female %
Relative (NET)	13	12	14
Spouse	2	*	3
Father	3	3	3
Mother	1	1	1
Brother or sister	2	2	2
Children	*	*	*
Another relative	7	6	7
A friend	14	17	10
No one	76	74	78
Don't know/Refused	*	*	*
Number of Interviews	(1016)	(515)	(501)

*Less than one-half of one percent.

Source of above tables: *New Jersey Residents' Attitudes and Behavior Regarding Gambling*, prepared by the Gallup Organization, Inc., for The Council on Compulsive Gambling of New Jersey, Inc., Princeton, NJ, 1993

to spend money gambling," 57 percent agreed that gambling "can make compulsive gamblers out of people who would never participate in illegal gambling," 61 percent thought it "open[ed] the door for organized crime," and 59 percent believed "gambling can erode young people's work ethics." The respondents were evenly split on whether "gambling teaches children that one can get something for nothing," with 49 percent agreeing and 48 percent disagreeing.

Where Do You Go for Help?

The researchers asked the New Jerseyites if they knew where to go for help. About half (48 percent) claimed they knew where to go for help, and half (52 percent) did not. Among those who did know where to go, most (38 percent) indicated Gamblers Anonymous. Another 18 percent would go to the telephone book. About 12 percent would call 1-800-Gambler, the helpline set up by the Council on Compulsive Gambling of New Jersey, Inc. to assist those addicted to gambling. (See Table 11.15.)

TABLE 11.14

AGREEMENT WITH STATEMENTS

- Is immoral -

	Total %	Age 18-34 %	35-49 %	50-64 %	65+ %	<$25K %	$25K-$39.9 %	$40K+ %
Agree	22	20	21	20	30	28	25	17
Disagree	75	78	78	80	62	68	73	81
Don't know/Refused	3	2	1	1	8	4	2	2
Total	100	100	100	100	100	100	100	100
Number of Interviews	(1016)	(351)	(314)	(190)	(155)	(307)	(216)	(408)

TABLE 11.15

PLACE WOULD GO TO FIND HELP

All Who Say They Know Where to Find Help

	Total %	Age 18-34 %	35-49 %	50-64 %	65+ %	<$25K %	$25K-$39.9 %	$40K+ %
Gamblers Anonymous	38	31	42	43	33	31	35	42
1-800-Gambler	12	20	11	6	7	14	12	13
Hotline	8	8	6	11	5	5	12	8
Telephone book	18	23	12	15	21	18	25	12
Private doctor (Psychologist, Psychiatrist, etc.)	2	1	3	2	0	0	1	4
Through employer sponsored programs	2	1	2	2	2	0	1	3
Friends/family	2	2	3	1	3	4	0	2
Through county/state offices	5	1	8	5	11	9	4	4
Counseling centers (unspecified)	2	2	1	4	2	0	2	2
Other	4	4	2	2	6	7	3	2
Don't know/Refused	5	5	3	5	8	6	3	4
Number of Interviews	(492)	(163)	(158)	(109)	(58)	(116)	(114)	(217)

Source of both tables: *New Jersey Residents' Attitudes and Behavior Regarding Gambling*, prepared by the Gallup Organization, Inc., for The Council on Compulsive Gambling of New Jersey, Inc., Princeton, NJ, 1993

149

CHAPTER XII

THE INTRODUCTION OF GAMBLING IS A GOOD IDEA

TESTIMONY OF JEREMY D. MARGOLIS, FORMER ASSISTANT UNITED STATES ATTORNEY AND DIRECTOR OF THE ILLINOIS STATE POLICE, BEFORE THE HOUSE COMMITTEE ON THE JUDICIARY, SEPTEMBER 29, 1995

People often ask whether the presence of gaming in their community would cause an increase in street crime. The facts are these: Las Vegas, Nevada, the city that is synonymous with casinos, is among the safest cities in America. Illinois, the county's leading riverboat casino state, has experienced no increase in crime in some riverboat towns and measurable reductions in crime in others.

... Las Vegas' crime rate is significantly lower than many other tourist and convention oriented cities such as Miami, New Orleans, Los Angeles, Atlanta, San Diego and San Francisco. It has a lower crime rate than college towns like Ann Arbor, Michigan, and heartland towns like Lincoln, Nebraska, and Lawrence, Kansas.

Significantly, it has a far, far lower crime rate than Orlando, Florida, the home of Mickey Mouse.

... A number of points must be made. First, comparing the demographics of problem-ridden pre-casino Atlantic City to the stable, family-oriented, economically sound and socially responsible communities now considering casinos is like comparing night and day. Sadly, Atlantic City's problems of unemployment, drug use, extreme violence, and substandard public housing long predate the advent of casinos on the Boardwalk.

... The most exhaustive research on post casino crime in Atlantic City was conducted by the noted criminologist and sociologist Jay Albanese ("The Effect of Casino Gambling on Crime," *Federal Probation*, 39-44, 1985).... He found that the individual risk of victimization in Atlantic City was actually less than it had been before the advent of casinos, and that the crime rate for people actually present was less than it had been before visitors tripled the city's average daily population.

The Illinois experience has surpassed all expectations and crime has, simply put, not been an issue at all.... There is no better or more accurate way to say it; crime has not been a problem.... [C]rime in the six block area around the downtown Joliet boat decreased approximately 12 percent.

Most other Illinois riverboat towns have also reported decreases in crime.

... Probably no issue arouses more passion or poses more of a community concern than does the question of the potential involvement of organized crime in legalized gaming. Based upon a combination of history and Hollywood imagery, some people allege that organized crime will be able to infiltrate and exert control. Recent experience in Las Vegas and the total experience of Atlantic City and Illinois riverboats refute this belief.

For many years, organized crime has not been a factor in Las Vegas. Aggressive and thorough regulators, and a very vigilant FBI (whose retired agents continue that work throughout the gaming industry), and highly efficient and tightly-controlled publicly owned companies have seen to that. In Atlantic City, organized crime never touched the casino industry.

As legalized gaming spread[s] throughout the United States, we are seeing that those states with strong regulation and enforcement are not experiencing an influx of organized crime activity....

TESTIMONY OF FRANK J. FAHRENKOPF, JR., PRESIDENT AND CHIEF EXECUTIVE OFFICER OF THE AMERICAN GAMING ASSOCIATION, BEFORE THE HOUSE COMMITTEE ON THE JUDICIARY, SEPTEMBER 29, 1995

Forty-eight of the 50 states plus the District of Columbia and Puerto Rico have some form of legalized gaming. They have not taken that responsibility lightly.... The people and elected officials of each state know what is best for their own state.

I am not here today claiming that the gaming-entertainment industry does not have problems. We do, but the problems we have are no different than those of any large visitor-dependent entertainment industry.

... The American Gaming Association has met with prominent leaders in the field who tell us that the vast majority of Americans are social gamblers who can participate in a gaming activity without harmful effects. Some gamblers cannot, however, and are referred to as problem or compulsive gamblers. Prevalence studies conducted in fourteen states show that the percent of those with a problem ranges from 1.7 percent in Iowa to 6.3 percent in Connecticut. Our view is that one problem gambler is one too many, and as good citizens it is our responsibility to address the

problem through public education, corporate training, and basic research.

A number of our members have been working with state and national organizations for many years to develop proactive corporate policies, public service announcements, employee assistance programs, funding of hotlines, speaker's bureaus, and training of employees. The American Gaming Association will continue this effort. We have created an industry-wide task force to develop a long-range strategy to reduce gambling addiction, raise public awareness, and provide models for early intervention and treatment. Working in partnership with public and private organizations, we will promote industry-wide training programs and public outreach techniques.

... It is time the organized crime issue was put to rest. There is no showing anywhere, be it FBI reports or other law enforcement reports, of organized crime activity in today's gaming-entertainment industry.

... gaming-entertainment today is owned by the same people who own other major industries — stockholders. More than 75 publicly traded companies, all under the stringent scrutiny of the SEC [Securities and Exchange Commission, the federal regulatory agency which monitors publicly traded companies], own gaming interests.

... In addition to the quality of ownership, no other industry has stricter regulation within the states.

... In fact, Jim Moody, supervisory special agent, FBI Organized Crime Program, in Congressional testimony in 1992 said, "As legalized gaming spreads throughout the United States, we are seeing that those states with strong regulations and enforcement are not experiencing an influx of organized crime activity."

Critics and naysayers notwithstanding, there is absolutely no credible evidence that shows the introduction of legal gaming, because of the nature of the business, increases crime. An increase in the number of tourists in any community will bring more crime regardless of the venue. A perfect example of this is what has happened in Orlando, Florida. No one would argue that Mickey and Minnie Mouse cause more crime, yet according to the FBI, Orlando has a higher crime rate than Las Vegas. And when you consider the visitor-adjusted population, Orlando's crime problem exceeds both Las Vegas and Atlantic City.

For example, in Illinois, State Police records indicate that overall patterns of service calls and crime incidents remained stable or even declined after the riverboats began service in the state.

... don't take my word for it. Ask the more than one million men and women whose jobs directly or indirectly support the industry about the economic benefits. Or ask the state and local governments that receive billions of dollars of tax revenues. There is no question that, just as with any expanding industry, some areas of the country will do better than others, but in the overwhelming number of cases, gaming-entertainment has been a boon to the communities where it is established.

Another culprit that opponents trot out is known as the "substitution theory." Somehow opponents argue every dollar spent on gaming, apparently unlike any other new industry, results in the loss of revenue somewhere else. That same logic for some reason isn't applied to money spent purchasing entertainment from theme parks, or movies, or baseball games. The "substitution theory" is highly controversial, to say the least.

The bottom line is there is a net increase in jobs and tax revenues, two positive economic indicators, when gaming-entertainment is introduced into a community. In other words, the economic pie gets bigger. We will take the facts over the theory any time.

TESTIMONY OF REPRESENTATIVE FRANK A. LOBIONDO (R-NJ) BEFORE THE HOUSE COMMITTEE ON THE JUDICIARY, SEPTEMBER 29, 1995

While I respect my colleagues as thoughtful people, I fear that they are motivated by stereotypes and misinformation of the gaming industry....

I asked to come before you today in order to tell the other side of the story ...

I represent a district that includes Atlantic City, New Jersey. It was the collective decision of the people of the entire state of New Jersey to require a heavily regulated, strictly controlled casino industry to operate in one city of the state in return for making a financial commitment to the people of the state.

Atlantic City is a perfect example of how a state, with the approval of its citizenry, is the best entity to determine what, if any, type of gaming should be permitted and what conditions should be applied to that permission.

First, the law approving casinos in Atlantic City was approved by a statewide, binding referendum. Second, the law established two state government oversight agencies....

Third, Atlantic City casinos must contribute to the betterment of the state. In an age when cities and states provide tax breaks to attract new industries, Atlantic City casinos are not only subject to all state and local taxes, but must pay substantial additional taxes and fees....

Finally, New Jersey casinos directly generate 45,000 jobs, and, in fact, Atlantic City casinos provide roughly one-third of all jobs in Atlantic County. When related jobs are taken into account, another 35,000 New Jersey residents owe their employment to the gaming industry.

Gaming's opponents will tell you that Atlantic City's casinos have increased the crime rate. This is simply untrue. The visitor-adjusted crime rate, according to the WEFA group, a private consulting firm in Pennsylvania, is comparable to, and in some cases lower than, cities such as Atlanta, Nashville, and Orlando. Our crime rate nationally is far too high for my taste, but there is no indication that Atlantic City casinos have contributed to that crime rate.

Gaming's opponents will also tell you that Atlantic City's casinos have led to economic decline in other parts of the city. The fact is that Atlantic City's economy was on the decline long before the first casino opened in 1978. If anything, Atlantic City's casinos have brought a welcome economic stability to the city.

The point to all of this is that for Atlantic City and for the State of New Jersey, casino gaming was the right answer to some serious problems. That does not mean that it is the right answer for Virginia, or Illinois, or Indiana. What is right in those states is for the residents of those states to decide. It is not for Washington to say.

TESTIMONY OF WEBSTER FRANKLIN, EXECUTIVE DIRECTOR, CHAMBER OF COMMERCE, TUNICA COUNTY, MISSISSIPPI, BEFORE THE HOUSE COMMITTEE ON SMALL BUSINESS, SEPTEMBER 21, 1994

Historically, Tunica County has been known as "the poorest county in the Nation."

... Our community's jobs have all been based on agriculture prior to the legislation permitting dockside gaming. Large farms which grow cotton, soybeans, and rice provided jobs for our citizens. But due to the mechanization and new technology that has come into the farming industry, hundreds of our workers have been displaced.

Unemployment as recently as January of 1992 was as high as 26.2 percent, one of the highest in the State of Mississippi. Per capita income was $11,865, one of the lowest in the State. Fifty-three percent of all Tunica County residents received food stamps. We were known for our substandard housing, poor health care delivery, and sanitation problems caused by inadequate or antiquated sewage systems.

... studies all recommended basically the same thing: Government assistance. Due to this national attention, we received much needed government money and assistance. But that did not solve our problem — which was jobs for our citizens. It was not until the gaming industry came into our county that those jobs surfaced.

... Since the arrival of gaming, our once defunct planning commission, now very active, has issued over $1 billion worth of building permits.

In 1993, we had 12 major casino constructions — in the construction phase. This allowed, for the first time, our citizens to go to work in the construction industry at salaries of $10 and upwards an hour. Every able-bodied person in the county was afforded, for the first time, the opportunity to acquire as many overtime hours as they could withstand; therefore, they had a skill that they could take to other jobs once these facilities had been constructed.

... Nine casinos currently operate in our county, employing approximately 9,000 people. There have been more jobs in our county in 20 months than there were people.... Our unemployment rate ... was 26.2 percent.... It has gone as low as 4.9 percent. Child support collections have increased.... [T]he number of welfare recipients has decreased 42 percent. Food stamp recipients have decreased 13 percent ... and that trend continues....

Business in Tunica County is, in fact, booming.... We have new housing, RV parks, restaurants and motels.... In fiscal year 1994, our county recorded the highest percent increase of retail sales of all of Mississippi's 82 counties, a 299 percent increase....

... This new revenue source has allowed the county to continue the much-needed infrastructure improvements.

... Revenue from gaming has allowed our county to provide an additional $1.4 million of funding for this school year. This funding will go to new classes, much-needed equipment, and increase in teacher salaries.

... Our board of supervisors also recently voted to reduce its tax on property by 32 percent.

... gaming has had an extremely positive impact on our local economy.

PREPARED STATEMENT OF S. TIMOTHY WAPATA, EXECUTIVE DIRECTOR OF THE NATIONAL INDIAN GAMING ASSOCIATION BEFORE THE HOUSE COMMITTEE ON SMALL BUSINESS, NOVEMBER 28, 1994

Indian gaming enterprises have, by necessity, relied on and become partners with local small businesses in order to survive. Tribal gaming enterprises are large purchasers of local business services. It has been determined that for survival, Indian Gaming, by and large, requires partnerships with local construction and building supply firms, local restaurants, local hotels, local lounges, local cleaning firms, local clothing/uniform manufacturers, local law enforcement/security, local limousine, taxi, bus, and air transportation, local grocers and food distributors, local public utility companies, and positive relationships with the local population. There is no "Walmart Syndrome" [big conglomerate business taking the place of and pushing out small business] in effect in Indian Gaming because of the reliance on the local business community to operate most Indian Gaming enterprises and because Indian Gaming creates a new type of business in a community where no business of this type existed before.

Finally, when a tribal gaming enterprise opens, many new small businesses are also created in order to provide necessary service to the new business. These can include restaurants, hotels, convenience stores, gas stations, banks, other entertainment ventures such as boating or skiing, childcare ventures, gaming employment training and management programs, etc. Indian Gaming enterprises are the genesis for an entire support network of business ventures. Literally hundreds of new businesses nationwide have been created as a result of Indian Gaming.

Certain trends have developed in local economies with the proliferation of Indian Gaming enterprises. These trends are as follows:

Indian gaming enterprises

- Stimulate and create new businesses, both Indian and non-Indian;

- Increase local economic activity, particularly increasing spending and employment;

- Reduce local public assistance rates and expenditures;

- Increase tourism and stimulate visitor spending;

- Increase federal, state and local tax revenues;

- Result in decreased crime rates and increased local law enforcement and security expenditures;

- Result in lowered unemployment rates on the reservation and in local non-Indian communities;

- Increase Indian governmental services, economic development, and self-sufficiency;

- Nationwide, have created in excess of 100,000 direct jobs and an additional 110,000 indirect jobs, a total in excess of 210,000 jobs created as a result of the industry. These are generally jobs and work created in depressed areas where no previous employment opportunity was available.

... If Indian gaming seems an economic and social panacea, it is because the industry has been designed to be so.

... Indian Gaming has provided positive benefits to Indian Tribes and to the local, regional, and state areas in which the gaming is situated. This is particularly evident in counties which the U.S. Census has identified as the poorest in the U.S. All are Indian reservations. Unemployment is as high as 80 percent, a rate similar to Third World Countries. For these areas, Indian Gaming is the only economic development tool which has worked in 200 years.

Finally, it must be remembered that Gaming is an entertainment industry. People do this to have fun. The average loss at an Indian gaming enterprise is less than $20. Tribes fully support, and have even created, programs to assist those who have a problem with gambling. But, the ultimate message is that people are having a good time. Their good time shouldn't be legislated out of existence.

CHAPTER XIII

THE INTRODUCTION OF GAMBLING IS NOT A GOOD IDEA

PREPARED TESTIMONY OF TOM GREY, EXECUTIVE DIRECTOR, NATIONAL COALITION AGAINST LEGALIZED GAMBLING, BEFORE THE HOUSE COMMITTEE ON THE JUDICIARY, SEPTEMBER 29, 1995

A battle is raging across our country. Ambitious gambling promoters have been invited into our communities by some state and local officials under the guise of prosperity, economic development, jobs, and a painless new source of government revenue.

The recent, rapid spread of gambling was never the result of a popular movement. Rather, it was driven by self-interested gambling pitchmen with money, high-priced lobbyists, and pie-in-the-sky promises. Cash-starved municipalities and legislatures, eager for a way to increase revenue while avoiding voter backlash, were vulnerable to the prospect of something-for-nothing.

The tide turned [against gambling] not simply because all of the major conservative Christian groups oppose the expansion of gambling, although they do. It is not simply because mainline churches — liberal, conservative, and moderate — are almost universally opposed to more gambling, although they are. Resistance to government-sponsored gambling is growing because voters from every walk of life recognize that legalized gambling is, based on the facts, poor public policy.

... To many Americans, government's promotion of gambling is a cop-out and a double-cross.

We see public officials sacrificing our communities to a predatory enterprise — for money. Citizens see government living off gambling profits, taken from the poorest and weakest of our citizens, instead of facing up to rational choices regarding budgets and taxes.

... One could say that gambling has become the new national pastime.

... The pro-gambling initiatives must be stopped before our nation's economy, and its social fabric, are irreparably harmed.

... The expansion of legalized gambling is a major threat to business in the United States. The gambling enterprise cannibalizes existing businesses, stealing their customers and revenues. At the same time, gambling establishments bring new social costs that are inevitably paid by business.

... Pathological gamblers tend to engage in forgery, theft, embezzlement, and property crimes to pay off gambling debts. They are responsible for an estimated $1.3 billion worth of insurance-related fraud per year.

... According to a study by the Better Government Association of Chicago, "Law enforcement officials agree that the mob usually infiltrates ancillary services to the casinos. New Jersey law enforcement officials believe that organized crime has infiltrated legitimate businesses, such as those which provide the casinos with ancillary services including limousines, linen, meat, and vending machines."

... Increased crime costs state and local governments not only the salaries of more police officers, but prosecutors, judges, court personnel, court facilities, and prisons.

... Legalized gambling triggers the mental disorder of pathological (or "compulsive") gambling. Pathological gambling destroys the lives of thousands of Americans and devastates their families, friends, and employers. The most common argument in favor of gambling expansion is that it will yield government revenues, which can be used for programs to "help" people. But helping some people by exploiting and destroying others is bad social policy, and simply unethical.

It is important to understand that gambling addiction is just as real, and its consequences just as tragic, as alcohol or drug addiction.

... Individuals who become gambling addicts accumulate debts averaging $35,000 to $92,000 before they seek treatment, are arrested, or commit suicide. Family savings are lost, marriages end, children go unsupported. A majority of pathological gamblers turn to some form of crime to support their addiction.

... Any expansion of legalized gambling is likely to trigger thousands of new victims of gambling disorders.

PREPARED STATEMENT OF PROFESSOR JOHN WARREN KINDT, UNIVERSITY OF ILLINOIS AT CHAMPAIGN-URBANA, BEFORE THE HOUSE COMMITTEE ON SMALL BUSINESS, SEPTEMBER 21, 1994

In recent economic history, legalized gambling activities have been directly and indirectly subsidized by the taxpayers. The field research throughout the nation indicates that for every dollar the legalized gambling interests indicate is being contributed in taxes, it usually costs the taxpayers at least three dollars — and higher numbers have been calculated. These costs to taxpayers are reflected in: (1) infrastructure costs,

(2) relatively high regulatory costs, (3) expenses to the criminal justice system, and (4) large social-welfare costs.

... In the context of social-welfare issues, it is well-established that legalized gambling activities act as a regressive tax on the poor. Specifically, the legalization of various forms of gambling activities makes "poor people poorer" and can dramatically intensify many pre-existing social-welfare problems. Demographic analyses reveal that certain disadvantaged socio-economic groups tend to gamble proportionately greater amounts of their overall income....

From the business perspective, businesses are not naive. With the exception of the cluster services associated with gambling, new businesses tend not to locate in areas allowing legalized gambling because of one or more of the aforementioned costs. In areas saturated with legalized gambling activities, pre-existing businesses face added pressures that push them toward illiquidity and even bankruptcy.

... More subtly, traditional businesses in communities which initiate legalized gambling activities can anticipate increased personnel costs due to increased job absenteeism and declining productivity. The best blue-collar and white-collar workers, the Type-A personalities, are the most likely to become pathological gamblers.

... Legalizing various gambling activities increases the number of problems related to pathological gambling in the context of the workforce, and these costs are reflected in increased personnel costs — such as "rehabilitation costs," which can easily range from $3,000 to $20,000 (or more) per pathological gambler.

Gambling activities and the gambling philosophy are directly opposed to sound business principles and economic development. Legalized gambling activities also negatively affect education — both philosophically and fiscally. In states with legalized gambling activities which were initiated allegedly to bolster tax revenues to "education," the funding in "real dollars" has almost uniformly decreased.

Those states which embrace legalized gambling activities can expect enormous socio-economic costs and declines in the quality of life. Unlike traditional business activities, legalized gambling activities cater to a market consisting of addicted and potentially-addicted consumers, and most pre-existing traditional businesses will find it quite difficult to compete for "consumer dollars" which are being transformed into "gambling dollars."

... Each newly-created pathological gambler has been calculated to cost society between $13,200 to $52,000 per year. These costs are not just reflected in society as a whole, but impact on all businesses.

... Sociologists almost uniformly report that increased gambling activities which are promoted as sociologically "acceptable" and which are made "accessible" to larger numbers of people will increase the numbers of pathological gamblers.

PREPARED STATEMENT OF DR. VALERIE C. LORENZ, EXECUTIVE DIRECTOR, COMPULSIVE GAMBLING CENTER, INC., BALTIMORE, MD, BEFORE THE HOUSE COMMITTEE ON SMALL BUSINESS, SEPTEMBER 21, 1994

Let me make something very clear: ALL types of gambling can become addictive, regardless of whether one gambles on or with machines, races, tickets, or games. Fortunately, only certain people will become gambling addicts. However, the number of compulsive gamblers has been increasing at an alarming rate in the past twenty years — ever since the spread of casinos and state lotteries, which has turned this country into a nation of gamblers.

... Until the mid-1970s, the typical compulsive gambler was a white, middle-aged, middle-class male. A dozen years ago, a female compulsive gambler was a rarity. Lottery addicts were just beginning to surface. Teenage compulsive gamblers and senior citizens addicted to gambling were nonexistent.

The profile of today's compulsive gambler is truly democratic, all ages, races, religious persuasions, socio-economic levels, and education. Sixteen or sixty, the desperation and devastation is the same.

... Why? Because our governments are saying "Gambling is OK," and because gambling is now so readily available, with so very little regulation.

The formula is quite simple: Availability leads to more gamblers, which leads to more compulsive gamblers. Casino gambling ... is particularly onerous because of the allure of escaping into fantasy, the fast action, and emphasis on quick money, all of which are basic factors in gambling addiction.

Gambling addiction increases socio-economic costs far greater than any amount of revenue generated for the government by the gambling industry.... Maryland's 50,000 compulsive gamblers cost the state $1.5 million per year in lost work productivity and monies that are abused (stolen, embezzled, state taxes not paid, etc.).

Other costs resulting from compulsive gambling are broken homes, physical and mental health problems, increase in social and welfare services, indebtedness, bankruptcies, and crime. Each and every one of these are far-reaching, affecting neighbors, employers, entire communities, and generations to come. These direct and indirect costs are staggering.

Taking just the issue of crime alone, virtually all compulsive gamblers, sooner or later, resort to illegal activities to support their gambling addiction. After all, money is the substance of their addiction, and when legal access to money is no longer available, these addicts will commit crimes.

The crimes are typically of a non-violent financial nature, such as fraud or embezzlement or failure to pay taxes.

While in jail, the gambling addict is neither gainfully employed nor paying federal or state taxes. The family may be surviving on drastically reduced income or be on welfare. Well-paying jobs for felons are hard to come by, which means the gambling addict will most likely be earning less in future years, after he or she is released from prison.

... Ironically, while there are many education, prevention, and treatment programs for the substance abuser, supported by state and federal monies, what is there for the individual who becomes addicted to the government licensed or sponsored activity, gambling? Pathetically little in a few states, nothing in most.

... The casinos historically have failed to take any measure of responsibility for compulsive gambling, and only recently have a few Indian Reservations addressed this potential problem among their own people or among their customers. In short, the greed of the gambling industry is matched only by its lack of concern for its customers or the community in which it operates. That is not good business.

... First of all, it must face the fact that the problem exists, instead of continuing to ignore it or minimize it. Secondly, it must stop believing the deceptions perpetrated by the gambling industry, that legalization of casinos or race tracks or lotteries are the answer to governments' fiscal woes, the answer to unemployment, or the way to stop tax increases.

... The number of compulsive gamblers in this country today runs into the millions. Who will provide the treatment, and who will pay for it? Not the gambling addicts — they have neither the money nor the health insurance — that was spent at the casinos or on other gambling.

This country can ill afford to ignore the problems caused by the proliferation of gambling and the resultant increase in compulsive gambling. We do not need the economic ruin, broken homes and crime brought on by this industry, which encourages instant gratification, something for nothing, while making a mockery of family, work and community.

TESTIMONY OF ROBERT GOODMAN, DIRECTOR, THE U.S. GAMBLING STUDY, LEMELSON PROFESSOR OF ENVIRON-MENTAL DESIGN, HAMPSHIRE COL-LEGE, AND PROFESSOR OF REGIONAL PLANNING, UNIVERSITY OF MASSACHU-SETTS, BEFORE THE HOUSE COMMIT-TEE ON SMALL BUSINESS, SEPTEMBER 21, 1994

In the process of studying and debating the economic consequences, I have come to understand why gambling industry executives and politicians were disturbed by criticism of this industry. Clearly, from the industry perspective, having a government monopoly — essentially, in many cases, government-sanctioned monopoly — gives them an immensely profitable position, and criticism can be seen as threatening to those profits.

But I think from the political perspective, criticism is also always threatening, but I think for more complex reasons, and these stem from, really, the limited opportunities for economic development in many parts of this country, and the introduction of gambling is really a symptom of that problem rather than a long-term solution to it.

Having to deal with downsizing by major private firms, having to bear the brunt of reduced Federal aid and other problems that you are familiar with in the cities, any new enterprise which promises large numbers of jobs and revenue can give the appearance of salvation and economic revival. With constituents hurting, with more productive solutions very hard to come by, even desperate solutions can seem better than no solution....

That model of gambling as economic development does no longer exist in this country. Unfortunately, many communities are looking toward that model that no longer exists as a source of creating jobs and revenue.

... what you are finding in this convenience gambling economy is that essentially that money, discretionary dollars that are being spent on other forms of entertainment and consumer expenditures, are now being shifted into casinos. That is not economic development in any real sense of the word. It is basically shifting dollars, and this is creating an onerous financial burden on future generations by simultaneously undermining what remains of America's productive economy.

... These governments are developing new partnerships with businesses in some of the most unproductive sectors of the economy, helping to expand an industry whose success increasingly depends on cannibalizing dollars from other businesses and whose expansion will create serious future problems for other businesses and governments to deal with in the future.

... it seems to me the Federal Government has done little to protect American businesses, especially small businesses, against the predatory industry or process. I should call it, not simply an industry but a predatory process at home, those State and local government partnerships with the gambling industry whose monopolistic powers will have a devastating effect on large portions of the existing economy.

In the process of doing this kind of quick relief, quick-fix economic development, we are creating some enormous problems. Potential investment capital is being reduced. Existing businesses are losing consumer revenues, being pushed closer to decline and failure.

Using our own research findings, we have conservatively estimated that each problem gambler costs government and the private economy $13,200 a year. [In Iowa that would mean $73 million and in California $780 million.]

What do those costs have to deal with? This includes such costs to the private economy as money which problem gamblers borrow and don't pay back, work time lost to private industry by problem gamblers who are ineffective on the job, salaries lost by problem gamblers laid off as a result of their problems, private insurance losses as a result of fraud by problem gamblers, losses that result from embezzlement, check fraud.

In addition, there are the public costs of processing public gamblers through the criminal justice system, including the cost of keeping some of those people in jail for some period of time.

TESTIMONY OF EARL GRINOLS, PROFESSOR OF ECONOMICS, UNIVERSITY OF ILLINOIS, BEFORE THE HOUSE COMMITTEE ON SMALL BUSINESS, SEPTEMBER 21, 1994

The essence of the gambling debate from an economic perspective can be understood by asking the question: Does America need another form of entertainment so badly that it is willing to add another social problem to the list that it already deals with, such as crime, alcoholism, teen pregnancy, illegal drug use, and so on?

From the Federal Government's perspective, a good analogy might be the following: Imagine if a pharmaceutical company invents a new pharmaceutical. There are already other drugs available for the same purpose. The product works extremely well for 98.5 percent of the people who use it. However, for 1.5 percent of the people who use it, the drug completely ruins their life. Would the FDA license this drug?

To see how gambling differs from other entertainment, we can ask, how would gambling have to be "sanitized" to make it like other forms of entertainment? I think at least three things are needed.

First, we would have to eliminate the 1.5 to 5 percent or so of the population who we know will become pathological or compulsive or addicted gamblers.

Second, we would have to eliminate those who gamble beyond the point of recreation or entertainment. Though gambling is a sterile transfer of money from one pocket to another, it does use time and resources. Gambling for nonrecreational or nonentertainment purposes reduces national income.

Third, we would have to eliminate the massive concentration into the hands of a small group in the gambling industry of money and influence, and especially its effect on the legislative process in statehouses and city councils across America.

... Were the Nation to introduce gambling everywhere, the damage would equal the costs of an additional 1990/91 recession every 8 to 15 years. Equivalently, this would be like the costs of an additional Hurricane Andrew, the most costly natural disaster in American history, or two Midwest floods every year in perpetuity.

... [Gambling draws] money away from other businesses, creating no economic development, but leaving social costs in its wake.

IMPORTANT NAMES AND ADDRESSES

American Gaming Association
555 13th St. NW, Suite 430 West
Washington, DC 20004-1109
(202) 637-6500
FAX (202) 637-6507

American Greyhound Track
Operators Association
1065 NE 125 St., Suite 219
North Miami, FL 33161-5832
(305) 871-2370
FAX (305) 893-5633

American Quarter Horse
Association
1600 Quarter Horse Drive
Amarillo, TX 79104
(806) 376-4811
FAX (806) 376-8364

Association of Racing
Commissioners International, Inc.
2 Paragon Centre, Suite 200
2343 Alexandria Drive
Lexington, KY 40504-3276
(606) 224-7070
FAX (606) 224-7071

Colorado Division of Gaming
720 South Colorado Blvd.
Denver, CO 80222
(303) 205-1300
FAX (303) 757-8624

Compulsive Gambling Center, Inc.
924 East Baltimore St.
Baltimore, MD 21202-4739
HELPLINE (800) 332-0402

Council on Compulsive Gambling
of New Jersey, Inc.
1315 West State St.
Trenton, NJ 08618
(609) 599-3299
HELPLINE 1-800-GAMBLER
FAX (609) 599-9383

Gamblers Anonymous
International Service Office
P.O. Box 17173
Los Angeles, CA 90017
(213) 386-8789
FAX (213) 386-0030

Gaming and Wagering Business
BMT Publications
Seven Penn Plaza
New York, NY 10001-3900
(212) 594-4120
FAX (212) 714-0514

Harrah's Casino Hotels
1023 Cherry Road
Memphis, TN 38117
(901) 762-8600
FAX (901) 762-8637

Illinois Gaming Board
101 West Jefferson St.
P.O. Box 19474
Springfield, IL 62794
(217) 524-0226
FAX (217) 524-0228

Iowa Racing and Gaming
Commission
Lucas State Office Building
Des Moines, IA 50319
(515) 281-7352
FAX (515) 242-6560

Mississippi Gaming Commission
P.O. Box 23577
Jackson, MS 39225-3577
(601) 351-2800
FAX (601) 351-2817

Missouri Gaming Commission
1616 Industrial Drive
Jefferson City, MO 65109
(573) 526-4080
FAX (573) 526-4084

National Association of Fundraising
Ticket Manufacturers
Ten South Fifth St., Suite 810B
Minneapolis, MN 55402
(612) 335-3590
FAX (612) 335-8244

National Coalition Against
Legalized Gambling
110 Maryland Ave. NE
Washington, DC 20002
Phone and FAX (800) 664-2680

National Council on Problem
Gambling, Inc.

P.O. Box 9419
Washington, DC 20016
(410) 730-8008
FAX (410) 730-0669
HELPLINE (800) 522-4700

National Indian Gaming
Association
224 2nd St. SE
Washington, DC 20003
(202) 546-7711
FAX (202) 546-1755

National Indian Gaming
Commission
1850 M St. NW, Suite 250
Washington, DC 20036
(202) 632-7003
FAX (202) 632-7066

Nevada Gaming Control Board
P. O. Box 8003
Carson City, NV 89702-8003
(702) 687-6520
FAX (702) 687-5817

New Jersey Casino Control
Commission
Tennessee Ave. and the Boardwalk
Atlantic City, NJ 08401
(609) 441-3200
FAX (609) 441-3840

North American Association
of State and Provincial Lotteries
1701 East 12th St., #15-SW
Cleveland, OH 44114-3208
(216) 241-2310
FAX (216) 241-4350

South Dakota Commission on
Gaming
118 East Missouri
Pierre, SD 57501-5070
(605) 773-6050
FAX (605) 773-6053

U.S. Trotting Association
750 Michigan Ave.
Columbus, OH 43215
(614) 224-2291
FAX (614) 224-4575

RESOURCES

Gambling in America (Washington, DC, 1976), the final report of the Commission on the Review of the National Policy Toward Gambling, despite its age, continues to be the most complete government study on the subject. The commission requested the Survey Research Center of the University of Michigan to prepare this extensive study of gambling, which covers gambling from the founding fathers down to its publication.

The U.S. Bureau of the Census reports the population growth of states in *National and State Population Estimates: 1990 to 1996* (Washington, DC, 1997) and the growth of cities and metropolitan areas in annual releases. The Indian Gaming Management Staff of the Bureau of Indian Affairs monitors the status of tribal-state compacts and periodically releases its statistics. The Federal Bureau of Investigation maintains statistics on gambling arrests in its annual *Uniform Crime Reports — Crime in the United States*. The General Accounting Office (GAO) investigates all areas of government activity. The GAO recently studied Indian gaming activities and the revenues generated from them in its report, *A Profile of the Indian Gaming Industry* (Washington, DC, 1997).

International Gaming and Wagering Business (IGWB), a monthly magazine devoted to the international gaming industry, contains invaluable information on every aspect of the industry. *IGWB* periodically publishes special reports on particular types of gambling activity, such as lotteries and casino gambling. Martin Christiansen and Will E. Cummings of Christiansen/Cummings Associates, Inc. (CCA), prepare an invaluable annual survey of gambling in America. Information Plus again extends its sincere appreciation to *International Gaming and Wagering Business* and CCA for permission to use selected material from their publications.

The Association of Racing Commissioners International, Inc. (Lexington, Kentucky) in its annual report, *Pari-mutuel Racing*, summarizes statistics on horse racing, greyhound racing, and jai-alai events. Information Plus would like to thank the Association for permission to use material from its publication.

The American Greyhound Track Operators Association (North Miami, Florida) publishes *Track Facts* and the *Summary of State Pari-mutuel Tax Structures*, which focus on state taxing and revenue structure and greyhound racing. The *Greyhound Network News* is a quarterly newsletter of general information about the situation of the American racing greyhound. The *Official Handbook of the American Quarter Horse Association* provides an overview of quarter horse racing in America.

The Nevada State Gaming Control Board, the New Jersey Casino Control Commission, the Colorado Division of Gaming, and the Illinois Gaming Board each publish a detailed yearly report on casino gambling in their states. The South Dakota Commission on Gaming, the Missouri Gaming Commission, the Mississippi Gaming Commission, and the Iowa Racing and Gaming Commission also produce annual state-wide reports on casino gambling.

The National Association of Fundraising Ticket Manufacturers (NAFTM; Minneapolis, Minnesota) annually surveys bingo, charity gaming, raffles, and other forms of gambling in *Report on Charity Gaming in North America*. Information Plus would like to thank the NAFTM for permission to use material from the publication.

As always, Information Plus expresses its sincere appreciation to the Gallup Poll (Princeton, New Jersey) and the National Opinion Research Center at the University of Chicago (Illinois), for permission to use material from their surveys.

The annual *Harrah's Survey of U.S. Casino Gaming Entertainment* (Memphis, Tennessee) is designed to "identify how people feel about casino gaming and to develop a profile of who games in casinos, where they visit, and what they like to play." The majority of the findings are based on a survey questionnaire developed by the NPD Group, Inc. (Home Testing Institute), plus questions commissioned by Harrah's as part of the Yankelovich *Monitor* Callback, an annual national survey of American values and attitudes conducted by Yankelovich Partners, Inc. Information Plus would also like to thank *Lodging Hospitality* magazine and the Hotel & Motel Brokers of America for permission to use their survey of casino visits by frequent travelers.

The National Coalition Against Legal Gambling has prepared a useful packet of material opposing gambling. The American Gaming Association, which represents the gaming industry, has prepared information supporting gambling. The National Indian Gaming Commission, a government agency, and the National Indian Gaming Association, an association of the Indian gambling industry, supply information on Indian gambling. (See Important Names and Addresses.)

Information Plus would also like to thank The Council on Compulsive Gambling of New Jersey, Inc., and Ed Looney, the organization's Executive Director, for permission to use various materials. In addition, Mr. Looney permitted Information Plus to use material from the survey, *New Jersey Residents' Attitudes and Behavior Regarding Gambling*, prepared by the Gallup Organization, Inc., for The Council on Compulsive Gambling of New Jersey, Inc.

INDEX